Generis

PUBLISHING

Hungarian Lay Judges

A Socio-Legal Study

Attila Badó
Gábor Feleky

Title: **Hungarian Lay Judges**

A Socio-Legal Study

ISBN: 979-8-89966-026-9

Author: Attila Badó, Gábor Feleky

Cover image: www.pixabay.com

Publisher: Generis Publishing
Online orders: www.generis-publishing.com
Contact email: info@generis-publishing.com

Hungarian Lay Judges: A Socio-Legal Study

Attila Badó

Gábor Feleky

The research on which the book is based was carried out by a research group of the Faculty of Law and Political Science of the University of Szeged. Attila Badó, Gábor Feleky and János Lőrinczi participated in the research.

CONTENTS

INTRODUCTION

The lay judge, as we understand it, is an individual entrusted with the authority to resolve legal disputes, yet lacking the qualifications required to become a professional judge. Such a person carries out their duties either based on their own sense of justice or for the purpose of incorporating specialized, non-legal expertise into the process of adjudication. This definition indeed encompasses the majority of lay judicial forms, yet it excludes certain exceptional cases, such as when a retiring judge or a lawyer possessing the qualifications required to become a professional judge undertakes the role of a juror or, alternatively, serves as a justice of the peace. In our view, remuneration—whether a lay judge receives a salary, an honorarium, or merely expense reimbursement—does not fall among the criteria by which the boundary between lay and professional judges can be drawn, contrary to the approach taken by the *European Charter of Lay Judges*.[1] The defining boundary lies in the fundamental purpose for which lay judges are appointed: unlike professional judges, they are intended to rely not on legal expertise, but on their common sense, sense of justice, or specific non-legal expertise when resolving legal disputes. As will become evident in the following discussion, the essence lies in the non-professional status of lay judges, whose roles, in most cases, stem precisely from their lack of legal expertise—or, to put it differently, their "inexperience" in legal matters.

In debates concerning the role of lay judges, the concepts of quality and efficiency arise in a markedly different context than in discussions focusing on the work of professional judges who engage in the administration of justice as a vocation. When practising judges and academic researchers involved in the management of the administration of justice contemplate improving the quality of judicial systems in European member states, the role of lay judges is raised only marginally from the perspective of quality justice—and perhaps justifiably so. Although some form of classical lay participation exists in every EU member state except the Netherlands and Latvia, lay judges who contribute to judicial decisions now play only a minor role in resolving legal disputes, with few exceptions. The few exceptions are legal systems where independently acting lay judges—be they justices of the peace or honorary judges—differ little from professional judges beyond their qualifications, remuneration, and the gravity of the cases they

[1] European Charter of Lay Judges, Brussels, 11 May, 2012.

handle. In less significant cases, at the lowest level of the judicial system, they perform the same duties as their professional counterparts. In a somewhat different manner, another exception may be lay individuals who serve as jurors in criminal proceedings. Their situation is, for this reason, consistently addressed in judicial reforms aimed at improving quality. In contrast, in those Member States where laypersons typically participate in judicial proceedings alongside professional judges[2], serving as a "representative touch of the people," reformersdo not generally view the enhancement of the quality of justice as being tied to reshaping the role of laypersons. Although proposals for changes affecting the position of lay judges frequently come before legislatures—sometimes expanding but more often curtailing their competencies—such measures bear little connection to quality assurance in the administration of justice. More precisely, it could be said that such changes are driven by the perspective that laypersons neither enhance nor diminish the professional quality of justice. At most, their presence serves to reinforce other aspects, particularly the democratic character of society. Naturally, laws introducing or reforming lay adjudication cannot omit the aspect of quality justice. However, this is largely regarded as a "mandatory exercise," much like in the case of any other legislative proposal concerning judicial matters.

It is worth examining what motivates modern legal systems to maintain or even introduce these particular forms of popular representation. Is it merely out of tradition, the appeal of a grand democratic façade, or something deeper that laypersons are involved in deciding the affairs of their fellow citizens? Can the arguments used by legislators to justify the various forms of public participation truly stand up to scrutiny? To properly weigh the merits of lay adjudication, it is worth examining not only the customary legislative explanatory memoranda but also the arguments grounded in scientific discourse that define the role of laypersons in the administration of justice. It is equally important to assess to what extent the arguments underpinning such institutions hold true in light of practical experience and scientific findings.

In our analysis, we deliberately avoid addressing any explicit or implicit arguments that are clearly unrelated to the objective of improving the quality of justice. Thus, we shall not analyse those non-rule-of-law, ill-intentioned legal-political measures that place the institution of lay adjudication in service of

[2] Kutnjak, Ivkovic Sanja: An Inside View: Professional Judges' and Lay Judges' Support for Mixed Tribunals. In: Law and Policy, April, 2003. 93–122. p.

achieving a particular political goal.[3] Nor shall we address instances where the introduction of the institution is driven by considerations of cost-effectiveness.

We regard as an interesting and innovative piece of work one of the most comprehensive European studies in recent years, which approaches the significance of lay adjudication from the perspective of human rights, asserting that laypersons contribute to the more effective protection of these rights in criminal proceedings.[4] Here, however, we deliberately aim to confront with reality a few of the arguments that have now become classical, which generally underpinned the current forms of public participation.

The administration of justice undoubtedly still calls for the participation of individuals who are not professionally engaged in judicial work when it comes to deciding legal cases brought before the courts.[5] These participants in the legal system take on the role of adjudicators either due to a civic duty or interest prescribed by law, or perhaps as a means of supplementing their income. There are those who regard it as an honour to take on a role that shapes the lives of others, a sentiment perhaps best reflected in the German term for lay judges (*Ehrenamtliche Richter*), which translates to "honorary judges." In modern legal systems, it may seem strange and incomprehensible to many how those without specialised qualifications can play a role in decision-making alongside or even instead of a highly specialised legal profession. Legal science provides the

---

[3] Badó, Attila – Bencze, Mátyás: *Reforming the Hungarian Lay Justice System.* In: Cserne Péter [et al.] (Ed.): Theatrum legale mundi: symbola Cs. Varga oblata. Szt. István Társulat, Budapest, 2007. 1–13. p.

[4] Jackson, John – Kovalev, Nikolay Pavlovich: *Lay adjudication and human rights in Europe.* In: Colum. J. Eur. L. winter 2006/2007. 83. p.

[5] Devlin, Patrick: Trial by Jury. Stevens & Sons Limited, London, 1956. 164. p.; Goldbach, Toby Susan – Hans, Valerie: Juries, Lay Judges, and Trials. In: Bruinsma, Gerben and Weisburd, David (eds.): Encyclopedia of Criminology and Criminal Justice = Cornell Legal Studies Research Paper, 2013. 13–87. p.; Machura, Stefan: Fairness und Legitimität. Nomos Verlagsgesellschaft, Baden-Baden, 2001. 385. p.; Simon, Rita James – Marshall, Prentice: The jury system. In: Nagel, Stuart S.: The Rights of the Accused in Law and Action. Sage Publications, Beverly Hills CA, 1972. 211–233. p.; Antal, Tamás: Az angliai es- küdtszéki rendszer kritikája és reformja a 19. század elején. In: Jogtudományi Közlöny, 2/2015. 79–89. p.; Antal Tamás: Az angol esküdtszék történetének rövid foglalata. In: Acta Jur. et Pol. Szeged, FORVM Szeged, 2/2013. 5–29. p., különösen 21–26. p.; Antal, Tamás: A 19. századi brit laikus bíráskodás magyar szemmel: Szilágyi Dezső az angol esküdtszékről. In: Ünnepi kötet Dr. Tóth Károly címzetes egyetemi tanár70. születésnapjára. Acta Jur. et Pol. Szeged. Tom. 78. 2015. 339–353. p.; Antal, Tamás: Szilágyi Dezső és műve = Jogtörténeti Tár 4. Pólay E. Alapítvány: Iurisperitus K., Szeged, 2016. 87–109. p.

foundation for the resolution of legal cases. So why might a case involving specialised legal questions be entrusted to laypersons, who are not versed in legal science? After all, no one would think of placing unqualified citizens alongside a surgeon to decide what intervention is necessary for a patient's recovery. The answer, undoubtedly, lies in the unique nature of legal science and the administration of justice, which makes the above analogy not only misplaced but entirely senseless. Where, alongside technical questions, fundamental moral dilemmas and solutions to everyday situations inevitably arise, the involvement of laypersons may seem a valid consideration. Moreover, one need not search far to find a suitable parallel in fields similar to the administration of justice. For now, it remains accepted in every democratic legal system to involve laypersons in the legislative process through representation, with these individuals making the final decisions on key legislative proposals, including whether there is a need for lay participation in the administration of justice.

It would, of course, be too simplistic to attribute the persistence or occasional renaissance of lay adjudication solely to this fact.[6] The global societal demand is evidenced by the fact that the majority of the world's legal systems, including about three-quarters of the Council of Europe's member states, employ laypersons in some form within the administration of justice.[7] This remains compelling even in light of the fact that, from time to time, serious debates—of interest not only to lawyers—arise, questioning the foundations of lay adjudication, even in those countries where such courts have been in operation for centuries.[8] Due to the widespread nature of the concept, it is not difficult to list the well-known arguments that seek to support the role of laypersons, just as it is easy to identify those that, whether vehemently or more subtly, oppose the use of lay courts or lay judges. The majority of the supporting arguments are linked, either directly or indirectly, to the improvement of the quality of justice or the efficiency of the judicial system, asserting that the involvement of laypersons in decision-making contributes to a better, more democratic, more appropriate, and more efficient

---

[6] Thaman, Stephen C.: Europe's New Jury Systems: The Cases of Spain and Russia. In: Law and Contemporary Problems, Spring, 2/1999. 233–260. p.; Thaman, Stephen C.: Spain returns to Trial by Jury. In: Hastings Intland Comp. L. Rev. 21/1997–1998. 241. p.; Antal Tamás: Törvénykezési reformok Magyarországon (1890–1900). Ítélőtáblák, bírói jogviszony, esküdtszék = Dél-alföldi évszázadok 23. Csongrád Megyei Le- véltár, Szeged, 2006. 219–222. p., 259–261. p.

[7] Jackson – Kovalev 2006/2007. 6. p.

[8] Malsch, Marijke: Democracy in the Courts: Lay Participation in European Criminal Justice Systems. Ashgate Publishing, Farnham, 2009.

administration of justice. The counterarguments, on the other hand, seek to demonstrate that the involvement of laypersons brings no benefit in terms of either quality or efficiency.[9] Based on the review of legislative justifications and scholarly sources, we can thus compile a clearly defined list of the reasons for the involvement of laypersons and how they contribute to the development of the quality of justice.

Whether the arguments and counterarguments regarding the involvement of laypersons convince us that they are an indispensable component of democratic justice, or that they are unnecessary ballast, one thing remains certain. In legal systems around the world, we encounter laypersons in various forms, who, either independently or alongside professional judges, participate in judicial decision-making. This is also the case in Hungary, where lawmakers periodically debate the necessity, extent, and legitimacy of lay participation.

In 2016, the Ministry of Justice proposed a reform of the Hungarian lay court system as part of the criminal procedure reform. The intention, which from 2018 significantly reduced the role of laypersons without legal qualifications in the administration of justice, fitted into the broader process that has characterized the former socialist countries since the 1990s. During the one-party system era, the courts with lay judges, modelled after the Soviet example, scarcely fostered in lawyers the belief that public participation could serve any meaningful purpose.[10] In the article by Jackson and Kovalev, it is raised that in the countries of the Council of Europe, in the poorest or those legal systems that show the least respect for human rights, lay participation is either modest or non-existent.[11] Furthermore, the authors highlight that in the former people's democratic legal systems, the reduction of lay participation was a result of the negative experiences of the old regime. Their examples clearly show that the aforementioned factors can sometimes overlap. In his 2011 article on the Czech reform of lay adjudication,[12] Michael Bobek also outlines the legislative justifications for reducing the lay element, which include the passivity and limited involvement of laypersons, as well as the technical difficulties associated with operating the jury system.

---

[9] Badó Attila: Az angolszász típusú esküdtszék kritikai elemzése. In: Acta Jur. et Pol. Szeged, Tom. 50., Fasc. 1. Szeged, 1996. 52. p.

[10] Kulcsár 1971. 127. p.

[11] Jackson, J. D. – Kovalev, N. P.: Lay Adjudication in Europe: The Rise and Fall of the Traditional Jury. (2016) 6. p. = http://ssrn.com/abstract=2782413 (2016. 10. 10.).

[12] Bobek 2014. 12. p.

In the reform of the Hungarian lay judge system, particularly with regard to the reduction of participation, the legislator refers to previous—unnamed—negative experiences, the non-rule-of-law past of the lay judge system, and trends observed in other countries.[13] Lay participation has remained only in military criminal proceedings and in criminal proceedings involving juvenile offenders. The reform that was implemented in the meantime effectively led to the consequence that, in criminal adjudication, the legislator now seeks to "utilise" laypersons' specialised (military, educational, psychological) knowledge rather than their general life experience. Although the arguments supporting the significant limitation of lay participation seem rather uncertain, and the reference to historical roots appears forced due to the existence of similar mixed judicial systems in many democratic states, it is undeniable that the changes followed the expectations of a significant portion of the Hungarian legal community.

Before the intention behind this reform was known, our research team decided to conduct a comprehensive empirical study in Hungary, exploring the views of both lay judges and professional judges.[14] With our enquiry, we aimed to gain insight into the lay judge system, as no such research had been conducted in over fifty years. In the 1960s, a research group led by Kálmán Kulcsár carried out a singular sociological survey on the popular lay judge system, a pioneering study conducted within the confines of the one-party state. Although, based on the conclusions of this study, those interested in the topic would have been presented with an image of a rather dysfunctional system.

We believe that the frequent negative perception of the activity of lay judges has, over the past decades, been shaped not only by the general antipathy towards this practice observed within the legal profession in other countries but also by the impact of the Kulcsár investigation. At the same time, we also believed that since the political transition in 1989, changes have taken place in society and the judiciary that could potentially reveal significant and positive differences compared to the findings of the Kulcsár study, fundamentally influencing the perception of the institution. Conversations with lay judges and professional judges conducted even before the commencement of our research reinforced the

[13] "The jury system, introduced universally in criminal cases in 1949, stemmed from the consideration that the totalitarian state sought to fully subordinate the independent judiciary. Due to its original purpose, it cannot be maintained in its current form within the framework of the rule of law—taking into account Article U (1) and Article R (3) of the Fundamental Law.

[14] This volume was produced within the framework of the OTKA research project (120693, Ensuring Impartiality in the Judiciary: A Comparative Study).

impressions that ultimately led to the formulation of our research hypothesis. Nonetheless, we felt it timely to undertake an empirical study to gain insight into the opinions of those who, whether as laypersons or professional judges, have firsthand knowledge of the actual workings of the system.

The aim of the research was to obtain reliable knowledge about the current state of the lay judge system through the analysis of academic sources, legal provisions, and the opinions of lay judges and professional judges. Additionally, where appropriate, it sought to provide *de lege ferenda* recommendations for the legislator.

Instead of the general use of lay judges, it is necessary to define the types of cases where social participation, based on specific criteria, genuinely contributes to effective and just adjudication."

In 2015, when the research began, we had not anticipated that the legislator would be preparing to significantly weaken public participation as part of the criminal procedure reform.

Before presenting our research findings on Hungarian lay judges, this volume undertakes a comparative analysis of lay judicial systems. This approach allows readers to acquaint themselves with international examples and to evaluate the domestic situation in the context of foreign practices.

Throughout the research, we received invaluable support from court leaders and the heads of the Lay Judges' Association, for which we would like to express our heartfelt gratitude.

Klausa 1972. 72. p.

Machura 2001. 236. p.

Machura 2001. 128. p.

Klausa 1972. 72. p.

Glöckner, Andreas – Dickert, Stephan – Landsberg, Marie – Scholz, Selina – Schönfeldt, Kristina: *Entscheidungsverhalten von Schöffen: Forschungsbericht*. Max-Planck-Institut zur Erforschung von Gemeinschaftsgütern, Bonn Forschungsgruppe Intuitive Experten. 33. p.; https://www.coll.mpg.de/ Download/IntuitiveExperts/Schoeffenbericht.pdf (2016.02.08.)

II. THE THEORETICAL FOUNDATIONS, HISTORICAL BACKGROUND, AND METHODOLOGY OF THE EMPIRICAL SOCIO-LEGAL STUDY OF THE HUNGARIAN LAY JUDGE SYSTEM

II.1 THEORETICAL FOUNDATIONS, RESEARCH OBJECTIVES

In our comprehensive socio-legal study of the Hungarian lay judge system, which began in 2015, we sought answers to a wide range of questions. However, following the example of international studies, we primarily focused on two central questions. One of our key questions was to what extent the requirement of representativeness is upheld in the recruitment of Hungarian lay judges, and what the lay judges' and judges' opinions are regarding the selection process. Our other key research question focused on the role and significance of lay judges' activities in legal proceedings, based on the assessments of both lay and professional judges. The study of these two issues constituted the central focus of our research, as the noticeable negative domestic evaluation of lay judges' activities is largely based on these very problems. The view remains widespread among legal professionals that lay judges, representing the retired age group, play virtually no role in proceedings where their inclusion is mandated by law. However, international research[15] on mixed judicial systems presents a much more positive picture than this. It is reasonable to assume that the original intention behind the inclusion of Hungarian lay judges was not merely to use them as "decorative pieces," as they are commonly referred to by lawyers among themselves.

The method of selecting lay judges deserves particular attention from the perspective of the fundamental aim of lay adjudication. Depending on the purpose

[15] Például: Dubber – Pihlajamäki 2015. 230. p.; Kutnjak, Ivkovic Sanja: Ears of The Deaf: The theory and reality of Lay judges in Mixed Tribunals. In: Chicago-Kent Law Review, 2015. 1031. p.; Rennig, Christoph – Machura, Stefan: Die Zusammenarbeit zwischen Schöffen und Berufsrichtern. In: Lieber, Hasso – Sens, Ulla (eds.): Ehrenamtliche Richter – Demokratie oder Dekoration am Richtertisch? Kommunal- und Schul-Verlag, Wiesbaden, 1999. 65–70 p. (The Cooperation between Lay Assessors and Professional Judges.); Machura 2000. 111–116. p.; Casper – Zeisel 1979. 81. p.; Malsch 2009.; Machura 2001. 38. p.; Rennig 1993. 724.p.

for which the legislator intends to employ laypersons, the selection methods may vary.

If, for example, the primary objectives are to strengthen the legitimacy of the judiciary, raise the level of legal awareness within society, and ensure external oversight of the justice system, then lay judicial activity should be made a civic duty. In such a case, emphasis should be placed on random selection as a means of ensuring representativeness. If the aim is to integrate specific expertise into the decision-making process, then the foundation for selection should naturally lie within those social groups possessing the requisite specialised knowledge. When Goldbach and Hans attempt to present the selection mechanisms of mixed judicial systems, they primarily focus on emphasising that, much like the selection of jurors, there are now countless variations of lay judge recruitment.[16] The study by Kovalev and Jackson also alludes to the extraordinary diversity in this regard.[17] From politically driven selection to the enforcement of the representativeness requirement, and even to the prioritisation of specialised expertise, there are numerous variations.

Based on a comparative analysis of various selection methods and the empirical research focused on these methods, it must be emphasised that, unlike the global trend in the selection of professional judges, the issue of representativeness in public participation has become increasingly prominent in the 20th and 21st centuries, as a direct consequence of the essence of lay adjudication. This was explored in greater detail in the first chapter of the book. The main reason for this is that, with proper representativeness, lay participants in the judiciary can uphold the values, norms, and sense of justice of their own group. Moreover, the social legitimacy of the courts can be enhanced by ensuring that societal control is exercised through the involvement of lay judges. While we witness the strengthening of merit-based systems in the selection of professional judges, with the demand for representativeness only faintly appearing, primarily in academic literature[18], in the case of lay judges, we can observe a gradual strengthening of the significance of the latter aspect in practice. All of this has been taken increasingly seriously in recent decades, both in light of the typical legislative goals[19] of public participation and to ensure impartial, unbiased adjudication.[20]

[16] Goldbach – Hans 2013. 13–87. p.

[17] Kovalev – Jackson 2006/2007. 9. p.

[18] See: Malleson 2006. 151 p.; Malleson – Russel 2007. 126–140. p.

[19] Badó 2016,.3–15. p.

[20] Maute 2006. 387–423. p.

The issue of social representativeness is becoming increasingly significant in relation to peace court, jury, and "mixed judicial" systems. In the case of mixed courts, there is likewise a discernible effort to enforce the requirement of representativeness through random selection and, in some cases, other means.

In the case of the Anglo-Saxon type of jury, where lay jurors are typically responsible for determining questions of fact and possibly deciding on sanctions, their decision-making freedom can also be considered nearly complete. In this case, the investigation into the operational mechanisms of the jury is less concerned with its dependence on professional judges and more focused on the influence of external factors on the decision-making group. These factors include the roles of lawyers, prosecutors, the media, and even the attractiveness of the defendants, all of which invite the scrutiny of researchers.[21] The situation is notably different in the case of mixed courts, where laypersons, theoretically endowed with decision-making authority equal to that of the judge, often find themselves confronting a significant imbalance. The professional judge, vested with the powers of presiding over the judicial panel, wields a level of expertise that inherently limits the laypersons' ability to participate as equal members in the decision-making process. As previously indicated, international research also confirms that the involvement of laypersons in lay judge-type courts is generally minimal.[22] However, we believe that the extent and nature of this limited involvement are far from insignificant when considering the arguments that view the primary purpose of the lay judge system as channelling society's sense of justice, serving as a check on judicial processes, or expanding the deliberative elements of democracy.[23]

In the Hungarian judiciary, laypersons have been involved exclusively as part of judicial panels classified in legal literature as mixed courts for many decades, including during the era of the one-party system. The legal sociological survey conducted in Hungary during the 1960s under the leadership of Kálmán Kulcsár took place within the framework of the one-party state. Our hypothesis was that, due to the significant social changes that have occurred since then, only a small fraction of the insights gained during that time remain valid today. Although some of the questions from this earlier research, in slightly modified form, were used in

---

[21] Badó 1998. 479–481. p.

[22] 158 Kubicki 1970.; Klami – Hämäläinen 1966.; Kutnjak 1999.; Machura 2001.; Perron 2001.

[23] Badó 2016. 3–15. p.

surveying the lay judges serving during the research period, the design of the questionnaire relied far more on the insights gained from international studies.

The research conducted by Sanja Kutnjak Ivković on the Croatian mixed court system and Stefan Machura on its German counterpart served as both an inspiring force and a foundational starting point for our work. Sanja Sanja Kutnjak Ivković was particularly influential in this regard, as she provided a compelling theoretical foundation for empirical research on mixed court systems by applying the Status Characteristics Theory to interpret the activities of this task-oriented group.[24]

The starting point for applying the Status Characteristics Theory to mixed courts is that these courts, like other small, heterogeneous decision-making groups, involve members who exhibit a characteristic difference that is significant from the perspective of the task at hand. In addition to specific characteristics, other diffuse characteristics such as gender, age, race, etc., may naturally differ. However, it is the differences in specific characteristics that fundamentally shape the group's decision-making mechanism, the interactions among its members, and their expectations of one another. In the case of mixed courts, the difference in specific characteristics naturally lies in the knowledge-based superiority possessed by a trained judge, in comparison to laypersons who lack legal qualifications or prior judicial experience.

It has been demonstrated in numerous studies that a hierarchical relationship emerges between lay judges and professional judges, despite both being endowed with equal legal rights at the statutory level.[25] The *German* mixed court system is the closest to the Hungarian system and has the longest history. Studies on German lay judges also confirm that the dominance arising from the professional superiority of the professional judges manifests itself even without an authoritarian personality, and the influence of laypersons on decision-making is generally weak.[26] This fact was also corroborated by Kulcsár's studies on Hungarian lay judges, where he observed their passivity and marginalisation, in contrast to the more active period driven by political goals in the past.[27]

In our empirical research, alongside measuring the representativeness of the institution, we also attempt to determine the actual extent of the involvement of

[24] Kutnjak 2015. 1031. p.

[25] 161 Klausa 1972. 235. p.

[26] Casper – Zeisel 1979. 81. p.; Kulcsár 1971. 127. p.

[27] Kulcsár 1971. 127. p.

Hungarian lay judges, in comparison to the lay judge courts that operated under the previous one-party state framework.[28] Our hypothesis was that the jury system in a political system based on a market economy and a multiparty system would result in greater lay participation than a lay judge system that has become consolidated in a dictatorial regime, one that has already lost its original political function, as was the focus of Kulcsár's study in the 1960s. This hypothesis still seemed plausible, even though, since then, there have been no significant legal changes regarding the selection and functions of lay judges.

We also made an attempt to contribute to a deeper understanding of mixed court systems by identifying the types of professional judge attitudes in the relationship between lay judges and professional judges.

It should be emphasized, however, that our research did not examine the relationships among lay judges, which, among other aspects, was explored in Machura's studies on the German jury system.[29]

II.2 THE ROOTS OF LAY PARTICIPATION IN THE HUNGARIAN JUDICIAL SYSTEM

II.2.1 Legal Historical Perspectives

In Hungary, debates took place as early as the 19th century in relation to the establishment of the jury system, presenting the most well-known arguments for and against the necessity of lay judges. As Tamás Antal pointed out in several instances, while theoretical jurists tended to support it, practising lawyers generally opposed it, or at the very least, strongly resisted it.[30]

The short-lived Hungarian jury system was essentially based on the French jury system, with German mediation, most notably reflected in its composition and the selection process. The jury court consisted of three professional judges and twelve jurors. After the selection of jurors from the original register, those called to serve

[28] Kulcsár 1971.127. p.

[29] Machura 2001/A.

[30] Antal 2006. 253–278. p.; Antal, Tamás: Szilágyi Dezső igazságügyi reformjairól (1890–1900). In: Jogtör- téneti tanulmányok VIII. Ed.: Kajtár István, et al. Pécs, 2005. 9–28. p.; Antal, Tamás: Hírhedt vádlottak a szegedi esküdtbíróság előtt. In: A Csongrád Megyei Honismereti Egyesület évkönyve, 2013– 2015. Ed.: Pálné Szabó, Zsuzsanna. Szeged, 2015. 241–249. p.

could be challenged by both the prosecution and the defence, each having the right to dismiss an equal number of individuals they found undesirable. What distinguished it from the contemporary French system was the population that formed the basis for the selection. In Hungary, both the relevant judicial ministerial decrees of 1848 and 1867, as well as Act XXXIII of 1897, excluded a broader section of the population from the possibility of becoming a juror compared to contemporary France.[31] However, the suitability of the groups selected for service was also questioned by many. Although there was consensus that the anomalies that arose were partly attributable to the unfortunate questioning rules of the 1896 *Criminal Procedure Code*. The normative reform of the domestic jury system took place in 1914; however, it occurred at nearly the last moment in its history, as the First World War, along with the liberal state concept, swept away the Hungarian jury system. The People's Republic might have preserved it, but thereafter, the conservative government of the public law provisional regime was never interested in a judicial form that, in certain cases, might disregard the law if something severely violated its sense of justice.

Thus, neither in 1919 nor after the abolition of exceptional powers was the jury system reactivated. Interestingly, during the Horthy era, the institution of the jury was technically only "suspended," and this was not done at the legislative level, but rather through a government decree.[32] The German-style jury system of adjudication did not exist in Hungary during the Dual Monarchy, and between the two world wars, it only left traces as part of the emerging labour court system.[33]

However, after World War II, lay judges once again played a significant role. Even before the communist takeover, the politicization of the Hungarian judiciary had already begun, and what was previously a relatively depoliticized sphere became a battleground for ideological conflict. Lay judges seemed to be an effective weapon in the ideological struggle for the communist party. Their use

---

[31] Badó 2000.; Badó, Attila: A francia esküdtszékkel kapcsolatos dilemmák. In: Acta Jur. et Pol. Szeged, Tomus 57., Fasc. 1. Szeged, 1999. 3–26. p.

[32] Bónis, György – Degré, Alaljos – Varga, Endre: A magyar bírósági szervezet és perjog története. (2. bőv. kiad.) Zala M. Bíróság, Zalaegerszeg, 1996. 245–252. p.; Stipta, István: A magyar bírósági rendszer története. Debrecen, 1998. 133–138. p.; Csizmadia Andor: Az esküdtbíróság Magyarországon a dualizmus korában. In: Csizmadia, Andor (Ed.): Jogtörténeti tanulmányok I. Közgazdasági és Jogi Könyvkiadó, Budapest, 1966. 131–147. p.

[33] Antal, Tamás: A munkaügyi bíráskodás történetének kezdetei Szegeden (1918–1920). In: Ünnepi kötet Dr. Czúcz Ottó egyetemi tanár 70. születésnapjára. Ed.: Hajdú, József. = Acta Jur. et Pol. Szeged. Tomus 79. Szeged, 2016. 13–19. p.

occurred across several platforms.[34] The most well-known of these were the People's Courts established to investigate war crimes,[35] as well as the people's lay judge system formed within the framework of regular courts. In 1948/1949, the socialist turn took place, when the communist party's takeover laid the foundations for a Soviet-type state structure. It was then that the new regime's demand to reorganise the judiciary became more pronounced, marking the beginning of the era of people's democratic legislation. The legislative process commenced, drawing on the Soviet model, in both substantive and procedural law. Gradually, the modern codes established during the civil era were replaced. The dismantling of the highly differentiated, four-tiered judicial system also began, allowing for the establishment of a Soviet-style judicial forum system aligned with the party organisation and the administrative structure.

The 1949 Act XI, which limited the possibilities for appeals in criminal cases, also provided for the introduction of the people's lay judge system. From that point on, in specific cases, professional judges formed a judicial panel together with lay judges at various levels of the court system.

Typically, these panels consisted of one professional judge and two lay judges, with the judges enjoying fully equal rights. This was essentially the adaptation of mixed judiciary practices, found in Germany and other European countries, to the Hungarian legal system. Interestingly, this often-criticised institution proved to be more enduring than anyone could have expected, as its essence remains in place to this day. According to the first law regarding lay judges, the introduction of this form of judiciary was intended to ensure that during trials and judgment, the "working people's" convictions, sound worldview, and natural sense of justice were represented, as well as to allow for the "democratic" oversight of the judges. It is not difficult to guess, given the political context, what objectives this latter task could have served. Certainly, it was not to ensure the independence or incorruptibility of the judge, but rather to control judges who had been socialised in the old system. After the communist takeover, efforts were made to intimidate or remove judges appointed under the old regime. One form this took was

[34] See, for example, Fleck 2001. 176–214. p.

[35] For example, József Ruszoly writes about the first People's Court decree:A Szegedi Nemzeti Bizottság részvétele a demokratikus államhatalom gyakorlásában (1944. december – 1945. január). In: Ibid: „és így is a mi korunk". Írások és források Magyarország alkotmánytörténetéhez, 1944–1949. Püski, Budapest, 2006. 11–31. p., regarding this, see: 21–31. p.; see also Lukács, Tibor: A magyar népbírósági jog és a népbíróságok, 1945–1950. Közgazdasági és Jogi K., Budapest, 1979.

assigning well-trained lay judges, loyal to the party leadership, alongside professional judges, who would report on or undermine the professional judges' work. This was possible because, from the outset, the law granted lay judges equal rights to the professional judges leading the panel. Where the law required lay participation, the decision-making was conducted together by professional judges and lay judges throughout the process—ranging from evaluating facts and legal questions to imposing sanctions. However, following the Stalinist period, the institution began to lose its political significance, and the dominance of professional judges became increasingly apparent. From the 1960s onwards, with the stabilisation of the communist regime, the judiciary gradually changed, and the political use of lay judges became unnecessary. With an increasingly technocratic and loyal judiciary, lay judges were relegated to the background.[36]

The socio-legal study conducted by Kálmán Kulcsár in the late 1960s stands as a testament to the process outlined above. It remains the only empirical sociological investigation into Hungarian lay judges, seeking to offer a comprehensive portrait of their activities. The research, based on a sample of over 1,000 individuals, explored a wide range of factors, from the distribution by occupation and demographic characteristics to gender ratios, the processes of selection and summons, and the lay judges' levels of engagement, legal consciousness, and knowledge of the law. The findings painted a picture of considerable passivity among the lay judges, with their involvement in the decision-making process being a rare and exceptional occurrence.[37] Although the study revealed numerous reasons for this passivity, one of the most significant factors could be traced back to the selection processitself. In general, those selected for lay judge duty were typically from the older, retired demographic, individuals who would not "disrupt" the work of the judges. Studies on jury-based legal systems in other Soviet bloc countries, modelled after the Soviet model, yielded similar findings to those in Hungary,[38] confirming the significant dominance of professional

[36] Badó – Bencze 2007. 1–13. p.

[37] 173 Kulcsár 1971. 127. p.

[38] See, for example, Pomorski, Stanislaw: Lay judges in the Polish Criminal Courts. 1975. (According to this research, while lay judges significantly overestimated their own role, lawyers and judges regarded the contribution of lay judges as minimal.)

judges and the marginal role of the lay jurors. This paradoxical situation was reflected in the ironic labels attached to the jurors, a trend that still persists today.[39]

II.2.2 The Lay Judge System Following the Transition to Democracy in Hungary

Following the free elections of 1990, calls for the reform of lay adjudication emerged almost immediately, with the chief objective being the introduction of a jury system.[40] This demand, in the wake of the dictatorship, appeared entirely logical to many, with arguments once again emphasizing the political advantages frequently championed in the apologetic literature on juries, from the writings of Lord Devlin onward.[41] However, despite the historical traditions, the proposals for introducing a jury system eventually faded from the political agenda. While there was a referendum initiative in the 2000s, spearheaded by a private individual, the National Electoral Committee (NEC) and subsequently the Constitutional Court intervened to thwart this attempt.[42]

The first comprehensive reform of the Hungarian judicial system following the political transition occurred, as is well known, in 1997. This reform included amendments to the lay judge system, many of which remain in effect to this day. According to the law, lay judges[43] continue to participate in judicial decision-making, securing their mandate through elections based on the principle of popular sovereignty. The law raised the minimum age for eligibility as a lay judge from 24 to 30, aligning this change with the increased age requirement for judicial appointments. The election process for lay judges has essentially remained consistent with previous regulations and continues to function in the same manner today. Lay judges are nominated by Hungarian citizens residing within the court's

[39] In the former Soviet Union and later in Russia, they were referred to as the "bodyguards of judges," in Croatia as "cabbage heads," and in China as the "deaf ears." See: Kutnjak 2015. 1. p.

[40] Botos, Gábor: Az esküdtbíróság újbóli bevezetéséről. Im: Rendészeti Szemle, 2/1992. 11–51. p.

[41] Devlin 1956. 164. p.

[42] Decision 30/2007 (V.24.) AB

[43] The term "people's lay judge," reminiscent of the socialist era, was changed to simply "lay judge."

jurisdiction who possess voting rights, by *local governments operating within the court's jurisdiction, and by social organisations*—excluding political parties.

Depending on the court level to which the lay judge is assigned, the municipal representative bodies carry out the election. The law maintained the provision that lay judges are appointed for a term of four years. The preparation for elections, as well as the determination of how many lay judges each court requires and which electoral body is responsible for selecting them, falls under the authority of the National Judicial Council (NJC), now replaced by the National Office for the Judiciary (NOJ). The President of the Republic sets the date for these elections, while the assignment of lay judges to judicial panels is carried out by the president of the court.

The law, compared to the previous regulations, provides detailed provisions regarding the circumstances and procedures for the termination of a lay judge's mandate. Lay judges are also subject to the rule that such a position may only be held until the age of 70. In judicial proceedings, lay judges continue to enjoy the same rights as professional judges.[44] Under the law adopted in 1997, the previously inadequate remuneration for lay judges was increased to reflect the level of responsibility associated with the judicial role.[45] Since the 1997 reform, no substantial changes have been introduced concerning lay judges. However, one notable adjustment has been made regarding impartiality: while Act LXVII of 1997 did not preclude party members from being elected as lay judges, Act CLXII

[44] However, these equal rights are not accompanied by equal obligations. A juror can be a party member as well, a fact supported by a Decision from the Constitutional Court: "The public law status of judges involves professional participation in the judiciary and the practice of adjudication. This public law status mandates political independence. The constitutional principle of the separation of powers, and the distinct nature of the judicial power, requires political independence even in the existential-public law status. People's lay judges do not participate in the judiciary as a lifelong profession, but temporarily, for the duration of their mandate. The constitutional justification for their temporary involvement is the inclusion of a lay element in the judiciary. Thus, their public law status involves temporary and non-professional participation in adjudication. Restrictions on their constitutional rights—such as the right to participate in public affairs as set out in Article 70 (4) of the Constitution—can only extend as far as is proportional to their temporary participation. A disproportionate limitation of rights, one that unnecessarily alters their 'lay lifestyle' status, would contradict the purpose of their involvement in the judiciary, which is to incorporate a lay element in adjudication." [Decision 51/1992 (X. 22.) AB]

[45] 180 181 Sections 122 to 128 of Act CLXII of 2011 on the Status and Remuneration of Judges (Act on the Status and Remuneration of Judges)

of 2011 established a prohibition similar to that applied to professional judges. Aside from this, only minor amendments have been made, none of which alter the fundamental features of the institution. The 1997 reform did successfully address one of the most pressing practical issues—the persistent shortage of lay judges.

Our investigation began within this historical and legislative context, with the aim of finding answers to the fundamental questions mentioned above.

II.2.3. The Methodological Limitations of the Research

Our original concept was to obtain a comprehensive understanding of the approximately 5,000-strong active jury community through an analysis of both the academic and legal sources, alongside a near-complete survey. For the survey, we intended to use a paper-based questionnaire (PAPI) technique, assuming that for jurors predominantly from the older age group, the online questionnaire (CAWI) would be less appropriate. Simultaneously, we planned to approach judges, who use computers on a daily basis, with an online questionnaire.

To conduct the research, we needed to request permission from the newly established, centralised body responsible for court administration since 2011 (the National Office for the Judiciary, or NOJ). In this regard, we were particularly encouraged by the Office's *Open Court Programme*, which promised to expand the possibilities for research within the judiciary. Based on the outlined research plan and the submitted questionnaire, we obtained the necessary approval to carry out the survey of lay judges. Our data collection approach was designed so that the lay judges attending the courts could pick up the questionnaires on-site, which they would fill out either individually or in groups, with our colleagues collecting the completed forms. The organisation of the data collection began through the county courts. In some counties, preparations were still underway, while in others, almost a full-scale survey was conducted. However, at this stage of the research, the President of the NOJ unexpectedly halted the data collection, citing that the leadership of the NOJ had not been aware of the questions included in the questionnaire.

After we pointed out that the significant preparatory work would be wasted due to this decision, the NOJ granted permission for the questionnaire to be completed in its online version. However, as expected, this only yielded modest results, thus thwarting our goal of conducting a full-scale comparison with Kulcsár's research.

In his study, a database of 1,223 respondents (based on a multi-step sampling method) was available, while we were only able to rely on a sample of 348 participants.[46]

However, we were given the opportunity to request professional judges to complete an online questionnaire regarding the evaluation of lay participation. We received completed questionnaires from approximately one hundred (109) professional judges. Many judges also shared their detailed opinions on the jury system, which, in itself, holds significant value.

As empirical social researchers, we are, of course, fully aware of the essential methodological distinction between data analysis based on a sample that accurately represents the population, and analysis relying on a sample that may be formed in a potentially arbitrary manner.[47] Therefore, we seriously considered the alternative of abandoning the data we had gathered during the research due to its partial explanatory power, forgoing any analysis of it. However, we ultimately concluded that, despite the methodological limitations, we would proceed with the analysis of this archive of lay participation – as a document of an era. In the meantime, the process of reducing lay participation in the Hungarian judiciary had already begun (whether one calls this process "strong restriction" or "phasing out" is a matter of perspective). This meant that our research could be the last report on the jury system of the "post-socialist era."

[46] 182 The sample included jurors who were active in the capital and ten selected counties, specifically those who were serving in October 1968 (Kulcsár 1971, pp. 10-12).

[47] Although the sample largely lacks proportional territorial representation, it reveals significant similarities among the counties in terms of age characteristics, gender composition, educational attainment, and employment status (with a notable overrepresentation of individuals over sixty, women, graduates, and retirees or inactive individuals). In light of this, we believe that our research, while not suited for presenting precise ratios or data, is still appropriate for illustrating the main correlations, and thus should not be regarded as merely a tentative search for answers.III. The Social Representation of Hungarian Lay Judges

III. THE SOCIAL REPRESENTATION OF HUNGARIAN LAY JUDGES

III.1 THE SELECTION OF LAY JUDGES AND SOCIAL REPRESENTATION

The selection of lay judges in Hungary, with the exception of political parties, takes place through the recommendations of various social organisations and the decisions of local government councils. It is likely that the representative bodies of court seats consider multiple factors in their decision-making process. However, based on our research findings, we can assert that the pursuit of social representation plays a minimal role, if any, in this process. Naturally, there are situations in which the number of candidates does not allow for meaningful selection, or where a different, deliberate selection strategy is employed. Whether this is the case or not, we can overall observe that the social composition of the selected lay judges differs markedly from that of Hungarian society as a whole. However, the representative bodies cannot be blamed for this, as there is no compulsory "quota system" in place during the application/nomination process. Those who apply or are nominated are considered suitable for the task based on their life circumstances, experiences, perceived readiness, and personal motivations. Therefore, we can already state that the selection procedure is not tied to any social representation requirements.

We were also curious to learn how the participants in the judicial system—on the one hand, the lay judges themselves, and on the other, the judge—evaluate the selection process. We asked them how they believe lay judges should be selected, whether the current system is effective, or if an alternative selection method would be necessary.

Table 1. Which is the best method for selecting lay judges?

Which solution do you consider the best for selecting candidates for lay judge positions?		
	Lay judges	**Judges**
	%	%
The decision on the selection should continue to be made by the local government representative bodies	40.1	20.4
The courts should decide on the selection	54.6	62.0
Some other professional organisation should decide on the selection	5.3	14.8
The selection should be carried out in another way	0.0	2.8
Total:	100.0	100.0

Figure 1. What is the best method for selecting lay judges?

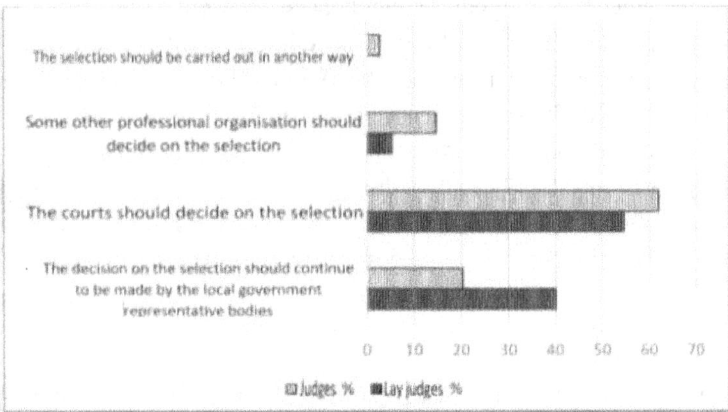

In both groups, the majority would prefer – 54.6% of lay judges and 62% of judges – for the courts to make the decisions regarding the selection of lay judges. However, the perception of this issue becomes notably divided within the lay judge community. According to the current regulations, the selection is carried out by local governments (representative bodies). At the same time, more than half of the respondents would prefer that the courts select the lay judges from among the applicants. Since all of them are currently "locally selected," the preference for court selection suggests an indirect criticism of the existing selection system.[48] Of course, there is support for the usual selection method as well (40 percent), but three out of five lay judges would prefer some other form of procedure. As we can see, judges are even more characterised by a critical stance towards the current practice: four out of five judges would prefer a different selection process. In connection with the most popular solution—that the courts should decide on the selection of lay judges—it is worth mentioning an observation made in the 1966 study, namely, that the already distorted composition of selected lay judges was further distorted by the courts' practice of calling them for specific cases, during which the courts' particular criteria prevailed. If this is still the case today, we can justifiably assume that, under the exclusive court selection of lay judges, the social representativeness of lay judges would be even more distorted compared to the current system.

We asked both lay judges and judges which three selection criteria they consider most important for those applying for lay judge positions – from the list below. We identified eight important **criteria for the selection of lay judges**, from which the respondents could choose. Four of these (***"qualities"***) referred to the attributes and qualities a lay judge brings with them (life experience, expertise, education, and independent thinking). Two (***"adaptability"***) concerned how well the individual could integrate into the organisation (knowledge of lay judge work and ability to adapt). Two (***"externalities"***) related to external factors concerning the candidate (public activity/acceptance and local recognition). The respondents were asked to rank these eight factors in order of importance: first, second, and third. The resulting rankings clearly indicate that the **quality-adaptability-externality sequence** also reflects a hierarchy of importance: both lay judges and judges clearly considered personal qualities the most important, and external factors were regarded as the least important. Therefore, the preferences of professional and lay judges in this regard hardly differ from one another.

The prioritisation of quality criteria also highlights that it aligns with the expectations of the judicial system if there is no strong emphasis on striving for strict social representation in the selection process.

---

[48] In our data analysis, we noticed that this critical stance is age-dependent: the proportion of those preferring judicial selection increases as one moves from the older to the younger age groups (60 years and older: 54%, 50–59 years: 65%, 35–49 years: 68%). There was also an interesting correlation with the lay judges' place of residence: the highest preference for judicial selection was found at the "ends" of the settlement hierarchy (among those living in the capital city and rural areas), where 66% and 72% respectively favoured judicial selection.

Table 2. The Three Foremost Criteria for the Selection of Lay Judges (%)

	Lay judges %	Judges%
The candidate’s life experiences	23.2	25.1
The candidate’s applicable professional expertise	18.3	23.5
The candidate’s independent way of thinking	18.3	18.6
The candidate’s level of education	16.0	15.2
The candidate’s familiarity with issues related to the role of a lay judge	10.7	8.4
The candidate’s adaptability and interpersonal skills	5.4	3.4
The candidate’s civic engagement, acceptance, and support within the community	5.9	3.1
The candidate’s local reputation	1.2	1.5
Other considerations	0.9	1.2
The optimal solution would be a random selection	0.1	0.0
Total:	100.0	100.0

Figure 2. The Importance of Criteria in the Selection of Lay Judges

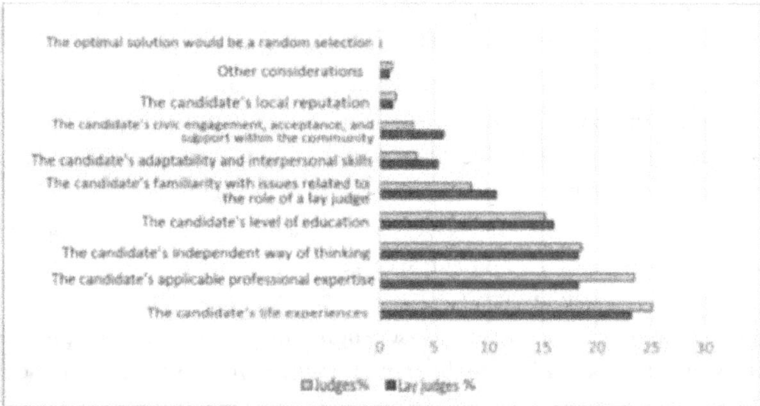

In light of these experiences, it may be worthwhile to engage in a professional debate on the method of selecting lay judges and to take a stance on the importance of social representativeness. If social representativeness is deemed significant, there should also be a discussion on how to select lay judges in a way that harmonizes the expectations of the judicial organization with the requirements of societal representation.

III.2 THE ACTUAL SOCIAL REPRESENTATION OF LAY JUDGES

In the case of the Hungarian lay judge system, it can be stated that there is no trace of an effort to achieve representativeness in the relevant selection laws, despite the fact that the current system of lay judges was specifically established to ensure social oversight. While the involvement of civil organizations and local governments in the selection process could theoretically lay the groundwork for some degree of representativeness, there are no technical mechanisms in place to enforce it. Since the study conducted by Kálmán Kulcsár, there has been virtually no research on this subject—a gap this analysis seeks to address.

Representativeness, in general, is, of course, difficult to define, and it must be emphasized that it is impossible to ensure fully representative representation from every perspective. As Kulcsár puts it: "The lay judge sitting on the judicial panel does not represent society as a whole, but rather a particular segment of society in multiple dimensions."[49] Accordingly, when exploring the social representativeness of lay judges, we must define the characteristics that are important from the perspective of lay adjudication, according to which we assess representativeness. These criteria largely align with those studied by Kulcsár, and thus, we will study the composition of lay judges in terms of gender, age, education, occupation, active-inactive employment status, as well as membership in national or ethnic groups, to understand how well these aspects reflect the social composition of the elected lay judges.

III.2.1 Representativeness by Age

In Hungary today, a lay judge may be a Hungarian citizen who is over 30 but under 70 years of age, has a clean criminal record, is of sound mind with legal capacity, and is not under any exclusion of public affairs. They must have taken the judicial oath and have proven their clean criminal record with an official certificate of good conduct.[50] This regulation inherently limits age-based representativeness by excluding individuals aged 18–29 and those over 70 from the possibility of becoming lay judges.

---

[49] Kulcsár 1971. 127. p.

[50] Sections 212(1), 214(3), 18(1), and 220(1)(d) of Act CLXII of 2011 on the Status and Remuneration of Judges (Act on the Status and Remuneration of Judges).

Therefore, from this perspective, we can only speak of a "limited" social representativeness. Naturally, there is a rationale behind why the regulation is structured this way, as Kulcsár also mentions: "To properly carry out the function of a lay judge, reaching a certain age is desirable. What is expected from lay judges in their participation in adjudication is precisely the experience of a layperson, in contrast to legal expertise, and acquiring such experience is, in itself, time-dependent."[51] Thus, the presence of life experience is important for lay judges, which implies an older age. However, Kulcsár, based on the results of his 1966 study, already noted that "the age distribution still skews too heavily towards the oldest age groups." He did not provide precise data, only stating that the proportion of those over 50 was higher than that of those under 50. In 2016, fifty years later, while we cannot claim that the age distribution of lay judges matches the data from our study (due to the lack of representativeness in the study), it is clear that the "lay judge corps" has not become younger over time. In fact, it may even be reasonable to state that it has aged compared to the situation in 1966. Although the lower age limit for being elected a lay judge is 30, not a single lay judge under the age of 35 responded to our survey, suggesting that there are likely few young judges in this age group. The proportion of those under 50 is only 6.4%, while those over 60 make up 72.5%, which shows a significant shift, even when assuming that older individuals (retirees) may have more free time and therefore a greater willingness to respond.

Table 3. Age Group Distribution of Lay Judges

<table>
<tr><th></th><th>Valid %</th><th>Aggregate %</th></tr>
<tr><td>35–39 years</td><td>0.9</td><td rowspan="5">27.5</td></tr>
<tr><td>40–44 years</td><td>1.8</td></tr>
<tr><td>45–49 years</td><td>3.8</td></tr>
<tr><td>50–54 years</td><td>6.1</td></tr>
<tr><td>55–59 years</td><td>14.9</td></tr>
<tr><td>60–64 years</td><td>38</td><td rowspan="2">72.5</td></tr>
<tr><td>65 years or older</td><td>34.5</td></tr>
<tr><td>Total:</td><td>100</td><td>100</td></tr>
</table>

[51] Kulcsár 1971.,127. p.

Figure 3. Age Group Composition of Lay Judges

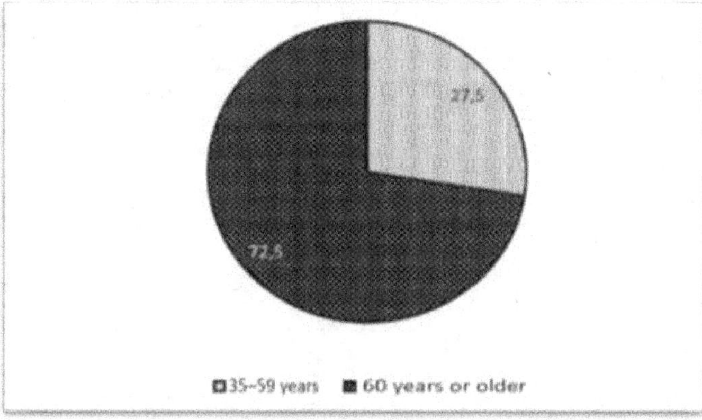

According to the 2011 census data[52], the proportion of the population in the 60–69 age group was 11.8%, which is significantly lower than the proportion observed in our study. Therefore, it can be confidently stated that, in terms of age composition, there is a strong distortion in terms of social representativeness, which reflects an underrepresentation of younger age groups and an overrepresentation of older ones.

III.2.2 A Labour Market Status: Active vs. Inactive Lay Judges

The age composition of the lay judges (with a high proportion of those over 60) already suggests a shift in the active-inactive ratio towards the inactive group. Of the lay judges who responded to the survey, 74.2% are retired, 16.9% are employed (working full or part-time or self-employed), 1.8% are occasional workers, 1.5% are unemployed, and for 5.6%, we have no information. However, it is likely that they also belong to the inactive group (e.g., homemakers, family helpers, etc.).

[52] 011 Census, National Data. Central Statistical Office KSH, Budapest, 2013. (http://mek.oszk.hu/11500/11517/11517.pdf)

Table 4. Composition of Lay Judges by Employment Status

	Valid %	Aggregate %
Works full-time	12.1	
Works part-time	3	
Works in own business	1.8	16.9
Works while receiving a pension	11.8	
Pensioner (old-age pension)	55.3	
Widow's pensioner	1.5	74.2
Partially disabled (with a disability pension), Disability pensioner	5.6	
Works on a contract or occasional basis	1.8	3.3
Unemployed	1.5	
Other	5.6	5.6
Total:	100	100

Figure 4. Composition of Lay Judges by Employment Status

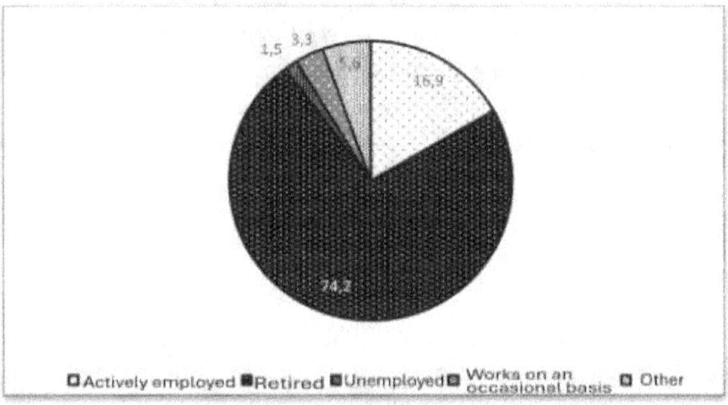

If we also take into account those who work while receiving a pension and thus cannot be considered "classically inactive," the proportion of inactive individuals—including the unemployed—still stands at 62.4%. Kálmán Kulcsár finds the high proportion of retirees in the lay judge system problematic for two reasons. First, "the value system, social views, etc., carried by retired lay judges, due to generational reasons, may already differ from those of other layers of society. The difference in itself is not necessarily a problem, but the proportion is, because it means that the perspective of retired lay judges [...] becomes reflected as the societal view within the court's environment.[53] As early as the late 1960s,

[53] Kulcsár 1971. 127. p.

Kulcsár warned of the differences in values, norms, knowledge, and worldviews between younger and older generations. He considered it dangerous if any particular group — in this case, the retirees — represented and asserted its views in court decisions to a significantly greater extent than their proportion in society.

If we examine generational differences today, we can confidently say that the gap between retirees and younger generations is much wider compared to the mid to late 1960s. In fact, we can even state that a strong differentiation has occurred between generations, with distinct groups such as Generation Y, Generation Z, and so on. The worldviews, values, norms, and knowledge of these generations differ from one another, which makes the issue of social representativeness even more pronounced today than it was at the end of the 1960s.

Kulcsár's other concern regarding the high proportion of retirees among lay judges is that "the 'aging' or 'retirement' of lay judges does not benefit the social prestige of the lay judicial function, and it also affects the 'feedback' of judicial work to the societal environment." If we accept Kulcsár's argument that the high proportion of retirees leads to a decline in the prestige of lay judges, and we examine the change in the proportion of retirees among them, we can state that the proportion of retirees among lay judges has increased since the 1966 figures (46–47%). Therefore, further loss of prestige for the lay judiciary remains a realistic threat.

III.2.3 Educational Qualifications

In the 1966 study, there is no data on the educational qualifications of lay judges, but we can infer it from the occupational data. In the capital, the proportion of industrial and agricultural workers among lay judges was 51.8%, while in rural areas, it was 63.9%. The majority of these individuals were likely unskilled or had vocational training. Kulcsár Kálmán determined the proportion of intellectual workers among lay judges to be 38.4% in Budapest and 19.7% in rural areas. However, we cannot be entirely certain that intellectual occupations corresponded to higher educational qualifications, as during this period, many individuals held intellectual jobs—sometimes even leadership positions—without the necessary formal education. In terms of the representativeness of educational qualifications, the current national data can serve as a useful reference. In 2015, the distribution was as follows[54]: among individuals aged 15 and older, 23.77% had no formal vocational qualification (either having completed only eight years of primary school or less), 23.98% had vocational qualifications (completed vocational or technical school), 32.02% had completed secondary education (graduated from secondary grammar school), and 20.23% held a university degree. In our study, the lay judges responding to the survey are comparable to the national data in only one educational qualification category—the proportion of those with a secondary school diploma is 31.5%, which is very close to the actual national figure of 32.02%. However, significant differences can be observed in the other two educational qualification categories when compared to national data. The proportion of those without a secondary school diploma (including those with no vocational training or with vocational qualifications) is 47.75% nationally (although in reality, this is slightly lower for the adult population, as those under 18 attending high school are counted with only 8 years of primary school education). However, there is a notable difference when it comes to the lay judges, as only 4.4% of them do not have a secondary school diploma. In terms of those with a university degree, the proportion among lay judges is 64.1%, compared to the national figure of 20.23%, which may actually be higher in the adult population, as university students may have a secondary school diploma instead of a university degree.

In terms of educational qualifications, the "middle" is representative, but the two "ends" show strong distortion: the proportion of those without a secondary school diploma is significantly lower, while the proportion of university graduates is approximately three times higher than the national average. Just as the argument regarding age suggested that a higher age among lay judges is somewhat justified due to life experience, the same reasoning may apply to educational qualifications. A higher level of education could also be seen as justifiable, as the meaningful execution of lay judge duties requires knowledge, the understanding of cause-and-effect relationships, and awareness, which higher educational qualifications may better provide.

[54] www.ksh.hu/docs/hun/xstadat/xstadat_eves/i_qlf015.html (2015.12.11.)

Table 5. Educational Qualifications of Lay Judges

	Valid %	Aggregate %	
Eight grades of primary school	0.9		
Vocational school, vocational training	0.9	4.4	Not graduated
Vocational training school	2.6		
Vocational secondary school diploma	14.7	31.5	Secondary school graduate
Secondary school diploma	16.8		
College diploma or higher vocational education	43.2		
University degree	20.9	64.1	Degree holder
Total:	100		

Figure 5. Educational Qualifications of Lay Judges

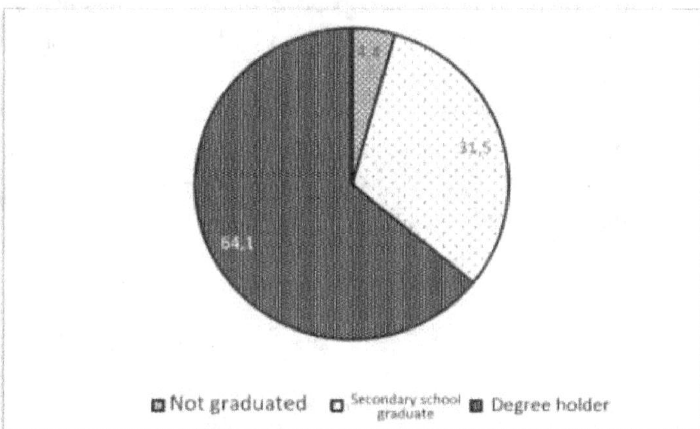

III.2.4 The Current Work Division Status – In the Case of Retirees, the Most Recent One

The educational qualification data (with 64.1% holding degrees and 31.5% having completed secondary education) suggests that, in terms of occupation, those with intellectual professions will constitute a strong majority compared to manual workers. In his 1966 study, Kálmán Kulcsár already observed that manual workers were underrepresented among lay judges, both in the capital and in the countryside, whereas those in intellectual professions were overrepresented in both regions. However, the distortions were by no means as pronounced as they are today. In Budapest, the proportion of manual workers was 59%, while among the elected lay judges, it was 51.8%. In the countryside, their proportion was 82.2%, yet only 63.9% of the elected lay judges came from this group. In contrast, the proportion of those in intellectual professions was higher among the elected judges than their actual societal representation would have justified. In Budapest, 27.3% of the population worked in intellectual professions, whereas among the elected lay judges, this figure was 38.4%. In the countryside, the proportion was 11.1% in the general population, while it stood at 19.7% among the elected lay judges. It is undeniable that we must consider the changes that have occurred in the occupational structure since then. Since 1966, a significant shift has taken place in the proportions of physical and intellectual workers in Hungary. The percentage of manual workers has decreased, while the proportion of those in intellectual professions has increased, though not to the extent observed among lay judges. When considering the occupations of the respondents, 73.2% are classified as intellectual workers, with the majority holding leadership positions – 28.9% in senior or middle management, and 17.3% in lower managerial or supervisory roles. The proportion of manual workers, however, is only 4.5%. This figure remains very low, even if we assume that all those who selected "other" are manual workers, which is unlikely, as there are certainly some intellectual workers among them as well.

Table 6. Occupation and Position of the Lay Judges

	Valid %	Aggregate %
Senior or middle manager	28.9	73.2
Lower-level manager, supervisor	17.3	
Administrative officer	19.9	
Clerical-administrative worker	7.1	
Skilled worker	3.9	4.5
Semi-skilled or unskilled worker	0.6	
Other	22.3	22.3
Total:	100	100

Figure 6. Occupations and Positions of Lay Judges

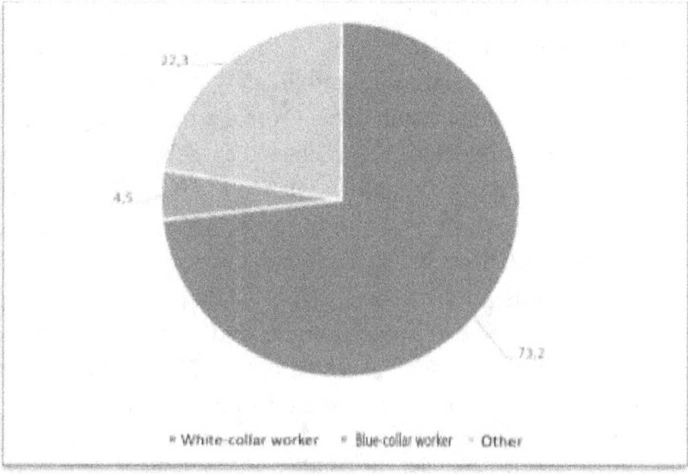

The trend observed by Kálmán Kulcsár in the 1966 study—where intellectual professionals were already overrepresented among lay judges compared to their actual proportion in society—has continued to this day. This was the case even during a period when political considerations emphasised the participation of worker peasants. While the exact ratios may differ from those revealed in this study—given its non-representative nature—it is highly likely that intellectual professionals are significantly overrepresented among lay judges, whereas physical labourers are substantially underrepresented.

Two occupational fields stand out among the professions (or former professions) from which lay judges are predominantly drawn: 1) public administration and politics (20.1%) and 2) culture, education, science, and the church (29%). All other occupational fields account for less than 10% each. Regarding employment sectors, the public sector (as public employees, civil servants, etc.) is dominant, representing 68.4% of lay judges. Those employed in the private sector (at corporations such as joint-stock companies, limited partnerships, or limited liability companies) constitute 28%, while only 3.6% are employed in the civil sector (e.g., at foundations, former public benefit companies, or associations).

III.2.5 Male and Female Lay Judges

The 1966 study revealed that men were overrepresented among lay judges both in Budapest and in rural areas. In Budapest, the proportion of male lay judges exceeded their actual societal ratio by approximately 8%, while in rural areas, the disparity was even greater, at around 19%. Over the past fifty years, the gender composition of Hungarian society has remained largely unchanged, with men accounting for roughly 47–48% and women 52–53% of the population—a balance that continues to reflect the ratios observed half a century ago. However, two significant shifts have occurred regarding the gender composition of lay judges. Firstly, in contrast to the 1966 figures, women are now overrepresented compared to their actual societal proportion. Secondly, this overrepresentation is substantial, as the survey data indicates that nearly 71% of the responding lay judges are women, marking a notable deviation from their societal ratio.

Table 7. Gender Distribution of Lay Judges

	Valid %
Male	29.2
Female	70.8
Total:	100

Figure 7. Gender Distribution of Lay Judges

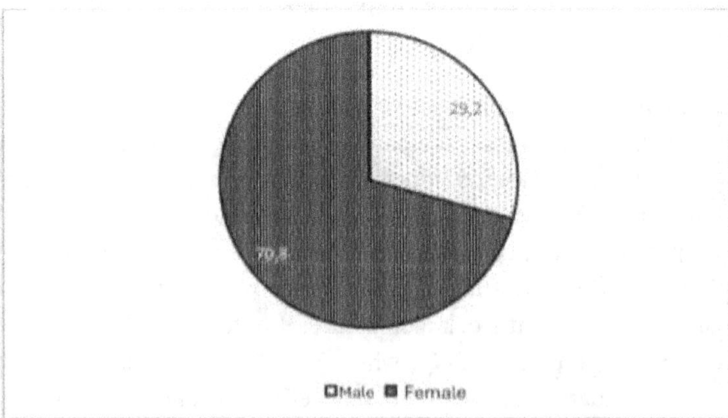

During his study, Kálmán Kulcsár made an observation regarding the gender composition of lay judges that extended beyond the mere data. He interpreted the distribution as an indicator of social activity, stating that, despite formal equality, the data pointed towards "the stabilisation of women's civic passivity."[55] Today's data reveal a significantly different gender distribution, reflecting a pronounced numerical dominance of women. But does this truly represent overrepresentation, and if so, can it be interpreted as an indicator of "activity"? From a demographic perspective, we can indeed speak of overrepresentation, even acknowledging that nearly three-quarters (72%) of lay judges are aged 60 or older, and that within this age group, the proportion of women slightly exceeds 60% (60.2%). However, this alone does not fully account for the 71% female composition among lay judges. Another key factor to consider is the prominent role of teaching qualifications and experience in lay judge work (and seemingly even in the nomination process). Nearly 30% (28.4%) of lay judges reported that their pedagogical knowledge and qualifications were most beneficial to their judicial responsibilities. Among those with such a teaching background, 77% were women. This feminisation of the teaching profession aligns with indirect evidence and comparable data from a representative survey conducted two decades ago.[56] From a purely demographic standpoint, the overrepresentation of women cannot yet be fully explained, but when we take into account the pedagogical factor, we can begin to understand the disproportionate number of women. The question remains, however, to what extent this reflects an increase in women's social activity. To determine this, a deeper understanding of the nomination process would be required.

III.2.6 Participation of National and Ethnic Minorities in Lay Judge Work

According to the 2011 census data, the proportion of national and ethnic minorities in Hungary was 6.5%[57], determined by the "self-identification" method for the 13 recognized national and ethnic minorities. Among the lay judges, 4.8% of respondents indicated belonging to a national or ethnic group, which at first glance does not differ significantly from the national rate of 6.5%.

---

[55] Kulcsár 1971. 55. p.

[56] A nationally representative survey conducted in 1996 (N=2411) found that 75.3% of teachers and educators working in primary and secondary educational institutions were women. In the age group of 20–39 years at the time (now 40–59 years), the percentage of women was 76.7%, while in the 40–59-year age group (now 60–79 years), the proportion of women was 74.3%. See Deák, Zsuzsa – Nagy, Mária: Társadalmi és szakmai mobilitás = http://ofi.hu/tudastar/tanari-palya/tarsadalmi-szakmai (2016. 09. 15.)

[57] Census, Central Statistical Office (KSH), Budapest 2013. (http://mek.oszk.hu/11500/11517/11517.pdf)

Table 8. The Lay Judges' Belonging to National and Ethnic Minorities

	Valid %
I do not belong	95.2
Yes, I belong	4.8
Total:	100

Figure 8. A The Lay Judges' Belonging to National and Ethnic Minorities

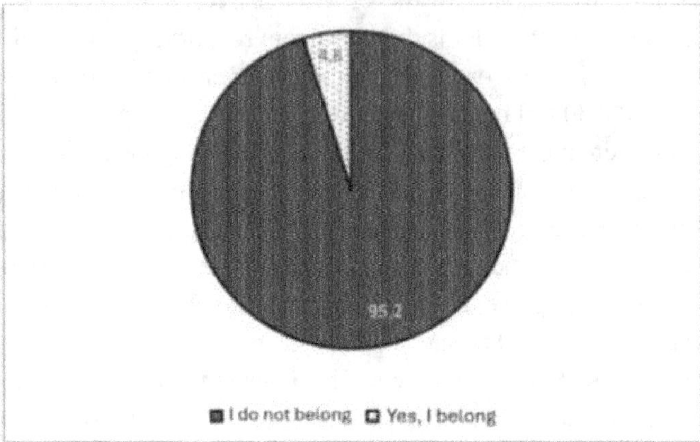

A more detailed regional analysis, however, revealed that out of the 16 individuals who identified themselves as belonging to a minority group, 10 were lay judges at the Békés County Court, while the remaining respondents were from four other counties (1 person from each) and 2 from courts in the capital. This suggests that there may be significant regional differences in this regard, which is naturally related to the territorial distribution of national minorities within Hungary. There are counties where, similar to Békés County, the number of respondents was high, but no one indicated belonging to a national or ethnic group. At the same time, in Békés County, which has a relatively significant Romanian and Slovak minority, 13% of respondents (10 individuals) identified as belonging to some ethnic minority (four of them Romanian and three Slovak).

What about the largest domestic minority, the Roma? In our sample, only two lay judges identified as Roma, which corresponds to a 0.6% representation (out of 348 respondents, 332 answered the question regarding ethnic minority affiliation). How should we assess this ratio? When it comes to the Roma population, we can refer to both the figures from the 2011 census, based on self-reporting, and research estimates. According to self-reporting, there are 315,000 Roma (3.2%), while research estimates suggest there are between 650,000 and 750,000 Roma (6.5–7.5%).[58] Since our research, by definition, was based on "self-reporting," for methodological reasons, we must examine the representation of Roma in the jury work based on the census data. Based on our calculations, considering the age structure of the Roma population[59] the age composition of those participating in lay judge work,196 the modest 0.6% representation found in our research is approximately half of the statistically "expected" 1.4% ratio. The "missing" 0.8% can clearly be explained by the fact that, in terms of the preferred level of education for lay judges, the educational indicators of the Roma population are significantly less favourable. As we have seen, 95% of lay judges have a high school diploma or a degree, while calculations based on the relevant data from the 2011 census show that only 7.0% of Roma (those identifying as Roma) in the 20–79 age group have completed secondary education or hold a degree.

Based on the data, we can say that representatives of national and ethnic minorities *are present* in the courts as lay judges and are not excluded from this role. However, their actual representation is likely somewhat lower than the approximately five percent we measured. This actual representation may show significant regional differences: "objectively," it could be linked to the ethnic composition of the region, but "subjectively," the practices (and preferences) of the institutional actors involved in the nomination process could also play a role, varying from region to region.

[58] There is no space to elaborate on the fact that, based on self-reporting, we significantly underestimate the proportion of Roma, nor to discuss the occasionally substantial differences in the magnitude of researcher estimates, which can be attributed to differing classification logics.

[59] The proportion of lay judges under the age of 60 is 28%, while the proportion of those aged 60 and older is 72%.

IV. THE PRINCIPAL CHARACTERISTICS OF THE STATUS OF A LAY JUDGE

We aim to present the status of a lay judge through several key characteristics: two **organisational indicators** (the ***judicial body*** and the ***area of law*** in which the lay judge operates), two **procedural indicators** (the ***number of terms served*** and the ***cases handled*** thus far), one **professional affiliation** indicator (membership in a lay judges' association), and one **expertise/qualification** indicator (relevant professional knowledge).

A key methodological challenge of the entire data collection process concerning lay judges was the failure of the planned comprehensive survey due to well-known reasons, such as administrative obstruction, suspension, or interruption. As a "result" of this, the sample suffered its most severe distortion in terms of regional distribution: in certain counties[60], the questionnaire never reached the organisations of lay judges, while in others[61], only a minimal number of respondents (1–6 individuals) provided answers. Although this offers a sociologically revealing snapshot of the "field of obstruction" at the time, it must be made explicitly clear that, from a methodological perspective, the data collection cannot be considered representative of the lay judge population.

IV.1 THE DISTRIBUTION BY JUDICIAL ORGANISATIONS/TYPES

Nevertheless, there is one fundamental indicator for which the composition of our sample, despite the regional distortion, closely approximates the composition of the lay judge community, and that is the issue of the judicial organisation. On the website of the Hungarian Association of Lay Judges, there was previously a report (titled The Number of Lay Judges in Hungary – The 2011–2015 Term), which listed, by county, the number of lay judges working alongside various courts (regional courts, district courts, Budapest-Capital district courts, and labour

[60] The counties of Baranya, Bács-Kiskun, Jász-Nagykun-Szolnok, Tolna, Vas, Veszprém, Zala

[61] The counties of Fejér, Hajdú-Bihar, Komárom-Esztergom, Somogy, Szabolcs-Szatmár-Bereg

courts)[62] with the caveat that data for thirty courts was not available. We were able to estimate the total number of lay judges and their distribution by judicial organisations based on this list by substituting the missing headcount data with the average value for the respective judicial organisation. According to our calculations, in the last "Belle Époque" term, 4,312,[63] lay judges were active, of whom 4,285 were reported as active[64]according to the website.

The distribution of lay judges across court organisations, when compared with the data from the questionnaire survey, revealed that our sample remarkably approximated the actual distribution. The proportion of ***district courts***[65] and ***Budapest-Capital district courts*** in the sample nearly mirrored the real figures, with district courts comprising 52 percent instead of 51, and Budapest-Capital district courts 5 percent rather than 6. However, a notable underrepresentation was observed for ***regional courts*** (15 percent instead of 23), while ***labour courts*** showed a similar degree of overrepresentation (29 percent instead of 19).

Table 9. Weighting of the Sample by Court Organisations

COURT ORGANISATION	Hungarian Association of Lay Judges Report (%)	Data Collection (%)	Case Number in Weighted Sample	Composition of Weighted Sample (%)
Regional Courts	23	15	73	23.6
Budapest-Capital District Courts	6	5	20	6.5
District Courts	51	52	158	51.1
Labour Courts	19	29	58	18.8
			309	

[62] A total of 149 courts were included in the study. Among them, 32 courts had missing data: 2 out of 20 regional courts, 28 out of 103 municipal courts, and 2 out of 20 labour courts. The national number of lay judges was estimated by substituting the missing data with the average for regional courts, municipal courts, and labour courts, respectively.

[63] 200 Nevertheless, the Hungarian Association of Lay Judges' website, in its "Facts and Interesting Information" section, noted that "there are currently around 4,800 lay judges." It cites a figure of 4,800 lay judges. http://www.ulnokok.hu/az-ülnöki-intézmény- története.aspx

[64] The inactivity is primarily explained by resignations, illnesses, and the deactivation due to a lack of cases.

[65] The Hungarian Association of Lay Judges' report still includes the term "municipal court."

Figure 9. The Distribution of the Hungarian Association of Lay Judges Register and the Sample by Court Organisations (Percentage)

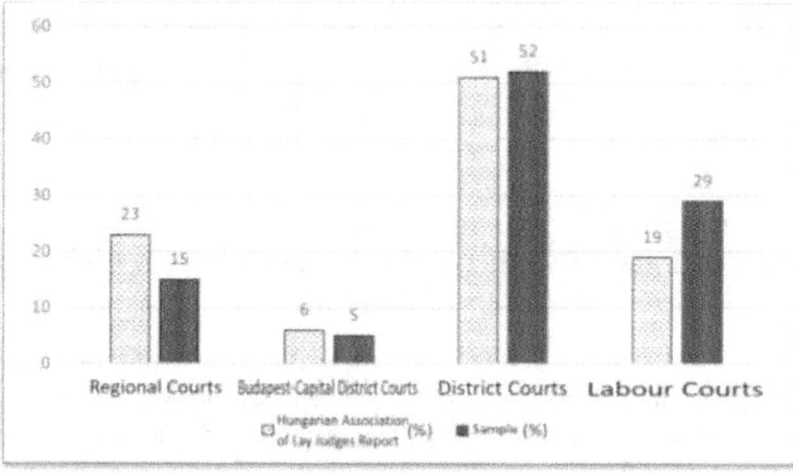

With knowledge of the extent of the discrepancies, we saw an opportunity to weight the sample to align with the figures in the Hungarian Association of Lay Judges" report. Therefore, in the analyses presented here, we use the data from the weighted sample, which reflects this **organisational representativity**.[66]

We must also address an additional methodological challenge that arises when we seek to explain the underlying causes of lay judges' opinions, votes, preferences, and so on. Instead of focusing on individual justifications, we explore the correlations with background variables (such as socio-demographic factors and indicators of lay judge status) as a form of explanation. In such instances, we are essentially conducting what is known as ecological analysis. Even if we uncover correlations of varying strength, we must not interpret these as causal explanations. Therefore, group-level data cannot be automatically used to explain the decisions of individuals within that group, as these decisions are inherently

[66] When presenting the research data, we must note that, due to the small sample size, discussing percentage distributions for certain subgroups may be problematic. Therefore, we adopt the solution of highlighting when the data pertains to small subgroups. Subgroups of 50–69 individuals are marked with one asterisk, subgroups of 20–49 with two asterisks, and those under 20 with three asterisks. In these cases, it is methodologically problematic to speak of percentage distributions; it is more realistic to state how many members of the small group belong to one category or another (e.g., an opinion group). The exact sizes of the sample subgroups are provided separately in the table on pages ... (APPENDIX).

multifactorial. Should we attempt this, we would be assuming the risk of what the literature refers to as ecological fallacy. Nonetheless, the "ecological" correlations we uncover remain valuable, particularly when they consistently align with the opinions we are investigating. In the following sections, we will first present the overall patterns revealed by the sample (the basic distributions), and then examine how these relate to the background variables featured in the questionnaire.

IV.2 ADDITIONAL INDICATORS OF THE LAY JUDGE STATUS: AREA OF LAW, NUMBER OF TERMS, AND NUMBER OF CASES HEARD

IV.2.1 At the time of the research, no official data (or unofficial report) was available regarding the distribution of lay judges by **area of law**. However, based on the responses received, the composition that emerged can be regarded as a good reflection of the actual situation. The proportions align with the principles of the legal regulation of the lay judge system, according to which lay judges primarily serve in criminal cases, labour disputes, and, in certain instances, civil cases. Of every five lay judges, four were involved in criminal cases, while their involvement in labour cases was considerably smaller (only a quarter), and their role in civil cases can be described as truly minimal.

There is a relatively small group of lay judges (approximately one in every seven in our sample, or 15 percent) who have served in multiple areas of law. Among them, the combination of criminal and civil cases accounts for nearly two-thirds of their cases.

Table 10. The Distribution of Lay Judges by Area of Law

AREA OF LAW	Percentage (%)[67]
Criminal	80.9
Civil**	10.7
Labour*	21.6
Other (Administrative)	1.8
MIXED AREAS OF LAW	
Criminal/Civil	24 individuals
Criminal/Labour	11 individuals
Criminal/Civil/Labour	4 individuals
Criminal/Other	3 individuals
Labour/Other	3 individuals

Figure 10. The Percentage Distribution of Lay Judges by Area of Lawa

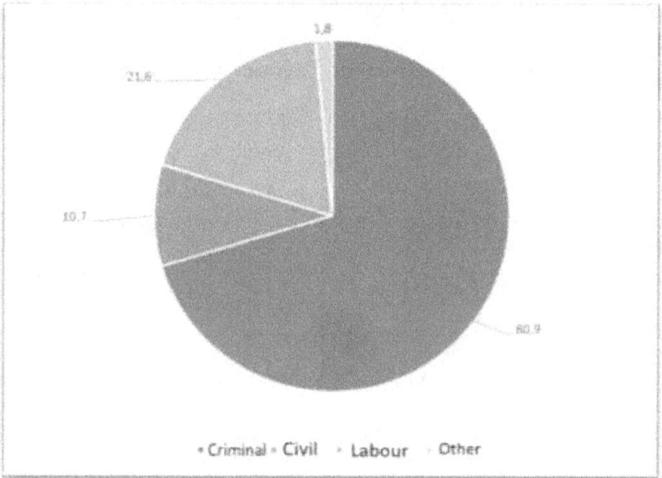

[67] 203 When presenting the research data, we must note that, due to the small sample size, discussing percentage distributions for certain subgroups may be problematic. Therefore, we adopt the solution of highlighting when the data pertains to small subgroups. Subgroups of 50–69 individuals are marked with one asterisk, subgroups of 20–49 with two asterisks, and those under 20 with three asterisks. In these cases, it is methodologically problematic to speak of percentage distributions; it is more realistic to state how many members of the small group belong to one category or another (e.g., an opinion group). The exact sizes of the sample subgroups are provided separately in the table on pages ... (APPENDIX).

IV.2.2 The mandate of a lay judge spans four-year ***cycles***. However, as some individuals have fulfilled this role for several decades, it is entirely plausible that they have served through six, seven, or even more such cycles.[68] Such longevity, however, is exceptionally rare, as the vast majority of lay judges serve for only two to three cycles, a trend reflected in the average number of cycles per lay judge, which stands at 2.3.

When examining the court organisations, the number of cycles is slightly below average among lay judges at the Budapest-Capital district courts*** (1.9), while it is somewhat above average (2.6) for those serving in administrative and labour courts*. The greatest deviation from the average is observed among lay judges participating the civil cases**, who have a relatively high value of 3.6 cycles.

In terms of the number of cycles served, the community of lay judges can be divided into three similarly sized groups.

Table 11. Duration of Lay Judges' Service Across Judicial Cycles

Number of Cycles Category	Proportion (%)
One cycle	31.1
Two cycles	36.1
Three or more cycles	32.9
Three cycles*	19.6
At least four cycles**	13.3
Average	2.3

Figure 11. Duration of Lay Judges' Service Across Judicial Cycles

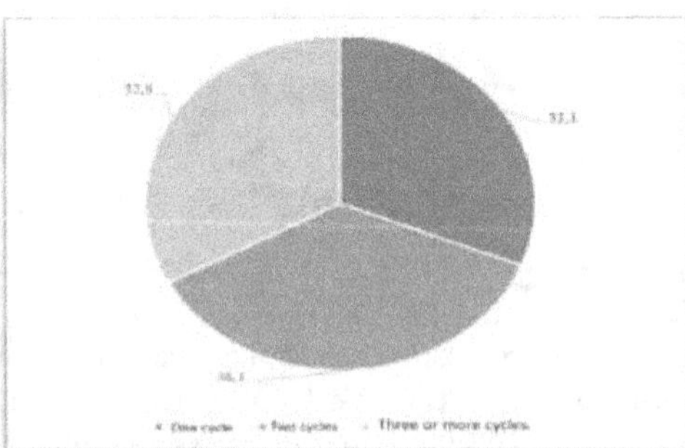

[68] In the sample, three individuals reported having served eight cycles, while one individual each indicated nine and ten cycles, respectively.

This tertile distribution is similar across nearly all lay judge categories, with the exception of those in the civil area of law**, where the majority are serving at least their third cycle.[69]

IV.2.3 The **number of cases** a lay judge has participated in can serve as a good indicator of their judicial experience. While it is unlikely that continuous statistics have been maintained on this, the lay judges themselves were able to provide relatively realistic estimates—excluding a few respondents[70] who reported improbably high figures. Based on these estimates, our calculations indicate that the average number of cases they have participated in approaches one hundred.[71]

Table 12. Judicial Experience of Lay Judges

Case Number Category	Proportion (%)
"Trainees" (1–10 cases)*	23.4
"No Longer Beginners" (11–30 cases)	30.5
"Experienced" (31–100 cases)	27.9
"Highly Experienced" (more than 100 cases)*	18.2
Average	~90

Figure 12. Judicial Experience of Lay Judges

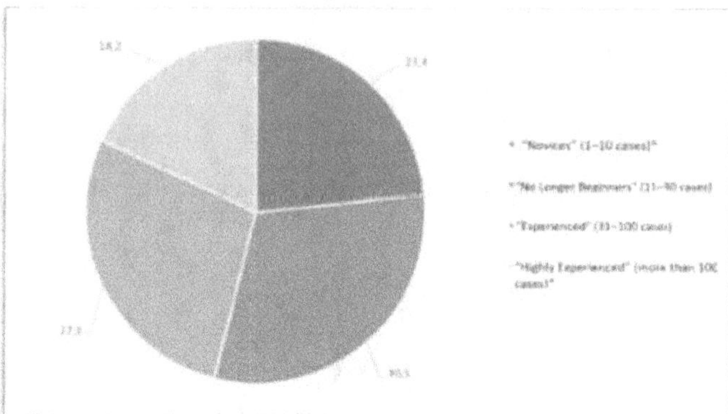

[69] 19 out of 32 individuals, approximately 60 percent.

[70] Those who responded in this manner were likely either joking or, fearing that providing accurate data might compromise their anonymity (as the survey was, of course, completed anonymously), entered figures in the thousands.

[71] By replacing the improbably high values with the average calculated without them, we determined an average of 90.

The distribution of lay judges based on experience differs strikingly in *administrative and labour courts** compared to other court types. Among these judges, the proportion of relatively less experienced individuals (those with a maximum of 30 cases) is remarkably low—just 13 percent compared to the average of 54 percent. Conversely, the proportion of highly experienced judges is exceptionally high—87 percent as opposed to the average of 46 percent. A similar pattern can be observed among lay judges specializing in the labour area of law*, with an experience ratio of 16 percent to 84 percent.

IV.3 THE ISSUE OF ROTATION

We considered it important to gain an understanding of the ***continuity*** of lay judges' work—specifically, the extent of rotation within the system during judicial cycle changes. Since our research was conducted during a cycle transition, we were able to determine what proportion of lay judges finish their service and what proportion wish to continue. It appears that lay judging requires a strong commitment, as the vast majority (83 percent) are eager to take on the responsibilities it entails.

Table 13. Lay Judge Rotation

Rotation	Proportion (%)
Departing * (52 individuals)	16.9
Continuing	83.1

Figure 13. Lay Judge Rotation

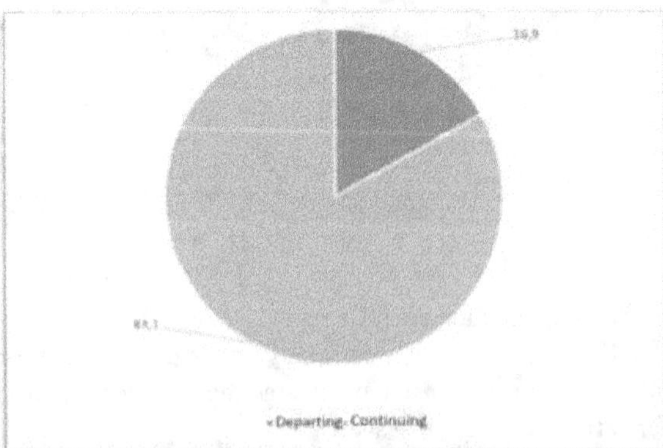

Despite the overall strong intention to continue, it is interesting to explore whether there is a group of lay judges where the desire to continue is less pronounced, meaning a higher proportion opts to conclude their service. From the perspective of those who decide to finish, we can observe that the average completion rate (17 percent) is somewhat higher (21 percent) among the youngest group, i.e., those aged 35 to 49***.

It is also higher among those with a secondary school diploma (25.5 percent), non-graduates (23.4 percent), those coming from the public administration and law enforcement sector* (25.0 percent), "one-cycle" judges (29.0 percent), as well as those with four or more cycles of experience** (24.4 percent), and "novices," that is, those who have only participated in 1–10 cases (23.2 percent).

The "attrition" may, of course, have a variety of personal reasons, but from the above, we can see that it primarily occurs among those who, relatively young, tried out lay judging for a single cycle and likely did not find the experience compelling enough to motivate further commitment. At the same time, this suggests that those who choose to continue[72] are increasingly becoming more committed to the role of lay judge.

IV.4 THE "BACKGROUND KNOWLEDGE" OF LAY JUDGES

Becoming a lay judge, of course, does not require **legal expertise**; however, it is undoubtedly advantageous if the individual has some level of knowledge or experience in the field of law. We found that two out of every five lay judges possess such a background. Upon examining this group, we see that their legal expertise primarily stems from two main sources: on the one hand, through their studies, and on the other, through the nature of their work (or workplace), which has provided them with legal knowledge.

Studies, of course, rarely represent a classical legal qualification (only six individuals in the sample had such a background). However, among the lay judges with some legal knowledge, we exceptionally find a law student who is about to graduate (2 individuals), someone with incomplete legal studies (1 individual), and a legal assistant qualification holder (2 individuals). A broader group consists of those who hold a relevant higher education degree in a field that pertains to

[72] Those who have felt the "sting of the locomotive's smoke."

legal knowledge (29 individuals). However, the largest group (64 individuals) consists of those who have had only brief encounters with law, which simply involved taking a legal subject during their studies.

There is a smaller group of lay judges (14 individuals) who acquired their legal knowledge through their work, such as those employed in judicial, prosecutorial, police, municipal, child protection, or similar roles, or through their activities as institutional leaders.

Table 14. Legal Expertise of Lay Judges

LEGAL EXPERTISE	%	
NONE	61.2	
YES	38.8	
Academic-based		87.9
Legal studies (lawyer, legal assistant)		8.1
Other[73](college – higher education) qualifications		25.1
Attended legal subjects		54.7
Work-related		12.1
	100.0	100.0

Among those with legal expertise in the broad sense, the proportion of men (49 percent), those living in the capital (48 percent), individuals under 60 years old (47 percent), graduates (46 percent), those previously or currently working in the public administration and law enforcement sector (73 percent), lay judges from regional courts (52 percent) and administrative and labour courts* (50 percent), as well as members of the Hungarian Association of Lay Judges* (49 percent), exceeded the average (39 percent). The cases in which lay judges participate not only require legal expertise but also **other specialised knowledge or skills**. The vast majority of lay judges (92 percent) described themselves as possessing such knowledge or experience. These were mainly acquired through their work or, quite simply, through life experience. The most prominent expertise (31 percent) is in pedagogy, which is one of the key aspects that can be useful in judicial work, particularly in certain case types (e.g., juvenile cases). Economic-financial (15 percent) and labour law (12 percent) knowledge also hold significant weight. The next most frequent categories include administrative (10 percent), military and law enforcement (8 percent), and technical (7 percent) expertise. Finally, there

[73] Labour, Social Security, Police Force, Public Administration

was a group of lay judges (16 percent) who classified their knowledge or experience under the "other" category but specified what it entailed.

Table 14. Areas of Lay Judges' Expertise

AREA OF EXPERTISE	Proportion (%)
Pedagogical	31.4
Economic, Financial	14.9
Labour Law	12.2
Administrative	9.8
Military, Law Enforcement	8.4
Technical	7.0
Other	16.3

Based on the foregoing, we identified three broad categories of non-legal knowledge or expertise considered beneficial to the work of lay judges: ***humanistic*** (including pedagogical, psychological, healthcare, social, interpersonal, and life experience-related skills); ***administrative*** (encompassing military, law enforcement, administrative, and employment-related knowledge); and ***technical*** (covering economic, financial, and technical fields).

Table 15. The Nature of Lay Judges' Expertise

TYPE OF EXPERTISE	Proportion (%)
"Humanistic"	37.7
"Administrative"	33.4
"Technical"	20.9
"I have no such expertise"	8.0

The ***"humanistic"*** knowledge and experience base is notably more prominent than the average (38%) among lay judges with higher education (48%), those hailing from the public sector (48%), those serving at municipal courts (51%), and among "trainees"* (48%).

The ***"administrative"*** knowledge and experience base is decidedly more prevalent than the average (33%) among lay judges in the capital (43%), those with secondary school qualifications (44%), those who have served for at least three terms (41%), the "highly experienced"* lay judges, and, unsurprisingly, those serving in administrative and labour courts* (59%).

Those possessing ***"technical"*** expertise were represented above the average (21%) among lay judges residing in the capital* (38%) and those serving at regional courts* (38%).

There is a particularly interesting *functional* relationship between "humanistic" and "administrative" expertise and the length of the lay judges' trial experience (the number of cases they have dealt with so far): the more experienced the lay judges are, the more the proportion of "humanistic" knowledge decreases, while the proportion of "administrative" knowledge increases.

Table 16. Rotation and the Nature of Expertise

	Proportion of Non-Legal Background Experts	
EXPERIENCE (Number of Cases)	"Humanistic"	"Administrative"
"Trainees"*	47.8%	19.4%
"No Longer Beginners"	45.3%	30.2%
"Experienced"	31.2%	35.1%
"Highly Experienced"*	25.0%	50.0%

The previously referenced Hungarian Association of Lay Judges (MÜE) report, alongside territorial (counties, cities) and organisational (regional courts, Budapest-Capital district court, municipal courts, labour courts) characteristics, also included two additional criteria. On the one hand, it indicated the number of ***teachers*** (in regional courts, Budapest-Capital district courts, and municipal courts) and ***military*** lay judges (in regional courts) among the elected lay judges. On the other hand, it provided data on the number of minority municipal lay judges (Roma, German, Ukrainian, Bulgarian, Armenian) serving at certain district courts. In the case of courts with missing data,[74] the missing values were replaced by the average, and in 2015, the following estimated distribution emerged, indicating a strong pedagogical dominance in the known specifications.

[74] 29 municipal courts and 3 regional courts.

Table 17. The Specification of Lay Judges

SPECIFICATION OF LAY JUDGES (according to the Hungarian Association of Lay Judges report)	individuals	%
Teacher Lay Judge	961	22.3%
Military Lay Judge	253	5.9%
Minority Municipal Lay Judge	23	0.5%
"General" (or unspecified) Lay Judge	3075	71.3%
Total	4312	100.0%

IV.5 MEMBERSHIP IN AN ASSOCIATION OR THE QUESTION OF COLLECTIVE ACTION

It is entirely self-evident that a working group operating within a particular organisational system has its own distinct interests, especially in the case of subordinate groups within hierarchical organisations. If the members of a group recognise their common interests and take steps to represent (protect, enforce) those interests, the group moves from a state of being "for itself" to a state of being "for the sake of itself," especially when this collective action takes an organisational form. The Hungarian Association of Lay Judges (MÜE) is such an initiative, with the aim of promoting and strengthening the social recognition of lay judicial activities within the justice system. It seeks to facilitate the enforcement of the rights of lay judges and the establishment of a unified practice necessary for this. Its founding was clearly motivated by the experience that the representation and protection of lay judges' interests were in need of support.[75]

Despite the entirely evident and well-intentioned support, only one in five or six lay judges chose to join the association. When compared to the membership of the judges' association (MABIE),[76] this may seem rather low. However, when we look further afield at membership in interest protection organisations (trade unions), it could still be considered quite respectable. For instance, according to a nationally representative survey[77] conducted in 2014, in which the authors

---

[75] There is also the Hungarian Judges' Association (MABIE), which aims to perform the tasks of collective representation and interest protection on behalf of judges.

[76] Of the approximately 2,800 judges, 1,600 are members (a 57% proportion).

[77] Dabis, Erzsébet – Feleky, Gábor – Lőrinczi, János – Rossu, Balázs – Ruzs Molnár, Krisztina: Elemző tanulmány – az új Munka Törvénykönyvének hatásvizsgálata (Független Szakszervezetek Demokratikus Ligája, TÁMOP-2.5.3.C-13/1-2013-0001). 2015. Https://docplayer.hu/4784032Elemzotanulmanyazujmunkatorvenykonyvenekhatasvizsgalata.html

participated,[78] union membership among employees in the private sector was a mere five percent (and even when including former members, the total did not reach twenty percent).

Table 18. Membership of Lay Judges in Associations

ASSOCIATION MEMBERSHIP	Proportion (%)
Hungarian Association of Lay Judges Member* (55 Individuals)	18.2%
Non-member	81.8%

For the sake of historical accuracy, it must be noted that the proportion of Hungarian Association of Lay Judges members is significantly overrepresented among the survey respondents, as in reality, it was at a level of only 2-3%. This overrepresentation in the sample can be attributed to the fact that the Hungarian Association of Lay Judges, recognising the importance of the research, provided substantial assistance with data collection.

Of course, the development of the membership ratio may also be influenced by the stage of organisation or structuring of the interest protection organisation. For example, the Hungarian Judges' Association (MABIE), which was reorganised in 1990, had already had a history of over forty years by the time of data collection, whereas the Hungarian Association of Lay Judges (MÜE) was a relatively new initiative, having been established in 2012. While membership is, of course, a personal decision, we identified several group-level factors within the sample that subtly influenced this choice. With one exception, this influence manifested primarily in slightly higher membership ratios in these subgroups, surpassing the 18% average, though not dramatically. As a result, notable differences emerged when compared to other subgroups.

For instance, among those under 60, the membership rate is 24%, compared to just 16% among those over 60. Among graduates, it is 23%, whereas only 9% of non-graduates are members. Among active workers, the membership rate stands at 30%, compared to 14% among retirees. In the field of human services (currently or previously employed), 14% are members, while 24-27% of those in other sectors (such as production, services, public administration, law enforcement) are members. Among regional court lay judges, 27% are members, compared to only 10% among district court lay judges.

---

[78] Gábor Feleky és János Lőrinczi

The most significant factor, however, was the urban context, which became strikingly evident in the exceptionally high membership rate of the Hungarian Association of Lay Judges (MÜE) among Budapest residents, standing at 49%. This meant that one in every two lay judges living in the capital was a member of the association, a stark contrast to the mere 5% membership rate among lay judges residing in county seats or cities with county rights. It seems almost self-evident to suggest that the Hungarian Association of Lay Judges' organisation was very much a "Budapest-centric concept,"[79] and this had an undeniable impact on recruitment. Yet, the political and organisational sociology behind why this process stalled at the county seat level remains a complex puzzle, particularly when one considers that in other cities, the membership rate among lay judges stood at a relatively strong 18%.

Among the regional court lay judges living in county seats,[80] there was not a single member of the Hungarian Association of Lay Judges, and among district court lay judges in county seats,[81] there were only three. The representation of lay judges living in Budapest is ten times greater than that of those residing in county seats!

Table 19. Residence and Association Membership

RESIDENCE TOWN	Capital	County Seat City	Other City	Village	Total
Membership Rate	49.1%	5.0%	18.1%	5.9%	18.0%

If we examine the membership of the Hungarian Association of Lay Judges based on the location of the courts rather than the place of residence (although, of course, the two are closely related), we observe that the representation from Budapest and Pest County is six times greater than that of other counties.

Table 20. The Court's Seat and Association Membership

THE COURT'S SEAT	Membership Rate (%)
Budapest	49.1
Budapest and Pest County***	49.3
Other Counties	7.4
Other County Seats*	1.5
Other Cities	10.1

[79] Of the 26 founding members, 24 worked at courts in the capital, with 18 at the *Budapest-Capital Regional Court*, 6 at district courts, and 2 at regional courts or municipal courts outside the capital.

[80] They represent one-tenth of the sample (n = 32).

[81] Nearly one-quarter of the sample (n = 71).

Our data suggest that there is no "trickle-down" effect in the search for an institutional form of collective action; the county seats—especially the courts located there—are not participants in this process. However, it is conceivable that this is not due to some organizational-sociological "wave-breaking/blocking" role, but rather can be explained by the known conditions of data collection.

IV.6 OPINIONS ON LAY JUDGE WORK

IV.6.1 The Role of Lay Judge Work

Perhaps the most crucial question of the research was how lay judges perceive the **role of their work** in the administration of justice. Based on the responses obtained, a more ***critical or dissatisfied*** attitude seems to prevail. Just over a third of the lay judges (37 percent) viewed the situation as ideal, supporting the opinion that lay judges play a *significant role* in the administration of justice. However, the majority (55 percent) believed their contribution was only *partial*, while a smaller group (8 percent) saw the system as more of *a formality*, with little substantive impact.

Table 21. The role of lay judge work in the administration of justice

	percentage %
Just a formality	8.1
Plays a role only partially	54.7
Plays a significant role	37.2

Figure 14. The role of lay judge work in the administration of justice

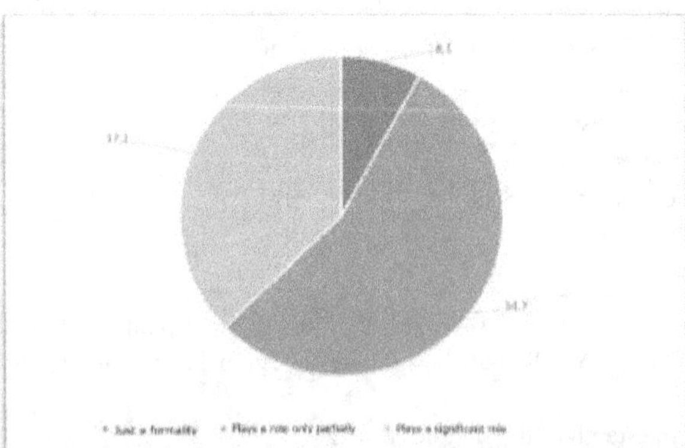

The latter group of opinions (the ***"skeptics"***) appeared at slightly higher rates in certain categories of lay judges: among those who have left lay judge work (16 percent), those working at courts in the capital city (15 percent), lay judges at courts in Pest County (14 percent), those considered beginners in lay judge work[82] (19 percent), and members of the Hungarian Association of Lay Judges (14 percent).

The proportion of those who view the system as functioning well (the ***"satisfied"***) is highest among the "old hands," with the percentage increasing as the length of the lay judges' career progresses: 28 percent among those in their first term, 39 percent among those in their second term, and 45 percent among those who have served at least three terms.

There are no dramatically differing proportions among the subgroups, but it does seem that the most experienced lay judges are considerably less critical compared to those who are new to lay judge work. As the "service time" in the role increases, so does the confidence in the proper functioning of the system.

However, between the skeptics and the satisfied, there is a third group of opinions, whom we can call the ***"moderates,"*** who believe that lay judge work is not merely a formality, but does have some role—albeit not a significant one—in the functioning of the administration of justice.

In fact, this viewpoint is also critical in nature, so it can be said that nearly two-thirds of the lay judges (63 percent) see some degree of problem in the realization of the lay judge function. At the same time, it is quite difficult to pinpoint exactly what fuels this assessment, as the lay judges expressed rather positive evaluations regarding the judges who oversee their work and the working conditions at the courts.[83] The criticism, therefore, seemingly does not stem from the nature of the judge–lay judge relationship, but of course, it cannot be ruled out that the lay judges present this relationship in a more favourable light for self-assessment reasons.

[82] Up until the data collection, they had participated in the hearing of one to ten cases.

[83] The judges' positive assessment is almost unanimous. According to 95 percent of the lay judges, they see the judges more as supportive colleagues rather than obstacles. Expressed in terms of a school grading system, they rated the human relationship between judges and lay judges at 4.7, and they gave the same rating to their satisfaction with the judges' professional work. Their satisfaction with the court facilities provided for lay judge work is also favourable, with an average score of 4.4.

We propose the hypothesis that, since the primary frame of reference for lay judges is the collaborative work with professional judges, any criticism regarding the role of lay judges in the system must stem from this joint work. It can be assumed that lay judges, for self-assessment reasons—seeking to demonstrate the respect they receive from the judges—present the judge–lay judge relationship more favourably than it truly is. However, when the system must be evaluated from an external or overarching perspective, the factors that limit the declared function of lay judges become more apparent to them.

It is worth reminding that nearly two-thirds of the lay judges (60 percent) also criticized the current ***selection method***, suggesting that the selection should be entrusted to courts or other professional organizations instead of local government councils. The typology created by considering both aspects (the selection method and the role of lay judges) reveals that there is a notable, though not insignificant, critical potential within the lay judge community.

Table 22. The typology of the method of selecting lay judges and the role of lay judge work

	CRITICAL TYPES	%
1.	The current selection method is good + lay judge work has a significant role	16.4
2.	The current selection method is good + lay judge work has no significant role	23.0
3.	The current selection method is not good + lay judge work has a significant role	21.1
4.	The current selection method is not good + lay judge work has no significant role	39.5

Figure 15. The typology of the method of selecting lay judges and the role of lay judge work

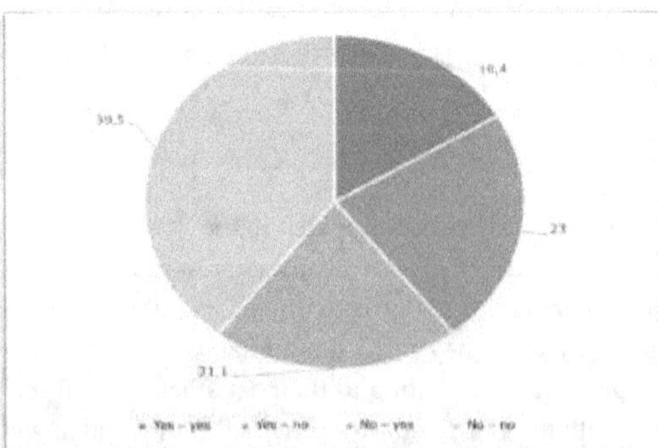

There are a few lay judge groups in which the critical (Type 4) attitude is notably more prevalent than the average, although these groups are not among the largest. These primarily include those who have left the role[84] (51 percent) and members of the Hungarian Association of Lay Judges[85] (14 percent). In both cases, an explanation is likely: dissatisfaction may play a role in the decision to leave, while membership in the Hungarian Association of Lay Judges may reflect a desire to improve the situation.

At the same time, there are some notable differences in proportions between the subgroups.

For example, there is a significant difference between those in their first term[86] (45.1 percent) and those who have already served at least their fourth term (21.1[87] percent). What is even more interesting is that women are distinctly more critical (44.4 percent) than men (27.1 percent), and lay judges in criminal law (41.0 percent) are also more critical than those in civil law[88] (27.3 percent), just as lay judges in district courts (43.1 percent) are compared to those in labour courts[89] (30.9 percent).

IV.6.2 How Can a Lay Judge Assist the Judge the Most?

In this regard, it is important to clearly distinguish between those working in criminal law and those in other areas of law (civil, labour, administrative). The vast majority of the latter group believes that they can most help the judicial work in *determining the facts of the case*. On the other hand, those in criminal law consider their contribution to be much more diversified: for them, determining *guilt (culpability)* takes the lead, followed closely by the *sentencing (sanction)* and, finally, the *establishment of the facts*. However, they are in complete agreement when it comes to the legal classification, which they view as solely the judge's prerogative, meaning they play no role in this aspect.

[84] Those not willing to take on another term, n = 51 individuals
[85] N = 54 individuals
[86] N = 91 individuals
[87] N = 38 individuals
[88] N = 33 individuals
[89] N = 55 individuals

Table 23. What does the lay judge help the judge with the most?

LAY JUDGE COMPETENCE	AREAS OF LAW	
	Criminal	other*[90]
Establishing the facts	***24.3***	**74.5**
Determining guilt (culpability)	**38.5**	7.3
Imposing sentence (sanction)	***25.9***	7.3
Legal classification	0.8	3.6
Miscellanea	10.5	7.3

Among lay judges specialising in criminal law, we explored whether any underlying factors might influence, even to a small extent, their perceived contribution across various areas of competence. The most significant discrepancies emerged in the ***determination of guilt***. Compared to the average of 39 per cent, markedly lower proportions of competence attribution were observed among those who *had left lay judging* (29 per cent), those *serving in the capital* (likewise 29 per cent), *members of the Hungarian Association of Lay Judges* (28 per cent), those who *did not undertake lay judging with particular enthusiasm* (23 per cent), those who were *not motivated by a sense of vocation* (26 per cent), and those who were *not entirely satisfied with* the human relations between lay judges and professional judges (32 per cent). Overall, these contributing factors suggest that the perceived limitations in involvement in determining guilt may indicate a tendency towards the development of a more detached attitude.

It is quite striking that, unlike in the determination of guilt, no such differentiating factors emerge in the perceived extent of contribution to ***sentencing***—save for a single exception. Compared to the overall average of 26 per cent, only 15 per cent of lay judges who were not entirely satisfied with the human relations between lay judges and professional judges felt that this was the area in which they could provide the greatest assistance to the judge.

IV.6.3 Attitude Towards Lay Judge Work

The critical attitude manifesting at a systemic level is accompanied by remarkably strong positive perceptions at an "operational" level. The vast majority of lay judges regard their role as a vocation, undertake it willingly without exception,

[90] 227 N = 55 individuals

are satisfied with their working conditions, and, as we shall demonstrate in the following chapter, perceive their relationship with judges to be highly favourable.

Lay judges can be divided into two groups based on their interpretation of their role. The largest group,[91] comprising four out of every five lay judges (79 per cent), perceives their work as a vocation, with a small subset (8 per cent) also viewing it as a source of income. The second group (21 per cent) attributes a different kind of significance to their role: the majority within this group regard it primarily as a useful way to spend their time (16 per cent), while others (5 per cent) ascribe it a distinct form of importance.[92]

Table 24. Lay Judges' Opinions on Lay Judging

WHAT DOES LAY JUDGING MEAN?	%
It is a special role, a vocation	82.1
It is just like any other job	1.2
It is not a job but a useful way to spend time	18.6
It is an additional source of income	9.2
It means something else	9.7

The cluster variable derived from the responses indicates that, despite the possibility of multiple answers, only the combination of vocation and income-generating opportunity formed a distinct—albeit relatively small—mixed group.

Table 25. Clusters in the Perception of Lay Judging

WHAT DOES LAY JUDGING MEAN?	%
It is a special role, a vocation	70.4
It is both a vocation and an income opportunity	8.4
Vocation-focused group (total)	***78.8***
It is a useful way to spend time	16.5
It means something else	4.8
Other motivation group (total)	***21.3***

[91] Respondents were allowed to select multiple answers, so the total percentage exceeds 100 per cent.

[92] The content analysis of the textual responses under the "Something else" category revealed that respondents primarily referred to their personal sense of contributing usefully and gaining insight into the judicial system. As one respondent phrased it, it provided "a glimpse into a unique segment of social existence."

The proportion of "***vocation-focused***" lay judges approaches or even exceeds 90 per cent in certain categories. This is particularly evident among "veterans"[93] who have served for at least four cycles (93 per cent), the "highly experienced"[94]who have participated in over a hundred hearings (87 per cent), and those serving in civil law cases[95] (91 per cent). By contrast, the lowest proportions are found among lay judges at regional courts and those with a background in public administration or law enforcement, both at 71 per cent.

Comparing the various subcategories, the most significant differences emerged in two areas: the number of cases handled and the sector of the lay judges' current or former workplace. In terms of experience, 77 per cent of "novices" in their first cycle identified as vocation-focused, compared to 93 per cent of "veterans." Regarding professional background, 71 per cent of those from public administration and law enforcement fell into this category, whereas the proportion was notably higher (83 per cent) among those working in human services.

There is a clear correlation between the perception of the role of lay judging and the motivation behind it. Among those who believe that lay judges play a *meaningful* role in the functioning of the judiciary, 90 per cent adopt a *vocation-focused* approach to their work, compared to 73 per cent in the more critical group.

Among *vocation-focused* lay judges, the proportion of those who believe their work plays a meaningful role in the judiciary is twice as high (42 per cent) as among those with *other motivations*[96] (19 per cent).

Nearly 60 per cent (58 per cent) of vocation-focused lay judges take a critical view of the role of lay judging, compared to more than 80 per cent (81 per cent) of those with other motivations.

---

93 N = 40 individuals

94 N = 54 individuals

95 N = 33 individuals

96 N = 64 individuals

Table 26. Motivation and the Perception of the Role of Lay Judging

Motivation for Lay Judging	*The Role of Lay Judging*		
	No meaningful contribution	Meaningful contribution	
Vocation	57.9	**42.1**	100.0
	72.8	**89.4**	
Other motivations	**81.2**	18.8	100.0
	27.2	10.6	
	100.0	100.0	

IV.6.4 The Motivational Background

How willingly do lay judges perform their work? To paint a comprehensive picture, there is no need to distinguish between different response groups, as this question exhibited perhaps the highest level of respondent uniformity. Expressed in terms of school grading, the result corresponds to a very strong "excellent" (almost "outstanding") average rating.

Among the five-point scale response options, none of the respondents selected the first three grades ("one," "two," or "three").[97] Instead, only "four" and "five" were chosen, with the latter overwhelmingly dominant. The "four" rating was almost an exception (13 per cent) compared to the vast majority (87 per cent) who awarded the highest score. The resulting picture is so overwhelmingly positive that, at first glance, searching for differentiating factors influencing responses might seem unnecessary. However, analysis suggests that it would be a mistake to merge these two response groups and treat them as a single entity.[98]

Table 26. How Willingly Do Lay Judges Perform Their Work?

(1) Not willingly at all	0.0
(2) Rather unwillingly	0.0
(3) Somewhat willing, somewhat unwilling	0.0
(4) Rather willingly than not	13.4
(5) Explicitly willingly	86.6

[97] "One" = "Not at all willingly"; "Two" = "Rather unwilling than willing"; "Three" = "Somewhat willing, somewhat unwilling."

[98] 235 In empirical social research, it is both possible and common practice to consolidate the response categories of a symmetrical five-point scale into a three-point scale for the purpose of correlation analysis—particularly when this allows for the formation of larger groups of a suitable size for analysis.

Figure 16. How Willingly Do Lay Judges Perform Their Work?

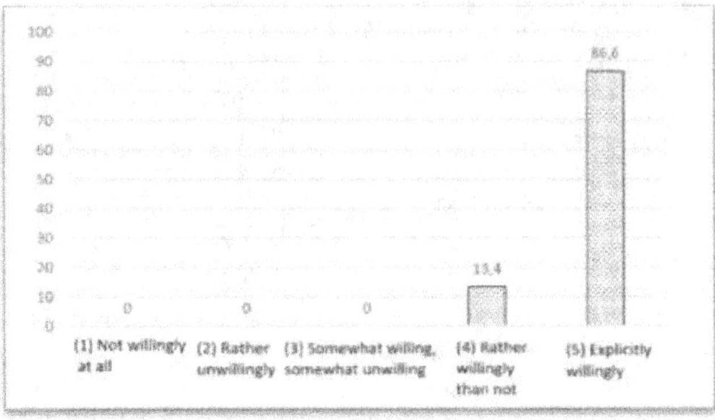

The correlation analysis revealed that the "four" rating ("rather willingly than not") was primarily given by those who, firstly, viewed the role of lay judges ***critically***, secondly, ***did not approach their work with a vocational motivation***, and thirdly, were ***less satisfied*** with their working conditions. While it is important to note that only a small group awarded this rating, it is nevertheless striking that, compared to others, they were more likely to believe[99] that lay judges do not play a meaningful role in the justice system, were less driven[100] by a sense of vocation, and expressed greater dissatisfaction[101] with their working conditions.

If this smaller group so clearly differs from the others and yet claims to perform its work with almost the same level of enjoyment, then this contradiction calls for an explanation. One possible interpretation is that we are witnessing an attempt to avoid a self-assessment trap. If someone perceives various aspects of their work as problematic and is dissatisfied with certain conditions, how do they justify their continued involvement— especially when they are no longer novices[102], persist in their role[103], and even commit to serving additional terms? In such a situation,

[99] 34 out of 41 individuals (~83 per cent), in contrast to the 60 per cent rate observed among the others.

[100] 23 out of 42 individuals (~55 per cent), as opposed to the 83 per cent rate among the others.

[101] Their average satisfaction rating of 3.9 stands in contrast to the 4.4 average of the others.

[102] There is no clear correlation suggesting that the "four" rating is more commonly given by novices or less experienced lay judges. However, it is true that the "five" rating appears most frequently among those in at least their third or fourth term—so-called "veterans"—as well as among highly experienced lay judges.

[103] Among lay judges serving their final term—those not seeking reappointment—the proportion of those awarding a "five" rating remains high at 79 percent, only slightly below the

they cannot simply say, "I do not enjoy it," as this would create an internal conflict, forcing them to either quit or disengage. Thus, the response "rather willingly than not"—corresponding to a rating of "four"—should not be grouped together with the "explicitly willing" response (a rating of "five"), as it likely signifies not mere proximity but a considerable distance, effectively serving as a carefully packaged form of criticism

IV.6.5 A Question Regarding a Symbol: The Wearing of the Robe

In Hungarian judicial practice, the issue of wearing robes[104] has periodically resurfaced in the wake of civil transformation, but for a long time, it did not become a general practice. Supporters of its introduction viewed it as attire that enhances and symbolizes the dignity of the judiciary and the authority of the courts. Ultimately, the wearing of robes became a standard element of judges' courtroom appearance in 1999[105], once again justified by references to dignity and authority. However, in a 2012 directive issued by the President of the NOJ[106] it was explicitly stated—again in reference to these prestige factors—that "this must also be reflected in the attire of lay judges, clerks, and judicial secretaries participating in procedural actions." While this directive did not mandate the wearing of robes, it did not exclude the possibility either. The key requirement was that courtroom attire should uphold the judiciary's esteemed status. As of 2015, there was no mandatory robe-wearing requirement for lay judges, nor is there one today, though they do have the option to wear formal attire.

That is why we asked them for their views on the issue of wearing judicial robes. We expected that, overall, they would support the wearing of robes as a way to outwardly express their status as associate judges. However, we were surprised to find that this was not the case, as nearly two-thirds (60 percent) did not consider it important for lay judges to wear robes.

---

88 percent recorded among the rest. This suggests that factors such as age, family circumstances, or health conditions likely play a role in their decision to step down.

[104] Bódiné dr. Beliznai, Kinga: Talár vagy díszmagyar? Adalékok a bírói uniformis történetéhez.https://birosag.hu/sites/default/files/201902/beliznai_kinga_talar_vagy_diszmagyar.pdf

[105] The Statutes of the NCJ (National Council of Justice) addressed this issue.

[106] 243 Directive No 9/2012 (V. 8.) OBH of the President of the National Office for the Judiciary

Indeed, those who identified themselves as supporters of the wearing of robes (40 percent) did not view it primarily as a factor enhancing their personal prestige (6 percent), but instead as a means to bolster the authority of the judicial panel (62 percent) and, secondarily (25 percent), to elevate the status of the lay judges' work. This reasoning structure seems entirely understandable: naturally, it is of great importance to them that they be perceived as possessing an authority akin to that of judges, even in outward appearances. However, in order to achieve this, they wisely elevate their argument to a higher level, invoking "divine justification" primarily in terms of enhancing the authority of the *judicial panel* and, secondarily, the prestige of *lay judging* as a whole.

It is a well-known phenomenon that employees in subordinate positions within a high-prestige institution—a hierarchical organisation—are often eager to "borrow" the prestige of the organisation, aimed at the outside world.[107] However, in the case of lay judges, this is not entirely the case, as they do not merely work in high-prestige courts, but occupy a status of co-judges, with formal authority and at the same level as the members of the institution who confer prestige. The demand for wearing robes, therefore, constitutes a legitimate claim. This is why we expected that there would be an almost unanimous expectation from their side for being "clothed" with this symbol. However, this did not occur.

We cannot provide a conclusive explanation for why the majority took a more reserved stance on this issue. However, we can examine which groups of lay judges are represented above the average (40 percent) among those who support the wearing of robes. This investigation, however, reveals only three factors in connection. The association is not particularly strong for lay judges in regional courts (58 percent) and in Budapest (60 percent), but somewhat stronger for members of the Hungarian Association of Lay Judges* (73 percent). The connection between these last two categories of lay judges is close; it is worth noting again that the initiative and recruitment of the Hungarian Association of Lay Judges are fundamentally organised in the capital. Based on these correlations, we can infer that in somewhat more critical lay judge groups, the proportion of robe supporters is higher than average. Since the difference is not dramatic, it is also likely that lay judges in this case based their stance on personal impressions and feelings.

---

107 They define themselves as performing physical work or office tasks by saying things like "I work at the university," "I work at the clinic," "I work at the Academy of Sciences," etc.

V. THE RELATIONSHIP BETWEEN LAY JUDGES AND JUDGES

The role of the lay judge, in practice, is far more than what is visible to the outside world—namely, mere participation in court proceedings. It extends well beyond this, as such participation is accompanied by various preparatory and follow-up tasks. Nevertheless, at the heart of the role lies the collaborative work with the judge. This is, without doubt, a rather peculiar working arrangement: while it is formally structured around the participants' ostensibly equal status, it is nevertheless embedded in an inherently asymmetrical relationship—a dynamic of authority. Though the lay judge holds a position that, in formal legal terms, proclaims equality with the professional judge, the very nature of the judicial profession inevitably places them in a subordinate role. The judge's expertise, which effectively consecrates their authority, ensures this hierarchical distinction. At the core of the relationship between the two—the "ordained" and the "lay"—lies the judge's inherent and unspoken power, woven into the fabric of their position.

It goes without saying that within such a setting, multiple interpretations of the lay judge's role may coexist. At one end of the spectrum, one might find a fundamentally passive and acquiescent stance—marked by acceptance, adaptation, and submission. At the other extreme, one may assume an activist disposition, actively seeking recognition and influence. To borrow the terminology of Albert O. Hirschman,[108] the former aligns with "loyalty," while the latter corresponds to "voice"—the act of expressing dissenting opinions. Naturally, between these two poles, various other role perceptions may emerge. Hirschman identifies a third fundamental reactive type: "exit," which typically becomes an option when "voice" fails to yield results. It would seem logical to equate this category with those who abandon their role as lay judges. However, our data suggests that departures are primarily driven by age rather than dissatisfaction. The majority of those leaving belong to older age groups, with individuals over 60,[109] accounting for two-thirds of departures and those over 65

[108] Albert O. Hirschman. 1970. Exit, Voice, and Loyalty: Responses to Decline in Firms, Organizations, and States. Cambridge, MA: Harvard University Press. ISBN 0-674-27660-4 (paper). In Hungarian: Kivonulás, tiltakozás, hűség. Osiris Könyvtár, Osiris, Budapest, 1995.

[109] 35 out of 52 individuals (~67 percent)

comprising half[110]). Thus, it is primarily advancing age, rather than any particular reaction to the judicial role, that plays the decisive role in their withdrawal.

Although one-third of those departing are under the age of 60[111], analysis has not revealed a significantly stronger critical attitude among them compared to their older counterparts. Their departure, therefore, appears to be a straightforward act of leaving—perhaps due to various personal reasons—rather than a deliberate act of "withdrawal" in the *Hirschmanian* sense.

We examined the relationship between lay judges and professional judges along two fundamental dimensions: firstly, the nature of their connection—whether characterised by partnership or personal ***rapport***—and secondly, the aspect of ***respect***. The latter encompasses both the lay judges' assessment of the judges' professional work and, conversely, the extent to which judges are receptive to lay opinions and the role these opinions play in judicial decision-making.

Diagram 1. Structural Framework of the Lay Judge–Judge Relationship

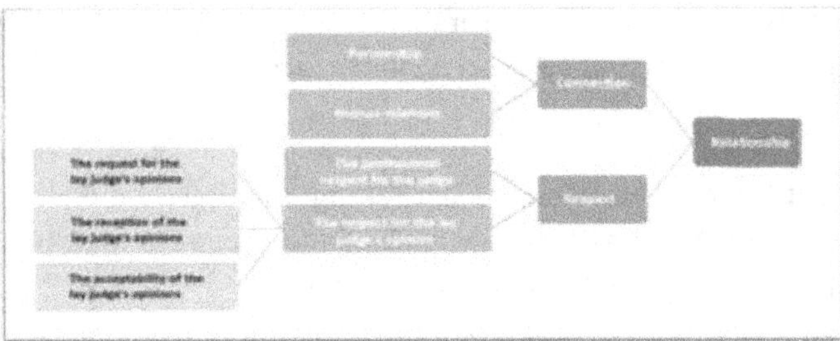

V.1 THE FUNDAMENTAL DIMENSION OF THE RELATIONSHIP

A distinctly positive picture emerges regarding the question of ***partnership***, as nearly all responding lay judges (95 percent) perceived that, based on their experience, judges generally regarded them as *supportive colleagues* rather than as *obstacles* to judicial work. Only a small minority (5 percent) held a different view. Higher levels of dissatisfaction with judges' attitudes towards lay judges were observed in only a few specific categories. Notably, this was the case among

[110] 247 27 out of 52 individuals (~52 percent)

[111] 248 17 out of 52 individuals (~33 percent)

those in the capital (16 percent), members of the Hungarian Association of Lay Judges* (~17 percent), and those serving their final term* (~15 percent).

The ***personal relationship*** between judges and lay judges also received a fundamentally positive evaluation, displaying a so-called J-distribution when measured on a five-point symmetric scale. Nearly four-fifths of lay judges (78 percent) reported being "*completely satisfied*" with this relationship. A further near one-fifth (17 percent) of respondents selected the option "*more satisfied than not.*" While it would be possible to merge these two positive categories, thereby presenting a 95 percent satisfied majority versus a 5 percent ambivalent[112] or dissatisfied minority, we chose a different interpretation. Given the distribution of responses, we regarded the "*more satisfied than not*" category as indicating that some underlying source of dissatisfaction still distinguished these respondents from those expressing complete satisfaction. Thus, we classified the responses as comprising a 78 percent majority expressing full satisfaction, alongside a 22 percent group exhibiting some degree of dissatisfaction. Further analysis revealed that in certain lay judge categories, dissatisfaction exceeded this 22 percent baseline. Notably, higher levels of dissatisfaction were observed among those serving in regional courts (33 percent), those in courts in the capital (47 percent), members of the Hungarian Association of Lay Judges* (46 percent), and those in their final term* (30 percent). Moreover, dissatisfaction was found to be above average among younger age groups, with 35 percent of lay judges under 55 expressing some level of discontent.

The cluster variable, which measures the relationship by integrating the two components—**partnership** and **personal rapport**—identified three distinct and well defined groups. Together, these groups formed a markedly J-distributed structure, with an overwhelmingly high proportion (80 percent) considering the situation to be optimal.

Table 27. Types of Relationship in the Lay Judge–Judge Interaction

RELATIONSHIP TYPES	group size (%)
Neither the partnership nor the personal rapport is fully satisfactory	5.5
Partnership is fine, but the personal rapport is not always	15.5
Both the partnership and the personal rapport are satisfactory	79.1

[112] Both satisfied and dissatisfied.

Figure 17. Types of Relationship in the Lay Judge–Judge Interaction

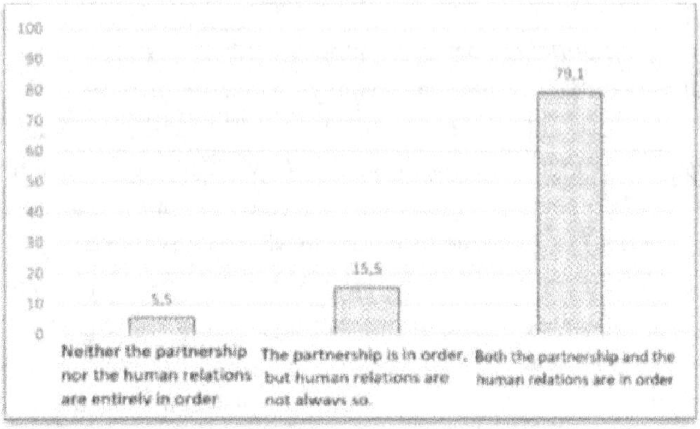

It is certainly reassuring that lay judges have rated the lay judge–judge relationship so positively. This suggests that, on a "phenomenological" level, the system is fundamentally stable, and that the vast majority of judges—perceptibly so to the lay judges—are fulfilling the work necessary for its operation. At the same time, however, for every five lay judges, there is one who has experienced a different judicial approach. While we can confidently assert that deviations from the attitudes and practices typical of the majority of judges are strongly dependent on individual circumstances, there are certain groups of lay judges that are more likely to encounter these "deviating" judicial behaviours than others. These include lay judges from regional courts (32 percent), courts in the capital (44 percent), members of the Hungarian Association of Lay Judges* (44 percent), those completing their term of office* (30 percent), and the youngest age group*** (42 percent).

It seems that a long lay judge career plays a significant role in how favourably the relationship is perceived by lay judges (of course, the reverse may also be true, as a good lay judge–judge relationship could contribute to the willingness to take on additional terms). Here is the "evidence": among those serving their third or more term as lay judges**, nearly a 100 percent (97 percent[113]) expressed satisfaction with the lay judge–judge relationship.

[113] This group consists of 40 individuals in the sample, with 38 responding to the questions regarding the relationship (they answered the questions related to the relationship). Of these, 37 individuals rated the lay judge–judge relationship as impeccable, and thus, by extension, the judges' approach as well.

V.2 THE FUNDAMENTAL DIMENSION OF RESPECT

As outlined above, we examined the question of respect in both directions (respect shown by lay judges towards judges and the perception of how much judges respect the work of lay judges). The lay judges' ***satisfaction with the judges' professional work*** also presents a picture that fundamentally follows a J-distribution. When measured on a five-point symmetric scale, the evaluations were predominantly positive. Two-thirds of the lay judges (68 percent) were "completely satisfied in every case," while nearly one-third (31 percent) were "satisfied in the majority of cases."[114]

We can see that the highly positive evaluation of the lay judge–judge relationship is accompanied by a similarly favourable evaluation, which, from the perspective of the functioning of the justice system, might even be more significant. The judge's professional work constitutes the most essential element of the system, and it is reassuring that this is regarded as impeccable within the lay judge environment. However, it is not necessary to engage in complex semantic discussions to state that an overall favourable evaluation does not mean that every lay judge considers the judge's professional work flawless. The category of evaluation that includes the phrase "in the majority of cases" necessarily contains some degree of critique (dissatisfaction). Using the language of school grading, a "good" grade means that, for some reason, it is not "excellent."

In a qualitative interview-based study, it would certainly be possible to clarify this reason, but the limitations of our questionnaire-based research did not allow for that. Thus, we could only use the tools of ecological analysis to examine which categories of lay judges exhibited partial dissatisfaction with the judicial work above the average (32 percent). We found only two such more critical groups, those with slightly more dissatisfaction than the others: lay judges from the capital (62 percent) and members of the Hungarian Association of Lay Judges* (58 percent). At the same time, it was striking that, within the very small (19-person) group of the youngest age group (35 49 years***), 11 individuals were among those who expressed some criticism of the judges' professional work. Compared to the average (68 percent), the lay judges from municipal courts (those not in

[114] The remaining 1 percent categorized themselves as "both satisfied and dissatisfied" (a mix of both).

county seats) showed significantly higher satisfaction (80 percent), as did those at the beginning of their lay judge experience (78 percent)[115].

We attempted to reconstruct the ***respect for lay judges' work by judges*** using several indicators. *One* such indicator was the practice, as perceived by the lay judges, of whether judges regularly ask for their opinions when making decisions in cases. The second indicator was an evaluation of how these opinions are received by the judges. The third indicator concerned the role that the opinions expressed by the lay judges play in shaping judicial decisions, according to the respondents. In the first and second questions, we once again encountered the classic J-distribution (i.e., the vast majority generally view the judicial practice in this regard as positive), but in the third question, the responses were more differentiated.

Table 28. The Respect for Lay Judges' Work by Judges

Do Judges Ask for Lay Judges' Opinions? (%)		Do Judges Willingly Listen to Lay Judges' Opinions? (%)		What Role Do Opinions Play in Judicial Decision-Making? (%)	
almost never	1.2	almost never	1.5	do not matter at all	1.5
mostly not	4.2	only very rarely	3.7	mostly do not matter	10.1
both	10.7	both, variable	14.2	both	5.3
mostly yes	33.9	mostly yes	40.4	matter, but judicial opinion dominates	58.3
always	50.1	always	40.2	matter very seriously	24.9

Figure 18. The Lay Judge's Work and the Respect Accorded by Judges

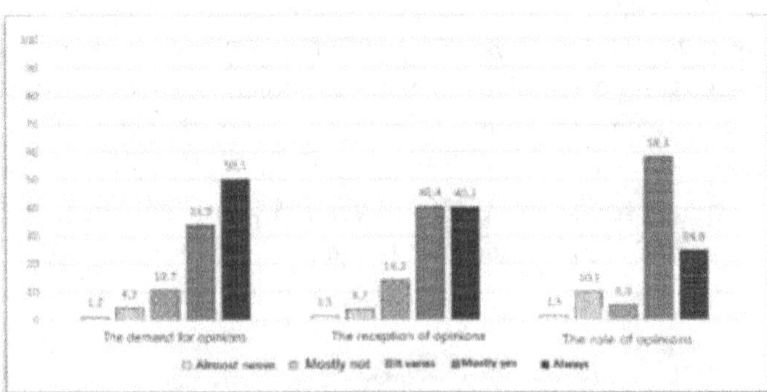

[115] Up to this point, they had participated in the proceedings of a maximum of 10 cases.

According to their content, the responses in all three areas – taken as a whole – present a favourable view of the situation.[116] Nevertheless, it is our opinion that the response categories which assess the situation as not entirely optimal (merely "suboptimal")[117] cannot be merged with those that evaluate it as optimal. If we construct a dummy-type variable ("not entirely optimal – optimal") for each of the three cases, using ratios of 50:50, 60:40, and 75:25, we obtain an intriguing group structure regarding the respect accorded to lay judges' opinions—one that exhibits a fundamentally "sloping" distribution.

The *largest* group (44 percent) consists of those who generally perceive respect in all three areas as good but did not award the judge the highest rating in any of them. The *second* group, of nearly the same size, is characterised by a mix of top and lower ratings—most often giving lower scores when they felt that lay judges' opinions played little significant role in judicial decisions. The *third*, smaller group, however, was entirely satisfied with all areas, awarding the judges the highest rating across the board.

Table 29. Lay Judges' Assessment of the Respect Received from Judges

Assessment of Respect Received from Judges by Lay Judges	%
Not entirely optimal in any area	44.0
"Mixed"	36.0
Optimal in all areas	19.9

[116] We merely note that in the non-representative data collection conducted within the same time interval, judges (N = 109) had a similar perception of the practice of seeking opinions. However, their attitude structure regarding the consideration of these opinions differed somewhat, and their view of the role such opinions played in their own decisions was markedly different.

[117] "Mostly yes" or "they matter, but..."

Figure 19. Lay Judges' Assessment of the Respect Received from Judges

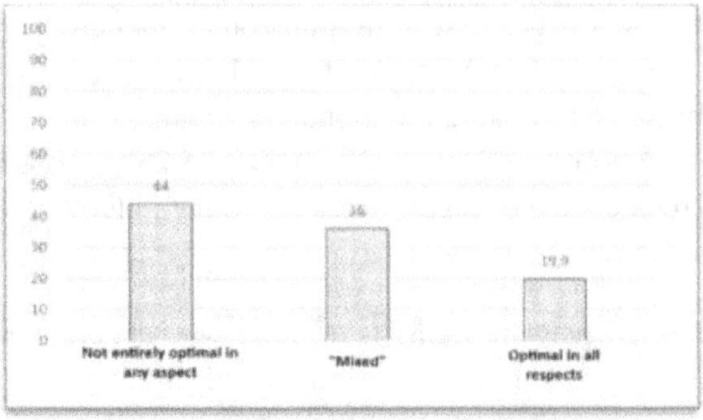

The attitude carrying a potential for dissatisfaction appears at a significantly higher rate than the average (44 percent) among lay judges from the *capital* (66 percent) and *members* of the *Hungarian Association of Lay Judges* (MÜE) (61 percent). It is also strikingly dominant in the small group of *those under 50****) (14 out of 18). Interestingly, we did not find any lay judge group in which the proportion of those fully satisfied with the respect received from judges was significantly higher than the average (20 percent).[118]

V. 3 THE "BALANCE" OF RESPECT

If we consider together the lay judges' assessment of judges' professional work and the judicial respect for lay judges' opinions (that is, how lay judges perceive the recognition granted by judges), we can distinguish three characteristic types of "balance." At one pole, we find those who view the situation so favourably that they award the highest rating to both aspects. In other words, they rate judges' professional work at the highest level and believe that judges fully respect lay judges' opinions.

At the opposite pole are those who perceive reasons in both aspects that prevent them from awarding the highest rating in either area. This reflects a generally mild sense of dissatisfaction and a partially critical attitude. Due to certain experiential reasons, they have some degree of concern regarding the judges' work and,

[118] Nowhere did this proportion exceed 25-26 percent.

moreover, feel that judges do not accord maximum respect to lay judges' opinions.

In the middle are those who awarded the highest rating in one area but gave a slightly lower grade in the other.

Table 30. Types of "Balance" of Respect

Types of "Balance" of Respect	%
Both dimensions optimal	18.4
"Mixed"	58.6
Neither dimension optimal	23.0

Figure 20. Types of "Balance" of Respect

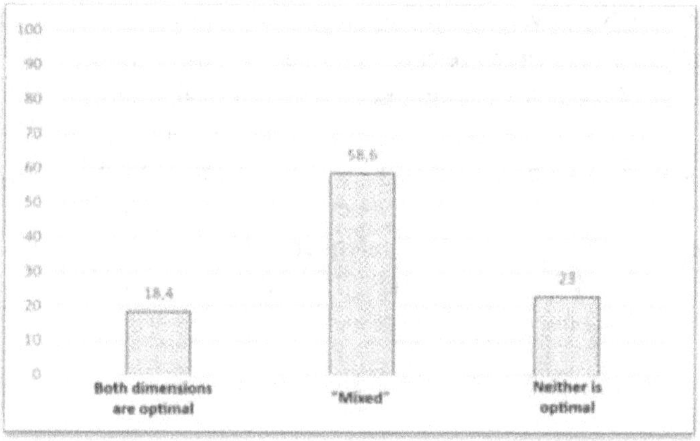

The ***"both optimal"*** type did not show a significantly above-average proportion (18 percent) in any subgroup of lay judges. The highest values were observed among those serving at least their third term (23 percent), the "highly experienced" who had participated in more than 100 hearings (25 percent), non-degree holders (24 percent), and those from the public administration and law enforcement sectors (24 percent).

The ***"neither optimal"*** type appears at a slightly higher rate than the average (23 percent) among those in their final term* (29 percent), judges at the regional courts (32 percent), those serving in courts in the capital (50 percent), members of the Hungarian Association of Lay Judges (MÜE)* (45 percent), university degree holders* (33 percent), and those coming from the service sector* (37 percent) or the private sector (32 percent).

V.4 THE "RELATIONSHIP": THE INTERPLAY OF CONNECTION AND RESPECT AS FUNDAMENTAL DIMENSIONS

The structure of opinions regarding the judge-lay judge ***relationship*** revealed a J-shaped distribution, presenting a very favourable picture. In contrast, the views on mutual ***respect*** between the participants depicted a more differentiated structure: the respect judges received from lay judges clearly followed a J-shaped distribution, while the respect lay judges received from judges displayed a structure more akin to an L-shape—"sloping," with decreasing favour from the less favourable to the more favourable.

However, overall, these two fundamental dimensions brought the structure of opinions closer to a normal distribution.

Using cluster analysis, we created the integral descriptive variables of the judge-lay judge relationship, which resulted in a nearly classic normal distribution of group structure. Among the lay judges, there is a critical group, approximately 20 percent in size, who have some concerns regarding both the relationship and respect. There is also a nearly equally sized (19 percent) highly satisfied group, who view both the relationship and respect as very favourable. Between these two groups, there is a large (61 percent) intermediate "cluster," characterised by the fact that, while they consider the judge-lay judge relationship to be entirely in order, they still have concerns about respect.

Table 31. The Interplay of Connection and Respect as Fundamental Dimensions

RELATIONSHIP (connection + respect)	%
Neither is flawless	20.4
The relationship is flawless, but there are issues with respect	60:8
Both the relationship and respect are in order	18:8

Figure 21. The Interplay of Connection and Respect as Fundamental Dimensions

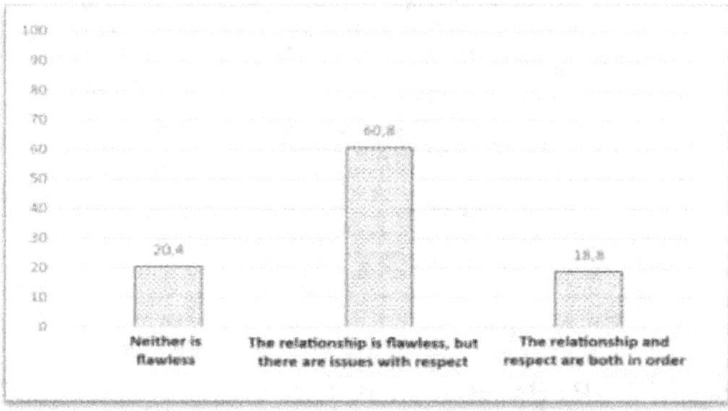

The *critics* are found in a proportion higher than the average (20 percent) among those in their final term* (31 percent), judges at the regional courts* (32 percent), those working in courts in the capital* (45 percent), newcomers* (25 percent), members of the Hungarian Association of Lay Judges (MÜE)* (46 percent), university degree holders* (34 percent), those coming from the service sector* (35 percent), and the private sector (32 percent).

The ***highly satisfied*** individuals are found in a proportion slightly above the average (19 percent) among those in at least their third term (23 percent), the "highly experienced"* (26 percent), non-degree holders (25 percent), and those coming from the public administration and law enforcement sectors* (24 percent).

At the same time, we found a very interesting correlation between satisfaction with the judicial institutions and attitudes towards the relationship. This means that those with a more critical stance are less satisfied with the functioning of these institutions compared to others, while the highly satisfied individuals are also more content with the judicial institutions.

Table 32. The Judge-Lay Judge Relationship and Satisfaction with Judicial Institutions

RELATIONSHIP Attitudes	Among those satisfied with the police	Among those satisfied with the prosecution	Among those satisfied with the court
Neither is flawless	10.2	24.1	62.1
The relationship is flawless, but there are issues with respect	40.9	68.5	85.0
Both the relationship and respect are in order	50.9	76.4	91.1

V.5 A NOTEWORTHY POINT: WHEN THERE IS NOT ALWAYS AGREEMENT BETWEEN THE LAY JUDGE AND THE JUDGE

There is no doubt that the judge-lay judge relationship has an asymmetrical basic structure, with the dominance of the judge inherently encoded within it. The formal legal equality of co-judges has professional competence limitations in its application/enforcement. Both parties are mutually aware of this: the lay judges tacitly accept subordination, which the judges compensate for by formally fulfilling their procedural obligations towards their co-judges (involvement in the proceedings, request for opinions, and hearing them).

In such a situation, it is inevitably confrontational if the co-judge indicates a disagreement with the professional judge's viewpoint. It could even be considered an act of rebellion ("a declaration of war") if the disagreement is expressed in the form of a dissenting opinion. Our data show that disagreement with the judge is far from common (for every five lay judges, two have never experienced this, and they are the ones *who always agree* and unconditionally accept the judge as the "master of the case"). Among those with differing opinions (three out of five lay judges), a smaller group (the "*hesitant ones*") has not yet voiced their differing views, while another group has followed a varied practice: sometimes they communicated their disagreement to the judge, at other times *retreating* into the "cover" of loyalty.

Almost a third of the lay judges described themselves as *systematically* and *consistently signalling their disagreement* with the judge's opinion. However, only a small group (the "warriors") took on the confrontation by formally expressing their dissent in the form of a dissenting opinion. Below, we present the frequency of these opinion groups in the sample.

Table 33. Lay Judges' Agreement with the Judge's Decision

TYPE	CONTENT	Size of the Groups (percentage of the total sample)
Always in agreement	has never had a differing opinion from the judge	**43**
Exceptionally disagreeing	one such case	**21**
Disagreeing multiple times	several such cases	**36**
"Timid"	even if there was, it was never signalled	**6**
Inconsistent	sometimes signalled, sometimes not	**20**
Consistent	was and always signalled	**31**
"Warrior" (convinced)	submitted a dissenting opinion	**4**

Figure 22. The Jury's Agreement with the Judicial Decision

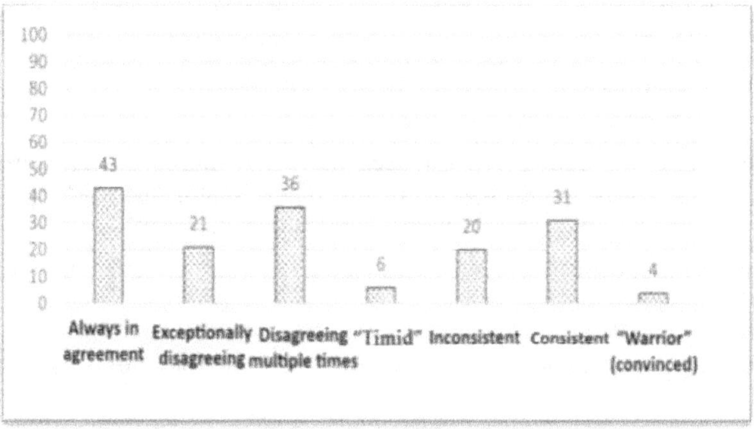

It seems like quite a challenging task to answer the question of what factors lie behind the opinions of lay judges regarding the judge's stance, what they say, or why they don't speak up, what actions they take, or why they refrain from acting. Indeed, the world of thoughts, attitudes, opinions, and actions is shaped by both personal inner traits and the social environment. Since we were not able to explore how personality traits might shape the behaviour of lay judges, we could only focus on examining the impacts of the background factors already known (indicators of the lay judge's status and their social background).

There are very few such factors that suggest personality traits and life experiences strongly shape the relationship with judicial opinions.[119] When it comes to the ***occurrence of differing opinions from the judge***, there is a naturally occurring, seemingly dependent relationship with the *length* of the lay judge's career. As the *number of cycles* and *cases increases, the frequency of opinions differing* from the judge's becomes more common.

Table 34. The Number of Cycles Spent in Lay Judge Work and the Occurrence of Opinions Diverging from the Judge's

NUMBER OF CYCLES NUMBER OF CASES	Occurrence of Diverging Opinions
One cycle	49.5
Two cycles	51.4
Three cycles	62.7
Four or more cycles	77.5
1–10 cases	43.3
11–30 cases	52.8
31–100 cases	59.8
More than 100 cases	77.4

In addition to the influence of career trajectory, only one *organisational* correlation emerged: the occurrence of diverging opinions was least prevalent among district court lay judges, while it was most commonly observed among those working in the capital city courts, as well as those in the labour court and labour law areas.

Table 35. Court Organisation and the Occurrence of Opinions Differing from the Judge's

ORGANISATIONAL INDICATOR	Occurrence of Opinions Differing from the Judge's
District Court Lay Judges	47.8
AVERAGE	**57.0**
Labour Court Lay Judges	72.4
Labour Law Lay Judges	74.6
City Court Lay Judges	70.0

[119] Naturally, we are not in a position to definitively call the picture that emerges from our sociological data a "reality." We are well aware that what people think, say, and do in real life does not necessarily follow from what they tell the social researcher—often with the intent of creating an impression.

According to their own admission, ninety percent of lay judges with differing opinions have ***already voiced their views***. However, not everyone follows a consistent practice in this regard, as there are those (35 percent) who only signal their differing opinion on occasion. Just over half of the opinionated group (54 percent) described themselves as always expressing their position when it differs from that of the judge.

Table 36. The Percentage of Those with Differing Opinions Among Those Who Disagree with the Judge's Opinion

VOICE GIVEN TO OPINION	Percentage Among Those with Differing Opinions
Has never done so	10.3
Has done so occasionally	35.4
Has done so every time	54.3

This tendency also highlighted the "reserve" of district court lay judges: they remained silent more frequently (21%) than the average, and a smaller proportion (43%) always expressed their differing opinions from the judge. The "loudest" were the regional court** lay judges: if the data is to be believed, none of them remained silent, and nearly three-quarters (72%) of them identified as always voicing their opinions.

Very few belong to the group of those who "rebel" with their dissenting opinions—only 11 individuals (almost 4%) in our sample fall into this category. They are mostly those who have continued their lay judge duties (9 individuals), those working in criminal law (8 individuals), graduates (8 individuals), and men (7 individuals).[120]

[120] For the sake of interest, it is worth noting that male lay judges show a noticeable difference in terms of differing opinions compared to their female counterparts. A slightly higher proportion of them express differing viewpoints (64%, compared to 54% among women), and more of them consistently voice their opinions (65%, compared to 49% among women). However, it is somewhat puzzling that the quietest group (those who have never voiced a differing opinion) is somewhat larger among men (14%, compared to 9% among women).

VI. LAY JUDICIAL PARTICIPATION IN COURT PROCEEDINGS

In the context of research on mixed court systems of the *Schöffen* type, Sanja Kutnjak Ivković's approach appears to be particularly useful to us. Drawing upon the status-characteristic theory developed by Berger and his colleagues,[121] she seeks to understand the internal workings and hierarchical relationships of mixed courts.

To understand the actions of the participants in the decision-making situation, it is crucial to clearly see the two structural elements of the situation. On one hand, there is a legal element arising from political intent, which suggests that the valid normative order formally provides equal status to both the professional judge and the lay participant. On the other hand, there is an organizational sociological element, which means that, in reality (latent, regardless of the participants' intentions), an asymmetrical relationship (the dominance of the professional judge, the subordination of the lay participant) is established between the two roles. In this situation, the lay participant faces the alternative of either accepting subordination or, in a "deviant" manner, attempting to assert the rights granted by formal law. At the same time, the professional judge also has several courses of action. They can fully adhere to the requirements of formal legal equality, or – by applying different techniques – they can assert the dominance stemming from the asymmetrical relationship.

Our assumption is that the lay judge system in a democratic society results in greater lay participation than a lay judge system in a dictatorship, which has become consolidated and lost its original political function, as was the focus of the previously cited Kulcsár study.

In the following, based on our investigations, we will demonstrate how the participants (the professional judge and the lay collaborator) navigate within the decision-making process's field of force, with particular attention to the strategies developed by the professional judge – as the "game master."

---

[121] Berger, Joseph [et al.]: Status Characteristics and Social Interaction (1977.); see also Berger, Joseph [et al.]: Status Organizing Processes. In: 6 ANN. REV. Soc., 1980. 479–508. p.

VI.1 THE PARTICIPATION OF LAY JUDGES IN THE HEARING AND DECISION-MAKING PROCESS

A fundamental question regarding the actual functioning of the lay judge system is whether the legal equality granted to them is realised in the context of case hearings and decisions. Naturally, we must be aware that this concerns formal legal equality, and the actual enforcement of the rights equivalent to those of the professional judge is highly dependent on the individual (personalised), meaning that it is a function of the *practices established by the respective professional judge*.

In our research, we examined four dimensions of lay participation from the judge's perspective: 1. preparation, 2. involvement in the hearing, 3. request for an opinion, and 4. influence (consideration of the opinion). Of these, the first two dimensions can be considered *procedural*, while the latter two are more *substantive (decisional)* in nature.

Diagram 2. Lay participation

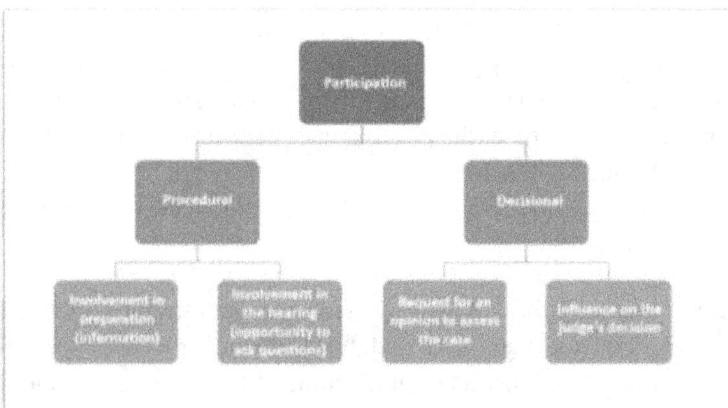

VI.2 THE PREPARATION

VI.2.1 A portrayal of the situation from the perspective of a lay judge

The "preparation" dimension was measured by assessing *what the lay judges considered to be the most characteristic practice of the judge during the past cycle*: whether the judge provided both the case materials and additional guidance, only the case materials without guidance, only guidance without the materials, or neither the materials nor any guidance.

The responses paint a generally positive picture: with very few exceptions (4%), judges seem to provide preliminary guidance on cases, likely not only due to formal legal requirements but also for professional reasons, aiming to facilitate collaboration with lay judges. They ensure that lay judges are well-informed about the cases at hand. However, differing practices are evident in this regard. The most common approach—experienced by two-thirds of lay judges—involves verbal briefing by the judge. Only a quarter of respondents reported receiving both a briefing and access to case materials for review. Nevertheless, a less favourable practice also exists, albeit on a smaller scale: in some instances, the presiding judge does not treat lay judges as partners and does not grant them the opportunity for prior familiarisation with the case.

Table 37. Briefing of Lay Judges

Briefing Type	Valid Percentage (%)
Received both case materials and briefings	25.9
Received only case materials	2.6
Did not receive materials, but received judicial briefings	67.6
Received neither materials nor briefings	3.9
Total:	100.0

Figure 23. Briefing of Lay Judges

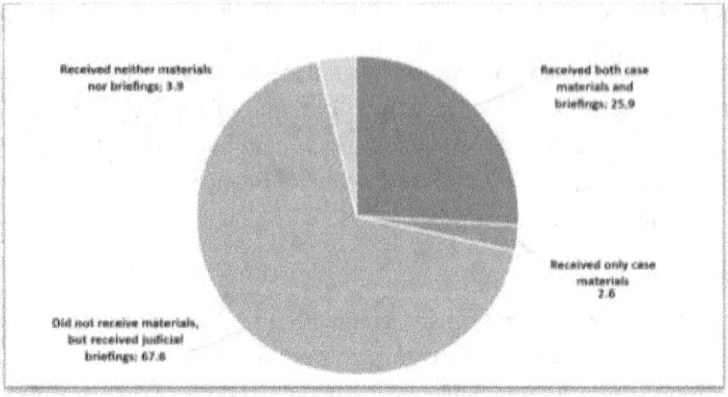

VI.2.2 As Seen by the Judges

As a point of interest, our (non-representative) online survey of judges (N=109) reveals a broadly similar picture, confirming the dominance of the briefing practice. According to the responses, 9.6% of judges provided both case materials and briefings, while 1.1% provided only the materials. The majority, 81.9%, offered only verbal briefings, whereas 7.4% neither provided materials nor gave any briefings.

VI.2.3 Background Factors in Lay Judges' Perception and Experience of Judicial Preparatory Work[122]

The extent to which lay judges are "brought up to speed" during their preparation process is evidently influenced by the judge's approach to their role. However, it is worth exploring whether certain conditions or circumstances affect the frequency of these judicial practices and how they are perceived. Regarding *the characteristics of the lay judge status*, the most favourable practice—where both briefings and case materials are provided—was experienced at a higher-than-average rate (26%) by certain groups.[123] This includes regional court lay judges (34%),[124] those serving their third or subsequent term (39%),[125] former lay judges who had completed their service (42%),[126] and those serving in Békés County (43%).[127] While social background factors did not show a clear correlation, some *attitudinal* differences were linked to the experience of favourable judicial practices. A higher-than-average proportion of *those satisfied with the recognition of their work as lay judges* (30%)[128] reported experiencing this practice. Similarly, it was more common among *those uninterested in politics* (37%)[129] and *those who do not consider themselves well-informed on political matters* (38%).[130] Some connection was also observed between this experience and satisfaction with the

[122] When designing the questionnaire, we assumed that, in assessing responses, the relevance of lay judges' personal attitudes would be as significant as their status and social background. Lay judge status was characterised by factors such as continuity (whether the respondent continues their role in the new cycle or discontinues it), organisational form (district court, Budapest-Capital district court, administrative and labour court, regional court), the number of cycles served, area of law (criminal, civil, labour, or other), the approximate number of cases heard, and membership in the Hungarian Association of Lay Judges (MÜE). Social background was measured by variables including gender, age group, education level, settlement type, employment status, job position category, sector of employment, and ethnicity. Personal attitudes covered satisfaction with personal life and institutional actors in society, trust in people, stance on legal issues in terms of strictness or leniency, and political engagement.

[123] Of these factors, we highlight only those correlations that proved to be statistically significant in a mathematical-statistical sense ($p \leq 0.05$).

[124] Out of 44 respondents, 15.

[125] Out of 100 respondents, 39.

[126] Out of 52 respondents, 22.

[127] Out of 74 respondents, 32. This is a particularly interesting and valuable data point, but it is important to note that the sample does not have territorial representation.

[128] Out of 228 respondents, 67.

[129] Out of 75 respondents, 28.

[130] Out of 40 respondents, 15.

institutions of the judiciary, though these correlations were not statistically significant.

The researcher considers it rationally understandable that favourable judicial practices correlate with the characteristics of the lay judge status, as well as with the various forms of satisfaction mentioned. In the latter case, this is likely because experiencing positive judicial practices enhances lay judges' sense of recognition and their satisfaction with the functioning of judicial institutions. However, there is no clear explanation for the correlation with an "apolitical" attitude.

VI.3 THE INCLUSION OF LAY JUDGES IN THE TRIAL PROCESS

VI.3.1 A Portrayal of the Situation from the Perspective of Lay Judges

The dimension of "involvement/inclusion" was measured by examining *whether presiding judges typically allow lay judges to ask questions during the trial proceedings, addressing individuals such as the defendant, witnesses, or experts*. Our focus was on identifying the prevailing practice—specifically, the frequency and extent to which this opportunity is granted.

Similar to the previous procedural aspect, respondents reported a relatively favourable picture in this case as well. Our classification of "favourable" simply means that the overall assessment is positive: when merging the original response options, we see that nearly two-thirds of judges grant lay judges this opportunity. However, this also implies that from the perspective of lay judges, the remaining one-third of judges follow a less favourable practice[131]—either inconsistently providing this opportunity or excluding it altogether.

[131]In a strict sense, we can only definitively label this practice as unfavourable if it can be demonstrably shown to contradict the needs of the lay judges. However, this particular need was not addressed in the questionnaire.

Table 38. Lay Judge Experiences: Does the Judge Provide the Opportunity for Lay Judges to Ask Questions During the Trial?

	Valid Percentage	
Almost never	6.9	18.0
Mostly not	11.1	
Sometimes, variable	19.4	19.4
Mostly yes	25.4	62.6
Always	37.2	
Total:	100.0	100.0

Figure 24. Does the judge provide the opportunity for the lay judges to ask questions during the trial?

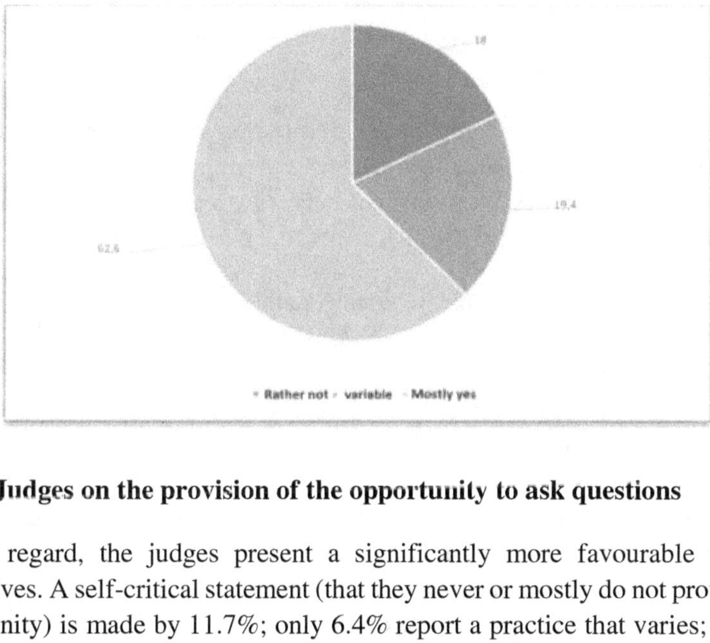

VI.3.2 Judges on the provision of the opportunity to ask questions

In this regard, the judges present a significantly more favourable view of themselves. A self-critical statement (that they never or mostly do not provide this opportunity) is made by 11.7%; only 6.4% report a practice that varies; the vast majority (82.0%) claim that they mostly or always provide this opportunity to ask questions.

VI.3.3 The contextual background of the lay judges' experience and perception of the judicial practice of providing the opportunity to ask questions

Here, too, it is primarily certain elements of the *lay judge status* that are linked to the judicial practice of providing the opportunity to ask questions. This means that, for instance, those serving their third or subsequent term (71%) experience this judicial *usus* at a rate somewhat higher than the average (64%). This is likely connected to the fact that the judges view them as experienced and proven colleagues, and do not see any risk factors in their involvement in the proceedings in this manner.

It is noteworthy (though not significant!) that members of the lay judge association (49 individuals in the sample) have encountered this judicial practice at a rate below the average (51%).

There is some variation in terms of areas of law as well. Among the different areas, lay judges working in the *civil law area* report above-average (75%) participation opportunities. However, since they are represented in the sample in low numbers (n=32), this correlation was not found to be significant.

However, the relatively marked regional (county) differences are significant, suggesting that the organisation *along different territorial units* may, to some extent, foster distinct judicial socialisation patterns. Our sample lacks territorial representativeness, and only a few counties are relatively well-represented (Békés: 75 individuals; Borsod-Abaúj-Zemplén: 55 individuals; Budapest and Pest: 75 individuals; Csongrád: 47 individuals). It is striking, however, that notable differences appear in the responses. On one hand, lay judges from Békés County (83%) and Borsod-Abaúj-Zemplén County (76%) report above-average participation rates, while their counterparts from Budapest and Pest counties together experience this procedural opportunity at only 47%, and those from Csongrád County at just 32%. We may venture to suggest that these differences are not random, but rather reflect patterns of judicial role perceptions that prevail within the same organisational contexts.

The *social background* of the lay judges does not show any significant correlation with the involvement or inclusion practice. Where such a connection was found, it actually reflects another influence: the *level of settlement* where the lay judges reside mirrors the regional differences mentioned earlier. While only 46% of those from Budapest report experiencing such practices, 70% of those living in county seat towns mention the same. It is particularly interesting that lay judges residing in small villages (population of 16) almost unanimously (15 out of 16) report this favourable participation opportunity.

There appears to be a correlation with *age groups* and *employment status* (whether someone is an active worker or a pensioner). However, the higher proportion among the older age group and pensioner lay judges actually reflects the previously mentioned aspect of the lay judge status: that judges are more likely to provide the opportunity to ask questions to experienced lay judges who are serving their third or subsequent terms.

Among the attitudes of lay judges, the most prominent is *their satisfaction with the recognition of their work*: 70% of those satisfied contrast with only 34% of those dissatisfied. Therefore, dissatisfaction is likely to stem, at least in part, from the fact that certain groups of lay judges are not afforded this opportunity for involvement (to ask questions). A similar correlation may be observed *in terms of satisfaction with the work of the courts*: 68% of judges express satisfaction, compared to 40% of those who are dissatisfied.

An interesting, though not significant, effect is observed in relation to the stance taken on issues such as *abortion* and *euthanasia*. The ratio between the proponents of leniency and those favouring stricter measures shows a difference of 61:74% and 60:84%, respectively, indicating that the two camps perceive the prevalence of the questioning practice in distinctly different ways, with the "lenient" group viewing it more negatively and the "strict" group more positively.

Although not significant, the mysterious *correlation with political attitudes* resurfaced. A more positive perspective is associated with political apathy: those who are uninterested in politics or claim to be uninformed on political issues perceive the prevalence of this practice more favourably than average (77% and 73%, respectively). On the other hand, those who stated that no current political parties or movements align more closely with their views show a higher proportion (67%) compared to those who express sympathy for a political organisation (57%).

VI.4 JUDICIAL DEMAND FOR LAY JUDGE OPINIONS

VI.4.1 The Portrayal of the Situation from the Lay Judge's Perspective

In addition to the two procedural elements, we also examined the two substantive ones. The opinion-seeking dimension directly measured the practice of *whether, according to the lay judges, the judges typically seek the opinions of lay judges in the assessment of cases*. According to the tables illustrating the prevalence of this practice, this substantive aspect is more strongly realised than the provision of the procedural opportunity, meaning it is more characteristic of a wider range of judges.

According to the lay judges, overall, four out of every five judges are characterised by seeking the opinions of lay judges in the assessment of cases.

Table 39. Does the judge typically seek the lay judges' opinions in the assessment of the case?

	Valid percentage
No (rather not or never)	5.4
Both (sometimes yes, sometimes no)	10.7
Yes (mostly yes or always	83.9
Total:	100.0

Figure 25. Does the judge typically seek the lay judges' opinions in the assessment of the case?

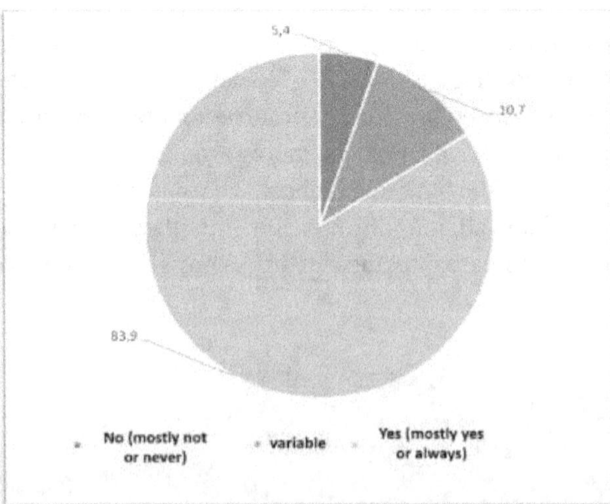

VI.4.2 Judges' Practice of Seeking Opinions

In this regard, lay judges' and judges' opinions largely align. Only 5.4% of judges report not requiring (or not particularly requiring) lay judges' opinions; 13.8% follow a fluctuating practice; the vast majority (79.8%) report a practice favourable to the lay judges.

VI.4.3 The Contextual Background of the Lay Judges' Experience of the Opinion-Seeking Practice

Given that this practice is widespread, occurring with a frequency of 84%, it was to be expected that relatively striking differences would be less pronounced compared to previous findings. Here, we adopt the approach of examining the factors associated with the 5% negative practice—namely, instances where lay judges perceive that the presiding judge *seldom* or *never seeks* their opinion—and identifying the contexts in which this tendency appears with greater prevalence.

Among the elements of *lay judge status*, one such factor proves to be the perspective of those departing from their role[132]—whether they have chosen not to continue or were not re-elected—at a rate of 14%. Additionally, the experiences of members of the lay judges' association also reflect this tendency, with a prevalence of 12%.[133] Among the elements of *social background*, the *type of municipality* and *age* show a correlation.

In smaller municipalities that are not county seats, residents report this negative (exclusionary) practice at an above-average rate of 9%. Similarly, younger individuals perceive different practices compared to their older counterparts, with 28%[134] of those under 50 and 9%[135] of those under 60 observing such tendencies). There is also a correlation with *employment status*, as 16% of actively employed individuals report experiencing this negative practice, though this is likely mediated by age. Additionally, some connection can be observed with

[132] Of 52 individuals, 7 report experiencing such practices.

[133] Of 49 individuals, 6 report the same.

[134] Of 18 individuals, 5 have encountered this practice.

[135] Of 86 individuals, 8 have reported experiencing it.

educational attainment[136] as well as with the sector of current or previous *employment*.[137]

Among lay judge attitudes, the perception of the recognition of their work plays a significant role in assessing the situation. Of those who are dissatisfied with the *recognition of their role* (58 individuals), 41% report experiencing exclusionary practices. There is also some correlation with satisfaction regarding the work of the courts: among *those who are dissatisfied* (53 individuals), 13% (7 individuals) report encountering exclusionary practices. No other attitudinal effects can be identified.

VI.4.4 The Frequency of Lay Judge Opinions Diverging from Those of the Presiding Judge

This aspect adds nuance to the picture of lay judge passivity or engagement. According to their own accounts, two in every five lay judges (42%) have never, in any case, held an opinion differing from that of the presiding judge.[138] A further one in five (21%) reports that this has occurred only once. This leaves two out of five lay judges (37.2%) who recall a few or a relatively significant number of such instances. The data provide a rational basis for arguments both in favour of a lack of lay judge autonomy—suggesting subordination to the professional judge—and in support of the persuasive and well-founded nature of the professional judge's reasoning. A more telling measure of lay judge engagement, however, is whether they voiced their differing opinions. Overall, we find that half (52%) of those with divergent views consistently expressed them in every instance. A substantial third (38%) adopted a mixed approach, sometimes voicing their dissent and sometimes remaining silent, while one in ten preferred to stay quiet. In terms of expressing dissent, the "*ancien régime*" lay judges were notably more passive, with 64% either rarely or never articulating their differing opinions.

---

[136] Among the 15 individuals without a secondary school diploma, three report encountering such practices.

[137] Among the small group (11 individuals) coming from the civil sector—compared to those from the public and private sectors—a higher proportion (3 individuals) report experiencing this negative (exclusionary) practice.

[138] According to our calculations based on Kulcsár's data (op. cit., p. 92), this characteristic was even more pronounced at the time, affecting 54% of lay judges.

By interpreting these two indicators together, we find that nearly half (151) of the 312 responding lay judges have either never held an opinion differing from that of the presiding judge or, if they have, they have chosen not to voice it. This practice was even more characteristic of earlier cohorts of lay judges, with three-quarters following the same pattern. At the same time, it appears that the most pronounced form of lay judge opposition—the formulation of a formal dissenting opinion—is exceedingly rare. Among 297 respondents, only five reported having done so on a single occasion, while another five had exercised this option multiple times. Given the small number of *dissenters*, any potential correlations between this form of activity and specific lay judge characteristics can only be suggested tentatively. We identified just one: while men constitute only 29% of the sample, they form the majority (six individuals) among those who have issued dissenting opinions.

VI.5 THE INFLUENCE OF LAY JUDGES ON JUDICIAL DECISIONS

VI.5.1 The Portrayal of the Situation from the Perspective of Lay Judges

The other key element—the dimension of "influence," or the extent to which lay judges' opinions are taken into account—can arguably be considered the most crucial factor from their perspective. Our inquiry focused on the *role that lay judge opinions play in shaping judicial decisions* (judgments). This is a comprehensive measure, as it assesses whether lay judges participating in proceedings perceive the impact and significance of their personal contributions and whether they feel they have played a part in shaping the decision that determines the outcome of a case.

If we take this as the basis for assessing the substantive role of the lay judge system, we can conclude that, in practice, the meaningful integration of the lay element into the judiciary is fundamentally upheld. The vast majority of lay judges (84%) report that their opinions matter in the assessment of cases. However, behind this positive evaluation lie two distinct experiential perspectives: 25% describe their role as akin to that of a "co-judge," while nearly 60% perceive their influence as ultimately subordinate to the professional dominance of judges. Overall, the perception that lay judges make no substantive contribution to case assessments is present to a lesser extent, accounting for only 16% of responses.

Table 40. Do Judges Take Lay Judges' Opinions into Account?

	Valid Percentage	
They do not matter at all	1.5	11.6
They have little weight and mostly do not matter	10.1	
Somewhat in between	5.3	5.3
They do matter, but the professional authority of judges prevails	58.2	83.1
They are taken very seriously (almost always)	24.9	
Total:	100.0	100.0

Figure 26. Do Judges Take Lay Judges' Opinions into Account?

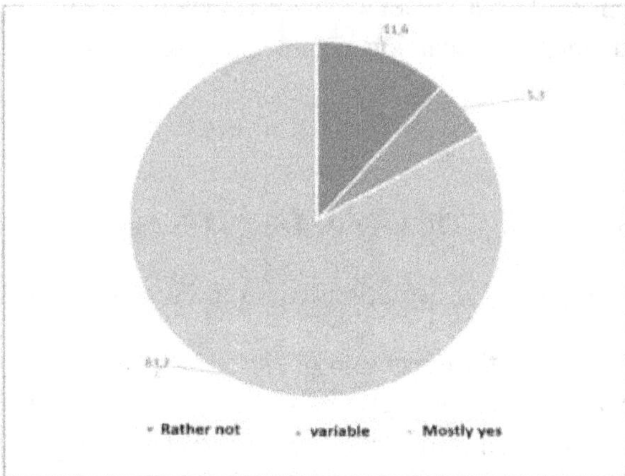

VI.5.2 Judges on the Influence of Lay Judges

In this regard, there is a stark contrast between the perspectives of lay judges and professional judges. Compared to judges, lay judges tend to view the influence of their opinions on judicial decisions in a significantly more positive light. This discrepancy may be explained through a socio-psychological approach. It appears that, at this point, lay judges are not merely assessing an external factor—namely, the judge's approach towards them—but rather evaluating a phenomenon that also involves an element of self-assessment. This may explain why lay judges tend to assess their own influence far more positively than professional judges do. After all, experiencing the disregard of their opinions could, to some extent, carry an element of self-devaluation. The majority of judges (70.5%) believe that the opinions of lay judges have little impact—whether negligible, minor, or inconsistent—on judicial decisions (judgments). A quarter of them (27.4%)

acknowledge that lay judges' views do matter, but ultimately, the professional authority of judges prevails. Only a very small proportion (2.1%) attribute a significant role to the opinions of lay judges.

VI.5.3 Factors Related to the Perception of Lay Judges' Influence

Overall, we found that one-quarter of the responding lay judges believe that their opinions play a significant role in shaping judicial decisions (judgments). We now turn to an examination of which groups of lay judges expressed a markedly different assessment.

Four key factors influence the perception of *lay judges' status*: *organizational position, geographical location, the number of terms served,* and *the area of law.*

This means that lay judges serving at Budapest-Capital district courts express a notably low level of satisfaction—only 1 out of 15 respondents gave a favourable assessment. In contrast, the figure is remarkably high in Békés County[139] where 44% of respondents rated their influence positively, while in Budapest and Pest County,[140] this proportion stands at only 12%. Among those serving their third or subsequent term[141] 35% reported satisfaction, and lay judges involved (also) in civil law cases[142] expressed a higher level of contentment (38%) compared to those in other areas of law.

Social background influences this perception in several respects, particularly in terms of place of residence, age, and level of education. Lay judges from the capital (60 respondents) are the least satisfied, with only 10% expressing a positive view, compared to the small group of non-urban lay judges (17 respondents), of whom 41%[143] reported satisfaction. Younger lay judges, specifically those under 50 (a group of only 18 respondents), stand out with a markedly different assessment—only a single individual (!) in this group expressed satisfaction with how their opinions are considered. It also appears that higher levels of education are associated with a more critical attitude.

---

[139] 75 individuals.

[140] 76 individuals.

[141] 101 individuals.

[142] 32 individuals.

[143] 7 individuals.

While respondents without a secondary school diploma (15 individuals) and those with a secondary school diploma (100 individuals) report above-average satisfaction levels (40% and 32%, respectively), this figure drops to 21% among university graduates (192 individuals).

The influence of *lay judges' attitudes* on their assessments manifests in two ways. First, there is a more direct, perhaps more professional effect. Among those who are *dissatisfied with the recognition of lay judges' work* (59 respondents), only 14% believe that lay judges' opinions carry weight in judicial decision-making, compared to 29% of those who are satisfied. Second, there is a more indirect effect, filtered through lay judges' broader perception of society. Those who view the *institutional functioning of society* more favourably tend to be more satisfied than average (25%). This includes individuals who express satisfaction with the government (32%),[144] the country's economic situation (37%),[145] the work of the police (36%)[146] and the prosecution service (31%),[147] the activities of the National Assembly (31%),[148] and local governments (32%),[149] political parties (*66.7%)[150] and the functioning of the European Union (40%).[151]

VI.6. SUMMARY OF JUDICIAL PRACTICES AS PERCEIVED BY LAY JUDGES AND AS RECOGNIZED BY JUDGES

VI.6.1 Lay Judges' Assessments Across the Four Examined Dimensions

The operationalized interpretation of lay judge participation is illustrated in the following framework, while the percentage distribution of judicial practices perceived by lay judges across four dimensions is represented in the accompanying diagram. Although judicial role perceptions may vary significantly between individuals and regions, lay judges are not merely passive spectators in the trial and decision-making process. Judges likely take care not to overtly undermine their formal status as associate members of the bench. However, a

[144] 93 individuals.
[145] 67 individuals.
[146] 100 individuals.
[147] 173 individuals.
[148] 70 individuals.
[149] 127 individuals.
[150] In total: 21 individuals.
[151] 76 individuals.

clear point of tension emerges between the lay and professional elements: in judicial decision-making, the influence of professional judges—marked by a sense of judicial aristocratism—is most perceptibly asserted, reinforcing their dominance in the process.

Diagram 3. The Operationalized Interpretation of Lay Judge Participation

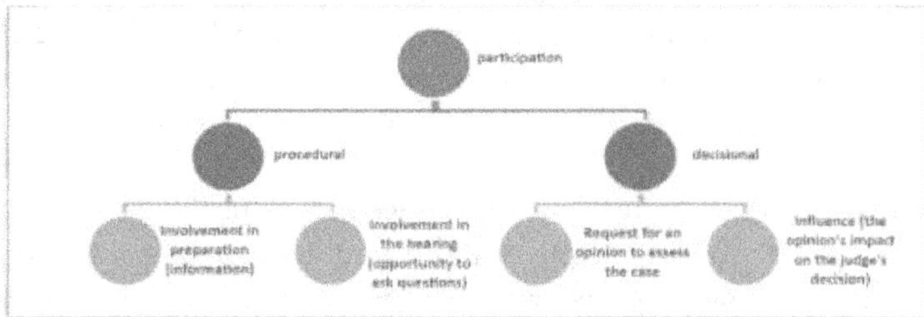

Figure 27. Lay Judges' Assessments Across the Four Examined Dimensions

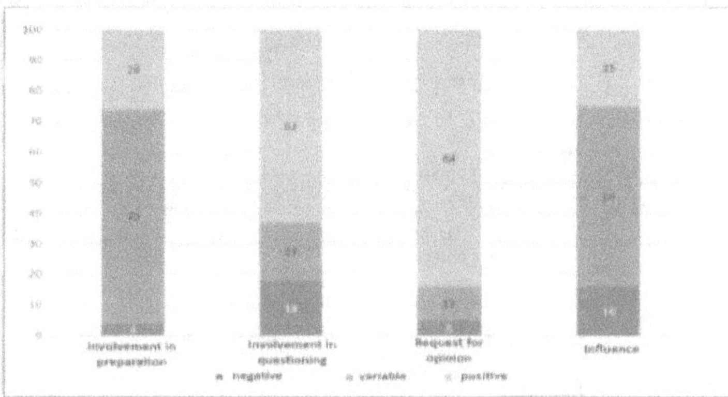

VI.6.2 Summary Types of Judicial Practices Emerging from Lay Judges' Assessments

We also attempted to provide a summary representation of the judicial practices perceived by lay judges across the four examined dimensions. To achieve this, we conducted a cluster analysis[152] to explore the interconnections between the

[152] We employed the SPSS K-means clustering method, incorporating all four variables (information provision, participation in questioning, solicitation of opinions, and the weight given to opinions) in a three-category format (positive, mixed, negative) into the classification process. Among the different clustering variations tested, we ultimately adopted the four-cluster model. This decision was based on the fact that, despite the relatively small sample size, all four

judicial practices observed in these four areas—preparatory involvement, participation in questioning, solicitation of opinions, and the weight given to opinions—using a scoring system (positive = 3, mixed = 2, negative = 1). The following table presents the average values measured across each dimension for the identified clusters. Considering these values collectively, four distinct judicial attitudes emerge: the collegial judge, who embraces a co-judge perspective; the fair aristocrat, who maintains a professional dominance while ensuring fairness; the ambivalent judge, who exhibits inconsistencies in their approach; and the distant judge, who remains detached from lay judge participation.

The overall picture, even in this summarised form, remains favourable, as nearly half of the lay judges (47%) unequivocally regard the judicial practices directed towards them as positive. Meanwhile, the practice that fails to ensure meaningful participation occurs in the smallest proportion.

Table 41. Types of Judicial Practices from the Lay Judge's Perspective – Overall Picture

	1.	2.	3.	4.
	Correct (Co-judge Perspective)	**Correct Aristocrat**	**Ambivalent**	**Detached Aristocrat**
	n = 142	n = 60	n = 57	n = 46
	46.6 %	**19.7 %**	**18.7 %**	**15.1 %**
Dimensions	**Averages (1–3)**			
Preparatory Involvement	2.20	2.70	1.98	1.93
Participation in Questioning	2.99	2.88	1.42	1.52
Solicitation of Opinions	2.98	3.00	3.00	1.65
Influence	2.45	1.65	2.18	1.48

The "*correct*" (*appearing to be* based on a co-judicial approach) judicial practice (47%) always provides the lay judges with information regarding the case (occasionally even materials); it consistently ensures the opportunity for questioning during the trial; it always seeks the *lay judges' opinions* on the assessment of the case; and, according to the lay judges, these opinions are taken into serious consideration when making decisions.

---

groups were sufficiently large and empirically well-defined. The program established this cluster structure based on responses from 305 lay judges through seven iterative steps.

Judges marked with the "*correct aristocrat*" label (20%) exhibit nearly the same characteristics, with one significant difference: in their decisions, they act autonomously. While they do listen to the lay judges, they ultimately do not take their opinions into account.

The "*detached aristocrat*" practice (15%) is the direct opposite of the "co-judicial" practice: it perhaps aligns most closely with the average practice in terms of providing information, but it does not prioritise allowing the lay judges the opportunity to question during the trial. It is not particularly keen on soliciting the lay judges' opinions regarding the assessment of the case; and accordingly, the lay judges' opinions play the smallest role in the formation of the judicial decision in this practice.

Alongside these three types, the analysis also identified a fourth: the "ambivalent" type (19%). This is characterised by fulfilling the duty to provide information, yet not supporting the idea that lay judges should have the opportunity to ask questions during the trial. Despite this, the judge always seeks the lay judges' opinions and appears to consider them to some extent.

VI.6.3 The comparison of the lay judges' and judges' perceptions of the situation

Since the judge data collection, conducted simultaneously with the lay judge data collection (although not representative), also included judges' statements about the practices they follow in terms of preparation, involvement during the trial, requesting opinions, and considering those opinions, we had the opportunity to compare the practices perceived (or possibly presented) by the lay judges with those emerging from the judges' self-description.

As we have seen, this four-component practice reveals both agreement and similarity, as well as clear differences. In terms of *preparation* (information), both sides view the judicial practice in a broadly similar manner; when it comes to *involvement* (the opportunity to ask questions during the trial), judges perceive their own practice as significantly more positive (and frequent) than the lay judges do; regarding the requesting of opinions, the two views are nearly identical; however, the greatest discrepancy arises in the most crucial dimension— the *inclusion* of lay judges' opinions in the formation of judicial decisions. The lay judges portray their *influence* on judicial decisions as considerably more positive, whereas the majority of judges hold the opinion—or rather report the actual situation—that the opinions of the lay judges do not play a meaningful role in this regard.

Figure 28. Comparison of the Lay Judges' and Judges' Perspectives

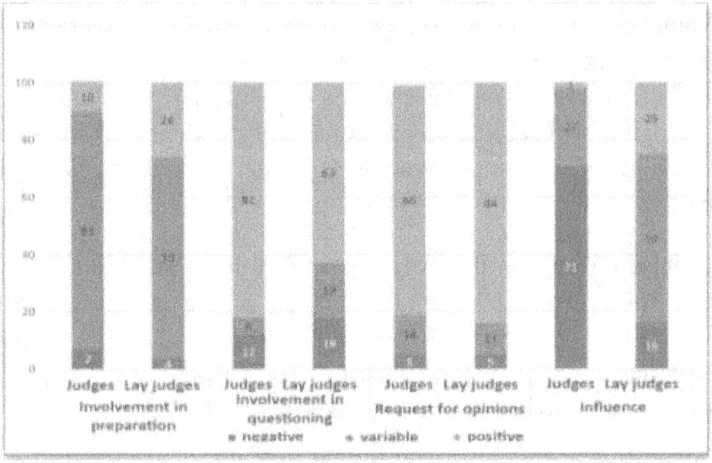

VI.6.4 The Summary Types of Judicial Practices Emergent from Judicial Self-Descriptions

Using the same set of variables, we conducted a cluster analysis on the database obtained from the judicial survey (N=109). After six iterative steps, the program grouped 93 responding judges into three empirically interpretable clusters (types).

Table 42. Summary Types of Judicial Practices from the Judges' Perspective

	1. **Correct**	2. **Correct aristocrat**	3. **Detached aristocrat**
	n = 26	n = 52	n = 15
	28.0 %	**55.9 %**	**16.1 %**
Dimensions	**Averages (1–3)**		
Preparatory Involvement	2.19	1.98	1.93
Participation in Questioning	2.96	2.94	1.40
Solicitation of Opinions	2.96	2.88	1.93
Influence	2.08	1.00	1.13

The "*correct*" type (28%) always informs the lay judges (even if no materials are provided); always offers them the opportunity to ask questions during the hearing; always solicits their opinions; and takes these opinions into account to some degree.

The "*correct aristocrat*" type (56%) differs from the previous one in that, although it provides every opportunity for the lay judges to participate and express themselves, it makes decisions essentially independently of the lay judges' opinions (with professional autonomy).

Judges classified as the "*detached aristocrat*" type (16%) almost always provide information, but do not favour the involvement of lay judges in the trial; their practice regarding soliciting opinions is highly variable; and in their decisions, they too distance themselves from the lay judges' opinions (influence).

Naturally, we do not encounter the "*ambivalent*" type, as formulated from the lay judges' perspective, since it was unlikely that any judges would characterise their own practice as inconsistent.

VI.7 THE CORRECTION OF THE PARTICIPATION MODEL

In light of the judges' statements, we must adjust our initial model: in addition to the two *procedural dimensions* (preparation and involvement), we have introduced two *decisional dimensions* (opinion request and influence). It appears that actual judicial practice overrides this structure at one point: the judges' demand for lay judges' opinions is, in fact, not a decisional, but a procedural element. The vast majority of judges formally meet the expectations by requesting lay judges' opinions, but in reality, they do not take these opinions into account when making decisions related to the case.

Diagram 4. Modified Participation Model

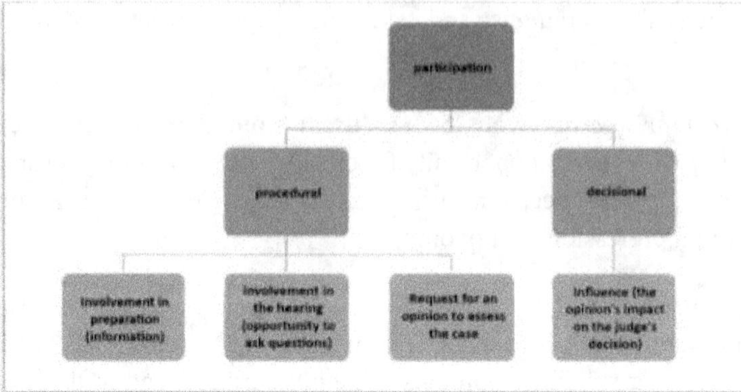

VII. The Lay Judges' Satisfaction with Their Position and Their Views on Societal Issues

Our opinions about the world around us can be seen as verbal expressions of the attitudes associated with them. These opinions reflect not only our emotional relationship and cognitive evaluation of the subject in question but also our "approach" to it. This study investigates how the opinions of responding lay judges can reveal their attitudes towards themselves, their lives, and the social environment. We examine the differences in attitudes between various groups and also explore whether there is a correlation between an individual's attitude towards themselves and their attitude towards the community.

Table 43. Averages and Standard Deviations of Satisfactions

	N	Average	Standard deviation
How satisfied are you with the country's economic situation?	280	2.80	0.996
How satisfied are you with the government's activities?	278	3.02	1.160
How satisfied are you with the activities of the churches?	273	3.10	1.024
How satisfied are you with your current financial situation and standard of living?	291	3.47	0.957
How satisfied are you with your social recognition?	287	3.82	0.899
How satisfied are you with the course of your life so far?	286	4.00	0.759
How satisfied are you with the recognition of your work as a lay judge?	288	4.08	0.910

On a five-point scale measuring satisfaction (1 – not at all, 5 – completely), the responding lay judges are least satisfied with the country's economic situation and most satisfied with the recognition of their work as lay judges. The pattern of the averages also reveals that the judges are much less satisfied with the country's economic situation, the activities of the government, and the churches, compared to matters concerning their own lives, such as their financial situation, standard of living, social recognition, the course of their lives so far, and the esteem of their work as lay judges. In other words, their opinions are far more favourable regarding their personal circumstances than concerning societal and community-related matters. In addition to the averages, it is also worth paying attention to the standard deviations, as they reveal how homogeneous the individual opinion averages are and whether they resulted from extreme responses. To interpret this, we use the relative standard deviation, which shows what percentage of the standard deviation the average represents. Therefore, if the relative standard deviation is larger, it indicates that the average was formed from more extreme responses. The following table shows the relative standard deviation for each opinion.

Table 44. Relative Standard Deviations of Opinions

	Relative standard deviation (%)
How satisfied are you with the country's economic situation?	35.60
How satisfied are you with the government's activities?	38.41
How satisfied are you with the activities of the churches?	32.99
How satisfied are you with your current financial situation and standard of living?	27.59
How satisfied are you with your social recognition?	23.52
How satisfied are you with the course of your life so far?	18.98
How satisfied are you with the recognition of your work as a lay judge?	22.30

The data show that the opinions of the lay judges are much more divided when it comes to social issues than regarding their personal circumstances. It is evident that while the satisfaction with the economic situation of the country, the activities of the government, and the churches – with generally lower averages – came with higher standard deviations, in the case of personal life circumstances – such as financial situation, social recognition, life satisfaction, and the recognition of the lay judges' work – the standard deviation is lower, indicating greater agreement among the respondents. To illustrate the difference, we present the distributions of the highest – related to the government's activities – and the lowest – regarding satisfaction with one's own life.

Table 45. Distribution of Variables with the Highest and Lowest Relative Standard Deviations

	%				
	Not at all	Rather not	Some-what	Rather yes	Fully
How satisfied are you with the course of your life so far?	0.7	1.7	19.4	53.1	25.1
How satisfied are you with the government's activities?	11.9	19.7	33.8	23.9	10.7

The low relative variance in satisfaction with one's life can be attributed to the fact that the majority of respondents fall into the group of those who are somewhat or fully satisfied—together, 78.2%. As a result, there is little significant variation in the majority's assessment. Almost no one is dissatisfied, with only 2.4%, and those who are moderately satisfied make up approximately 20%. In contrast, the evaluation of the government's activities shows much greater division, with the dissatisfied making up 31.6%, the moderately satisfied 33.8%, and the satisfied 34.6%.

In summary, two important conclusions can be drawn regarding the satisfaction of the lay judges. On one hand, satisfaction with social actors—the government, the church—and the country's economic situation is significantly lower than satisfaction with their personal lives—material situation, standard of living, social esteem, the course of their lives so far, and the recognition of their judicial work. On the other hand, while opinions about their personal lives are largely shared among the majority, views on social issues are much more divided.

For easier handling, we performed a principal component analysis using the seven indicators listed above, the results of which are shown in the table below.

Table 46. Principal Components

	Components	
	1	2
How satisfied are you with the development of your life so far?	.860	.103
How satisfied are you with your social recognition?	.811	.189
How satisfied are you with your current financial situation and standard of living?	.773	.128
How satisfied are you with the recognition of your lay judge work?	.502	.085
How satisfied are you with the government's activities?	.117	.904
How satisfied are you with the economic situation of the country?	.259	.863
How satisfied are you with the activities of the churches?	.087	.815

The result confirms that the indicators related to an individual's life – including financial situation, standard of living, social recognition, life's progression, and the recognition of lay judge work – form a distinct set, separate from those relating to society, the government's activities, the churches, and the country's economic situation. In the first principal component, therefore, the indicators of individual life are present, with the greatest weight being given to satisfaction with life's progression, social recognition, and financial situation, while the recognition of lay judge work appears with considerably less weight, suggesting that the appreciation of judicial activity is less significant when evaluating individual life. In the second principal component, the highest weight is given to the assessment of the government's activities, followed by the evaluation of the country's economic situation, and finally – with the smallest weight – the evaluation of the activities of the churches. The average score of the principal components is zero in the total sample for both components, so if a value is negative in any subsample, it indicates below-average satisfaction, while a positive value indicates above-average satisfaction.

In traditional variables known as "sociological hard variables" such as gender, age, educational attainment, occupational status, and place of residence, we found no significant differences. In other words, opinions do not differ along these variables, whether between men and women, young people and middle-aged or older individuals, those with higher education and those with less education, active workers and inactive ones, or between those living in the capital and large cities and those residing in smaller towns or villages. Although no significant differences can be identified along these variables, it can still be stated that men and residents of Budapest are more critical of the social environment than women and non-capital residents.

The only significant difference in satisfaction with personal life and social actors is between those with and without political party preferences. In the questionnaire, respondents who answered "yes" to the question *"Is there a current political party or organization that is closer to you?"* are considered to have a strong party preference, while those who answered "no" are considered to have no or only weak party preference.

- In terms of satisfaction with social issues, those with party preferences reported significantly higher satisfaction (0.364) compared to those without party preferences, who achieved an average score below the mean (–0.283) ($t = -5.336$; sig. <0.05).

Figure 29. Satisfaction with the government, the country's economic situation, and the activities of the church

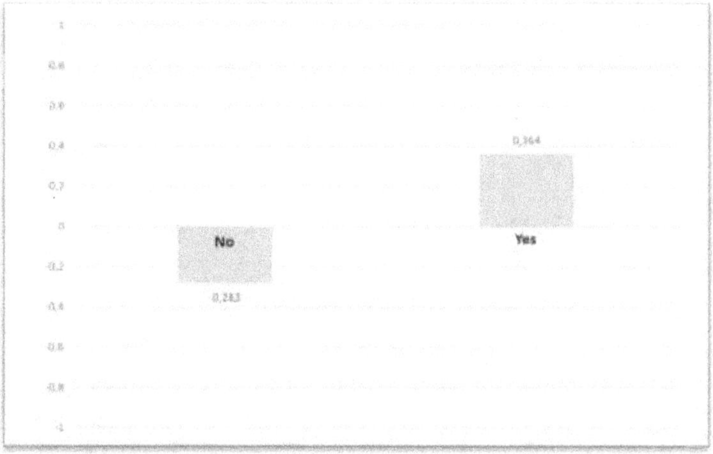

There are significant differences between the two groups on all three indicators – those belonging to this principal component – concerning satisfaction with the government, the assessment of the country's economic situation, and the evaluation of the activities of the churches. There are significant differences in satisfaction with the government's performance (Z = –5.502; sig. <0.05), the assessment of the country's economic situation (Z = –4.106; sig. <0.05), and the evaluation of the activities of the churches (Z = –4.043; sig. <0.05). Given that those with party preferences report significantly higher satisfaction both in the principal component score and on each of the associated indicators, we must assume that members of the group with party preferences are likely supporters of the ruling party or, at the very least, sympathisers with it.

- In terms of satisfaction with individual life, we found a result that is precisely the opposite of the previous one. Those with party preferences reported significantly lower satisfaction (-0.200) than those without party preferences, who achieved an above-average (0.159) score in satisfaction with their own life (t = 2.843; sig. <0.05).

Figure 30. Satisfaction with individual life

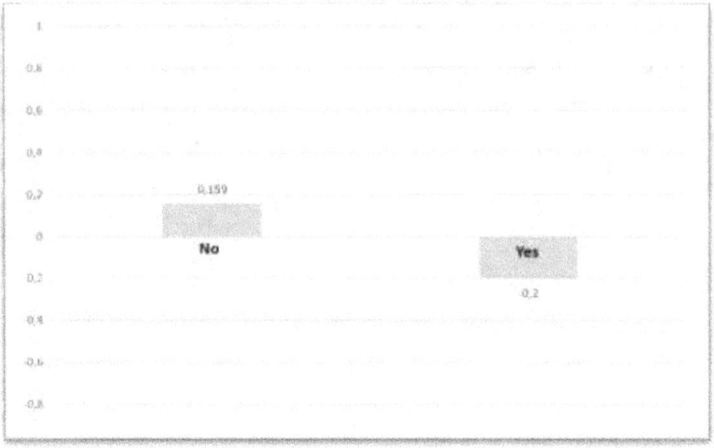

Among the four indicators belonging to the principal component, there is no significant difference in three cases—although the average for those without party preference is slightly higher in all three—but the fourth indicator, where the difference is significant, is the recognition of lay judge work (Z= -2.681; sig.<0.05). Therefore, the significant difference in the principal component score is attributed not only to the three indicators where no significant difference was found but also to the one indicator showing a significant difference, despite it having the smallest weight in the principal component.

VII.1 SATISFACTION WITH DOMESTIC POLITICAL ACTORS AND THE ADMINISTRATION OF JUSTICE

Table 47. Satisfaction with Domestic Political Actors and the Administration of Justice

	N	Average	Standard deviation
To what extent are you satisfied with the activities of political parties?	273	2.38	0.923
To what extent are you satisfied with the work of the National Assembly?	277	2.86	1.029
To what extent are you satisfied with the functioning of civil society organisations?	274	3.13	0.848
To what extent are you satisfied with the performance of the police?	283	3.24	0.805

	N	Average	Standard deviation
To what extent are you satisfied with the activities of your local government?	280	3.39	0.889
To what extent are you satisfied with the work of the prosecution service?	282	3.66	0.791
To what extent are you satisfied with the performance of the courts?	285	4.07	0.724

Measured on a five-point scale of satisfaction (1 – not at all, 5 – completely), lay judges expressed the lowest level of satisfaction with the activities of political parties and the National Assembly, while they were most satisfied with the work of the judiciary, the prosecution service, and the courts. Other social institutions (civil society organisations, the police, and local governments) occupied an intermediate position between the judiciary and political actors (the National Assembly and political parties). Beyond the averages, attention should also be paid to the standard deviations, as differences can be observed in the distribution of opinions. The following table illustrates the relative standard deviation for each opinion.

Table 48. Relative Standard Deviations of Satisfaction with Domestic Political Actors and the Judiciary

	Relative Standard Deviation (%)
To what extent are you satisfied with the activities of political parties?	38.78
To what extent are you satisfied with the work of the National Assembly?	35.98
To what extent are you satisfied with the functioning of civil society organisations?	27.09
To what extent are you satisfied with the performance of the police?	24.85
To what extent are you satisfied with the activities of your local government?	26.22
To what extent are you satisfied with the work of the prosecution service?	21.61
To what extent are you satisfied with the performance of the courts?	17.79

The data indicate that lay judges' opinions are far more divided when it comes to political issues—much like in the assessment of broader social matters—while their views are less fragmented regarding civil society organisations, the police, and local governments. The most uniform opinions, however, concern the two key actors of the judiciary: the prosecution service and the courts.

For easier interpretability, a principal component analysis was conducted using the seven indicators above. However, only six of these indicators appear in the two principal components. The reason for this is that satisfaction with the police was equally associated with both components, effectively "sitting" on both, and was therefore excluded from the analysis.

The results of the principal component analysis are presented in the table below.

Table 49. Principal Components

	Components	
	1	2
To what extent are you satisfied with the activities of political parties?	.846	.142
To what extent are you satisfied with the work of the National Assembly?	.775	.180
To what extent are you satisfied with the activities of your local government?	.707	.254
To what extent are you satisfied with the functioning of civil society organisations?	.643	.180
To what extent are you satisfied with the performance of the courts?	.157	.901
To what extent are you satisfied with the work of the prosecution service?	.292	.842

The six indicators were grouped into two principal components. The first principal component encompassed the evaluation of political actors—the activities of political parties, the National Assembly, local governments, and civil society organisations—while the second focused on the judiciary, comprising the assessment of the courts and the prosecution service. Within the first principal component, the indicators were weighted in descending order of importance: political parties, the National Assembly, local governments, and civil society organisations. In the second principal component, the evaluation of the courts carried the greatest weight, followed by that of the prosecution service, with a slightly lower significance. The average score of both principal components is zero across the entire sample. Consequently, a negative value within a subsample indicates satisfaction below the average, whereas a positive value signifies above-average satisfaction.

There is a significant difference in satisfaction with political actors (political parties, the National Assembly, local governments, and civil society organisations) between those who have a party preference and those who do not.

- Those with a party preference reported significantly higher satisfaction with political actors (0.199) compared to those without a party preference, who scored below the average (-0.156) (t = -2.841; sig. < 0.05).

Figure 31. Satisfaction with the Government, the Country's Economic Situation, and the Activities of the Church

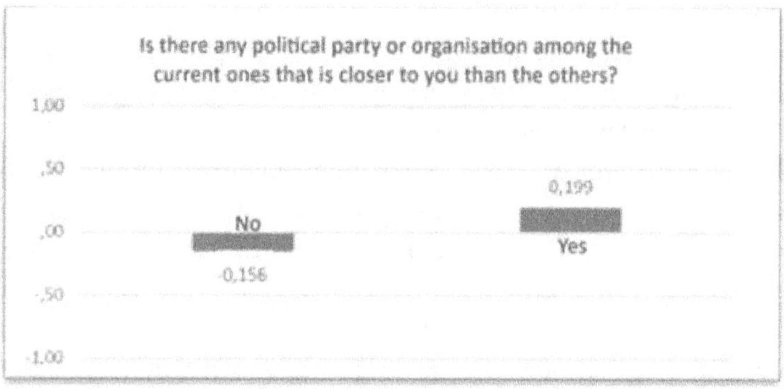

In three out of four indicators, there is a significant difference between the two groups in terms of satisfaction with political activities. These differences are observed in satisfaction with the work of the National Assembly (Z = –3.523; sig. < 0.05), the assessment of local governments' activities (Z = –3.155; sig. < 0.05), and the evaluation of political parties' activities (Z = –2.684; sig. < 0.05). Although the difference in satisfaction with civil society organisations is not statistically significant (Z = –1.041; sig. > 0.05), those with a party preference still express greater satisfaction with their activities than those without one.

- There is no significant difference in satisfaction with the judiciary (prosecution service and courts), either in terms of the principal component score or the individual indicator scores. Those with and without a party preference assessed the judiciary's activities in almost the same way.

While significant differences in satisfaction with the social environment—including government activities, the country's economic situation, and the work of the churches—as well as with individual life, were observed only between those with and without a party preference, in the case of the political environment and the judiciary, multiple differences can be identified.

By Gender

- Men are significantly more critical of the activities of political actors than women, expressing notably lower satisfaction ($t = -2.017$; sig. < 0.05).
- Men also report lower satisfaction with the judiciary's activities; however, the difference is not statistically significant.

By Place of Residence

- Satisfaction with the activities of political actors does not show any significant differences based on place of residence, nor does any clear trend emerge in the levels of satisfaction.
- However, in terms of satisfaction with the judiciary, residents of Budapest are significantly less satisfied than those living in small towns. Those in county seats and villages do not differ significantly from either Budapest residents or those in small towns. Nevertheless, a capital–countryside divide can be observed, with lay judges residing in the capital reporting below-average satisfaction (-0.491), while those in all other types of settlements express above-average satisfaction with the judiciary's activities.

By Age

- Satisfaction with the activities of political actors does not exhibit any significant differences across age groups, nor does any clear trend emerge. However, it is noteworthy that the youngest cohort (35–49 years) expresses the lowest level of satisfaction.
- In contrast, satisfaction with the judiciary's activities does show a significant difference, with the youngest group being notably less satisfied than older respondents. The average satisfaction score for the 35–49 age group is -0.607, while for those aged 50–59 it is +0.016, and for those over 59 it is +0.015. This indicates a statistically significant distinction between the youngest age group and the two older cohorts in their assessment of the judiciary's performance.

According to Educational Qualifications

It is methodologically challenging to produce a reliable result based on educational qualifications, given that a significant majority of the responding lay judges—approximately 65%—hold a degree, about 30-31% have completed secondary education, and around 4-5% lack a high school diploma. Consequently, this latter group is rather small, comprising just 14 individuals. The comparison of these groups is therefore methodologically problematic, and it would be more appropriate to apply a division between graduates and non-graduates, merging the groups of those with secondary education and those without—thus blurring the distinction between those who have and have not completed high school, while increasing the sample size.

1. If this latter classification is used—where the sample sizes are methodologically more accurate—there is no significant difference between graduates and non-graduates in their assessment of the political environment. In the less methodologically accepted breakdown, where those without a diploma are listed as a separate group, a significant difference will emerge: members of the group without a high school diploma are more satisfied with the political

environment than those with at least a secondary education. In other words, the least educated perceive the political environment more favourably, while there is no difference between the other two groups.

2. In terms of satisfaction with the activities of the judiciary, there is no significant difference either in the graduate–non-graduate or graduate–secondary school–non-secondary school groupings. However, in this area too, it is the least educated group members who are the most satisfied, while the graduates are the most critical.

VII.2 SATISFACTION WITH THE OPERATION OF THE EUROPEAN UNION

After considering satisfaction with domestic social and political actors, the domestic situation, and the judiciary, let us now turn to opinions regarding the European Union. Satisfaction with the functioning of the European Union was originally measured on a five-point scale (1 – not at all, 2 – rather not, 3 – mixed,

4 – rather satisfied, 5 – fully satisfied). We reduced this scale by merging the two dissatisfied and two satisfied groups, while leaving the mixed responses unchanged. The following figure shows that the satisfied and dissatisfied groups are nearly equal in size (26.6% and 27.7%), while the majority of respondents fall into the middle category (45.7%). In other words, nearly half of the respondents cannot be clearly classified as either satisfied or dissatisfied with the European Union's functioning, should they be required to make a decision.

Figure 32. How satisfied are you with the functioning of the European Union? (%)

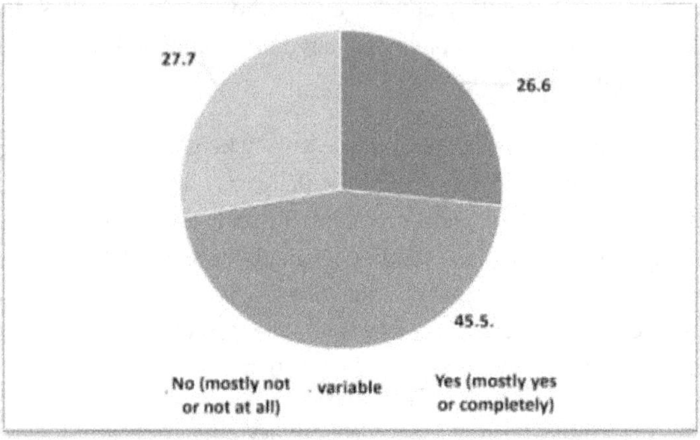

Satisfaction with the functioning of the European Union was also examined by asking the lay judges, "What would you say, in which direction are the affairs of the European Union moving now?" This was to be answered on a four-point scale (1 – definitely bad; 2 – rather bad than good; 3 – rather good than bad; 4 – definitely good).

Figure 33. What would you say, in which direction are the affairs of the European Union moving now? (%)

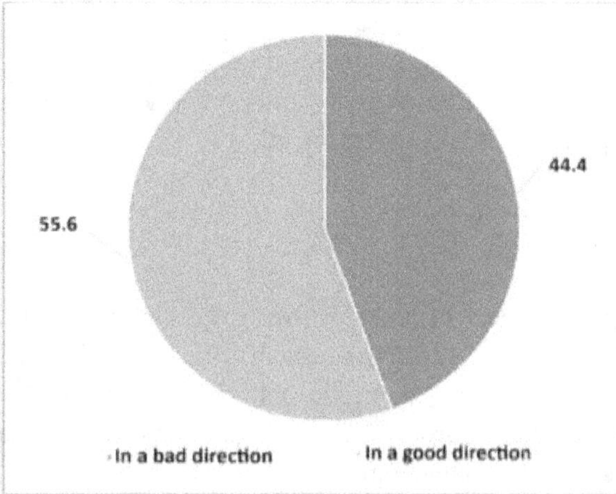

The relatively high proportion of respondents (45.7%) who answered "mixed" to the previous question regarding the functioning of the European Union rearranged their responses to this latter question—given that here, a neutral "mixed" option was not available, and they were required to take a stance. The majority of them (62.4%) expressed the view that "the affairs of the European Union are moving in the right direction." The above figure illustrates that, as a result, just over half of the responding lay judges (55.6%) believe that "the affairs of the European Union are moving in the right direction."

There is also a significant difference in satisfaction with the functioning of the European Union between those with party preferences and those without.

- Those with party preferences indicated significantly lower levels of satisfaction than those without party preferences ($Z = -2.108$; sig. < 0.05). In other words, individuals with party preferences are more dissatisfied with the functioning of the European Union than those without party preferences.

To summarise the points described so far, the following picture emerges:

I. Those with party preferences are significantly more satisfied than those without party preferences in both of the "domestic political" areas:

- the social (satisfaction with the government, the church, and the country's financial situation) and
- the political (satisfaction with political parties, the National Assembly, local governments, and civil organisations) areas.

II. On the other hand, those without party preferences are more satisfied than those with party preferences with regard to:

- their individual life and
- the European Union.

III. There is no difference between the two groups in their satisfaction with the actors of the judiciary, which suggests that the perception of the judiciary is not influenced by either "domestic political" factors or the perception of individual life or the European Union. The respondents appear to treat the judiciary as an independent entity.

VII.3 ATTITUDES OF LAY JUDGES TOWARDS THE SOCIAL ENVIRONMENT

We were intrigued to explore whether there exists a general attitude or stance towards the social environment that reveals the respondents' relationship with the surrounding societal context, shedding light on the pattern of this relationship.

To analyse this relationship, we used three indicators that assess the evaluation of the social environment:

- In which direction would you say the affairs of your town are moving now?
- In which direction would you say the affairs of the country are moving now?
- In which direction would you say the affairs of the European Union are moving now?

Regarding their own town, when asked, "What would you say, in which direction are the affairs of your town moving now?", 75.6% of the respondents answered that they believe things are moving in a positive direction.

Figure 34. In which direction would you say the affairs of your town are moving now? (%)

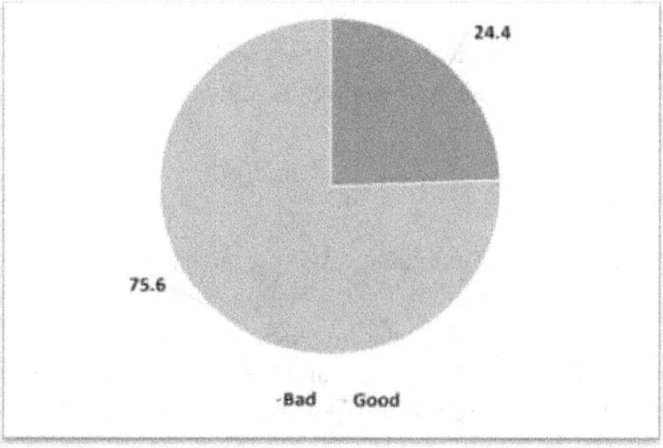

Regarding the affairs of the country, 57.4% of the respondents believe that the country's affairs are moving in a positive direction.

Figure 35. In which direction would you say the affairs of the country are moving now? (%)

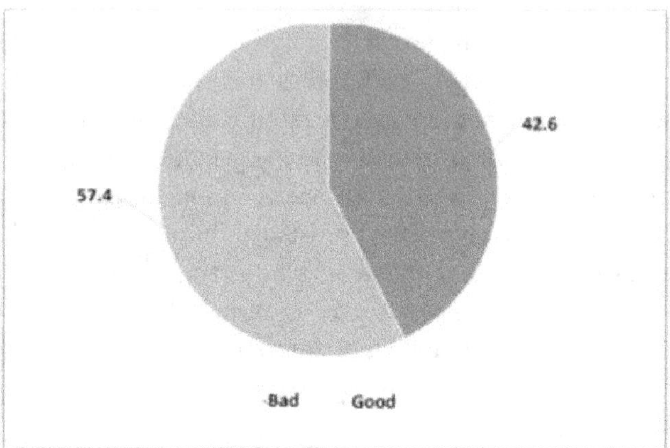

Overall, among the three entities surveyed, most respondents feel that things are moving in a positive direction in their own town, with 57.4% perceiving the same for the country, and 55.6% for the European Union.

To explore the attitudes in greater depth, we conducted a cluster analysis on the three variables mentioned above, resulting in the identification of three distinct groups.

1.Completely Satisfied

- This group consists of individuals who perceive that matters are progressing in a positive direction at all levels—within their own locality, the country, and the European Union. Regarding their own locality, all members of this group (100%) expressed a favourable opinion on the direction of developments, while 70% held a positive view concerning the country and 60% regarding the European Union. These individuals can be characterised as those who assess their social environment positively and maintain an optimistic attitude towards it. In terms of cluster size, this is the largest group, comprising 212 individuals, representing approximately 76% of respondents.

2.EU-Centric

- Members of this group believe that things are moving in the wrong direction both in their own locality and across the country. None (0%) of them expressed a favourable opinion regarding their locality, and only 16% considered the national situation to be heading in the right direction. However, when it comes to the European Union, all members (100%) view developments as positive. EU-centrists exhibit a negative attitude towards the Hungarian social environment, while their outlook on the European Union is overwhelmingly positive. In terms of size, this is the smallest cluster, comprising 27 individuals, approximately 10% of the respondents.

3.Completely Dissatisfied

- Members of this group perceive that things are deteriorating at all levels—within their locality, the country, and the European Union. None (0%) expressed a favourable view regarding their locality or the European Union, while only 21% considered the national direction to be positive. Thus, these individuals maintain a generally negative attitude towards all three social environments, embodying a classic “everything is bad” perspective. In terms of cluster size, this is the second smallest group, consisting of 39 individuals, accounting for approximately 14% of the respondents.

We believe that at least two of these three groups represent broader patterns of general attitudes, which extend beyond perceptions of the social environment and influence perspectives on various aspects of life. One is the "enthusiastic" mindset, typically characterised by a positive outlook, while the other is the "pessimistic" mindset, where individuals are largely dissatisfied with their surroundings—sometimes with everything.

VII.4 “COMPLETELY SATISFIED” VS. “COMPLETELY DISSATISFIED”

If it is possible to define a more general attitude—one that extends beyond perceptions of the social environment and influences other areas of life—then this attitude should also be observable in the lay judges’ views on matters unrelated to society.

VII.4.1 Civic Duty or Personal Choice?

We asked the lay judges whether they regarded participation in elections as a civic duty or a matter of personal choice. The majority (68.8%) held the view that the election of community leaders is a public affair in which members of the community ought to express their opinions, considering it, therefore, a duty incumbent upon them.

Figure 36. What is your position on civic participation in elections? (%)

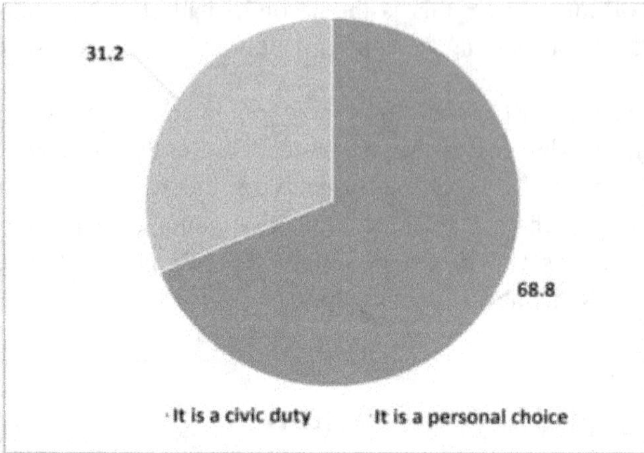

The various attitudinal groups perceive this form of social responsibility in markedly different ways. Among the Completely Dissatisfied, opinions are almost evenly divided between viewing voting as a personal choice and considering it a civic duty. Among the EU-Centric group, however, the balance shifts towards civic duty, with 64.3% believing that voting is an obligation of citizenship.

In the Completely Satisfied group, this stance is even more pronounced, with a decisive majority (73.3%) upholding the view that voting is a civic duty.

Figure 37. What is your position on civic participation in elections? By satisfaction groups (%)

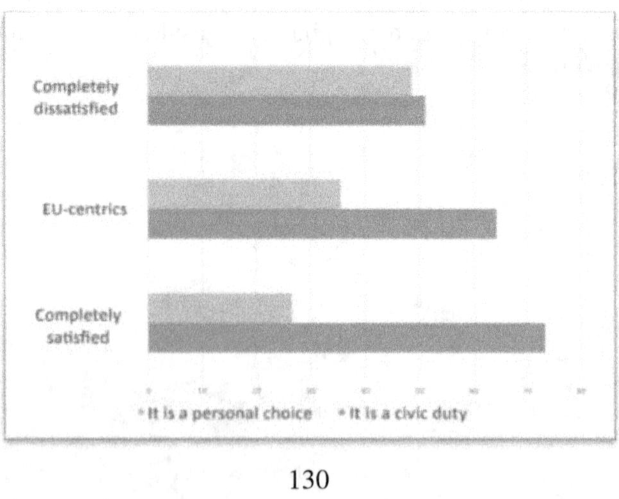

In terms of social responsibility, the Completely Satisfied group can be regarded as the most responsible, while the Completely Dissatisfied group exhibits the least sense of responsibility.

VII.4.2 Trust or Mistrust

Regarding trust in others, approximately one-third of the lay judges believed that most people can be trusted, while a little over one-fifth held the opposite view. The remaining 43.4% chose the "somewhat" response, indicating a more nuanced stance.

Figure 38. To what extent do you agree with the statement that most people can be trusted? (%)

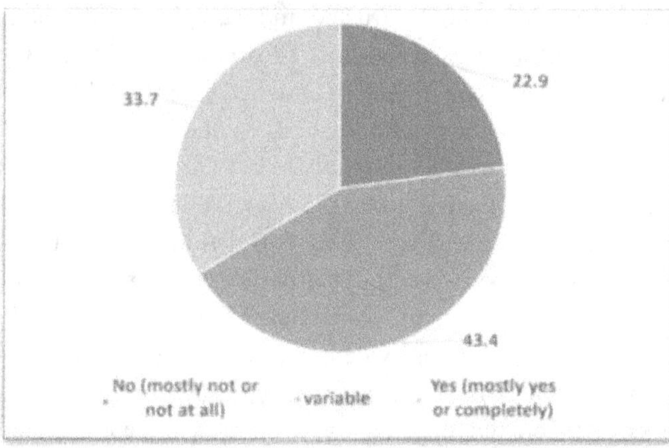

When comparing the three groups, it seems a logical conclusion that the Completely Dissatisfied are less trusting of others than the Completely Satisfied. Their dissatisfaction with their locality, country, and the European Union ultimately reflects a broader discontent with the actions and decisions of leaders and other individuals.

Figure 39. To what extent do you agree with the statement that most people can be trusted? By satisfaction groups (%)

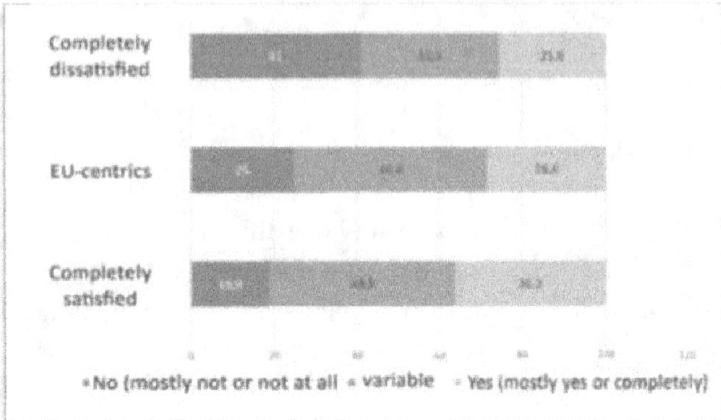

As illustrated in the figure above, 41% of the Completely Dissatisfied group believe that most people cannot be trusted, indicating a strong sense of mistrust towards others. In contrast, this proportion is lower among the EU-Centric group (25%) and lowest among the Completely Satisfied group (18.9%). The pattern is reversed when considering those who trust others: the lowest proportion (25.6%) is found among the Completely Dissatisfied, followed by a slightly higher proportion among the EU-Centric group (28.6%), while the highest share (36.3%) is among the Completely Satisfied*. This correlation clearly suggests that the Completely Dissatisfied group is significantly more distrustful of people than the EU-Centric group and even more so compared to the Completely Satisfied. However, while the relationship is evident, we do not claim it to be a direct causal link. It is possible that personal life difficulties lead to greater distrust in others, but it is equally plausible that negative experiences with people foster mistrust in the first place.

VII.5 SATISFACTION WITH THE SOCIAL ENVIRONMENT AND PERSONAL LIFE

The groups formed based on satisfaction with the social environment—those dissatisfied with everything, EU-centric individuals, and those satisfied with everything—allow us to explore whether personal life satisfaction is influenced by one's perception of the social environment. One possibility is that an individual's evaluation of their personal life remains independent of their assessment of the social environment, meaning that while they may be dissatisfied with society, they still consider their own life successful. In this case, we could conclude that the social environment has no bearing on the evaluation of personal life. However, it is also possible that dissatisfaction with either the social environment or one's personal life influences the perception of the other, creating a "spillover effect." In other words, those who view their social environment as unsuccessful may also be more inclined to perceive their own lives as unsuccessful, and vice versa. Our key question, therefore, is whether the correlation observed earlier in the context of trust—where those dissatisfied with everything exhibited greater distrust in people than those satisfied with everything—can also be identified here. If so, this would reinforce the assumption that these groups reflect not only specific attitudes toward society but also a broader, general outlook on life.

Figure 40. How satisfied are you with the course of your life so far? (%)

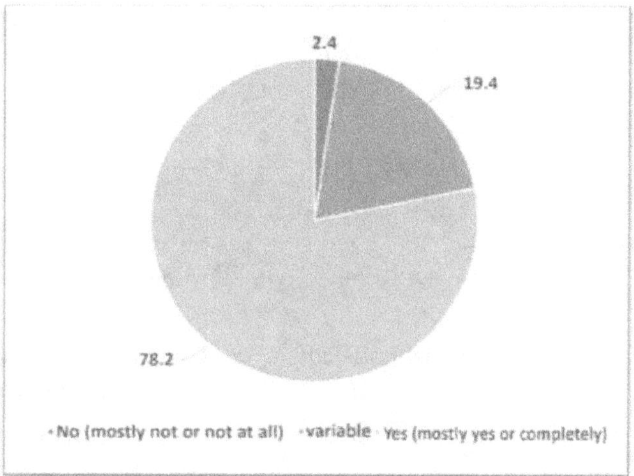

In response to the question, "How satisfied are you with the course of your life so far?" the overwhelming majority (78.2%) expressed satisfaction. Among those satisfied, most—53.1% of all respondents—consider themselves somewhat satisfied, while 25.1% are completely satisfied. A mixed response was given by 19.4%, and the proportion of those dissatisfied is very low, at just 2.4%. Among the dissatisfied, fewer than 1% indicated they are entirely dissatisfied with the course of their life thus far.

The following diagram illustrates the satisfaction with life among the three groups. Both the thoroughly dissatisfied and the European Union-centric groups exhibit strikingly similar patterns. In these groups, 68.4% and 69.2% respectively are "satisfied" with their lives, while 26-27% of both groups fall into the "somewhat satisfied" category, and it is only among the thoroughly dissatisfied that there is a slightly higher percentage (5.3%) compared to the European Union-centric group (3.8%) of those who are dissatisfied with their lives. Among the "completely satisfied," a much larger proportion (82.1%) express satisfaction with their lives so far, with considerably fewer being somewhat satisfied (15.9%), and only 1.9% of respondents are dissatisfied.

Figure 41. How satisfied are you with the course of your life so far? According to satisfaction groups (%)

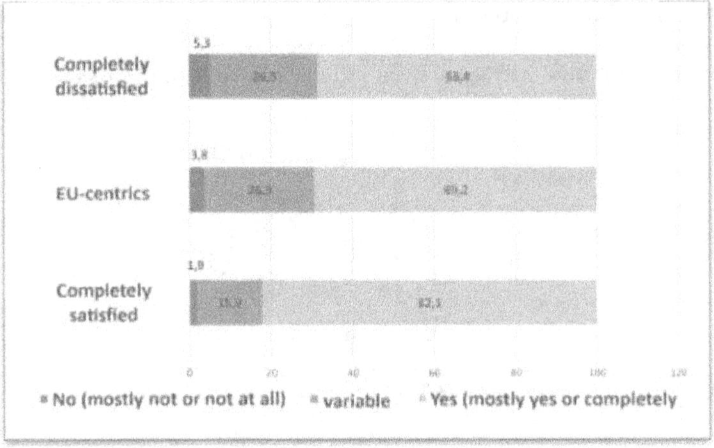

The above results suggest that satisfaction or dissatisfaction with the social environment is not independent of individual contentment with one's personal life.

When examining an individual's satisfaction with their own life from a different perspective, 84.3% of respondents answered the question, "In which direction would you say your personal life is currently heading?" affirmatively, stating that it is heading in a good direction. This figure closely aligns with the 78.2% who expressed agreement with the earlier statement, "I am satisfied with how my life has unfolded so far," particularly as the middle "neither-nor" response option was not included in the available choices. Among those who chose the "neither-nor" option to the previous question, the majority selected the response, "my life is currently heading in the wrong direction," with only 6.1% claiming their life is heading in a good direction. This led to the following distribution of answers: 84.3% of respondents felt their life was heading in a good direction, while 15.7% thought it was heading in a bad direction.

Figure 42. In which direction would you say your personal life is currently heading? (%)

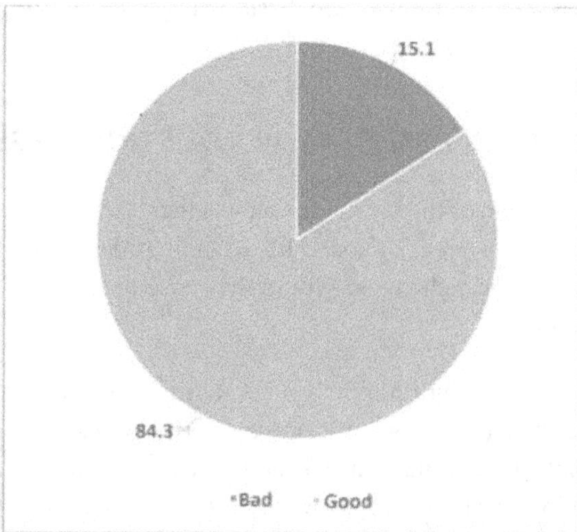

Among the group of those who are "dissatisfied with everything," and even fewer among the EU-centric individuals, there are those who believe that their personal lives are heading in the right direction (59% and 64.3%), whereas the proportion is significantly higher, at 91.4%, among the "content with everything."

Figure 43. What direction would you say your personal life is currently heading in? According to satisfaction groups (%)

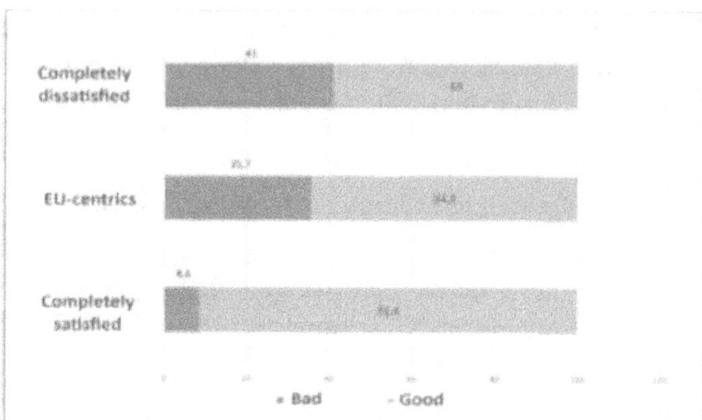

Overall, the responses to the questions "How satisfied are you with the course of your life so far?" and "What direction would you say your personal life is currently heading in?" reveal the same pattern: satisfaction with one's social environment is linked to satisfaction with one's personal life. Those who are content with everything are significantly more satisfied with both aspects than the EU-centric individuals and those who are dissatisfied with everything.

VII.6. THE REPRESENTATIVES OF STRICTNESS?

We also sought the opinion of the lay judges on whether they consider the relevant legal regulations in various areas of social life to be in order, and if not, in which direction they would suggest changes. Would they ease the regulations or, on the contrary, tighten them?

They were able to express their opinions on six items, two of which were related to biological life (euthanasia, abortion); one concerned the sanctioning of norm violations (judgments in criminal cases), and three were of an "immigration-related" nature (immigration regulations, acquiring citizenship, foreign ownership).

Overall, it can be stated that the majority of the lay judges were generally in favour of easing the regulations on euthanasia, would not change the rules on abortion, would tend to tighten the judgments in criminal cases, and would clearly advocate for stricter immigration regulations.

Naturally, these areas of life, which were the subject of evaluation from a *de lege ferenda* perspective, were selected by the researcher's discretion. Although only one of them is directly related to the work of lay judges, all of them are indirectly relevant, whether they concern personal life decisions, norm violations, or socio-ethical issues.

Table 50. Easing or Tightening of Legal Regulations?

	Easing the rules (-1)	Maintaining the status quo (0)	Tightening the rules (1)	AVERAGE
The Regulations on Euthanasia	**54.8**	34.7	10.5	-0.44
The Regulations on Abortion	16.0	**66.8**	17.2	0.01
The Sentences Imposed in Criminal Cases	2.9	38.4	**58.7**	0.56

The Regulations on Immigration	4.7	33.1	**62.2**	0.58
The Rules Governing the Granting of Citizenship	2.7	36.1	**61.2**	0.59
The Regulations on Foreign Ownership of Property	3.7	18.3	**77.9**	0.74

Figure 44. Easing or Tightening of Legal Regulations?

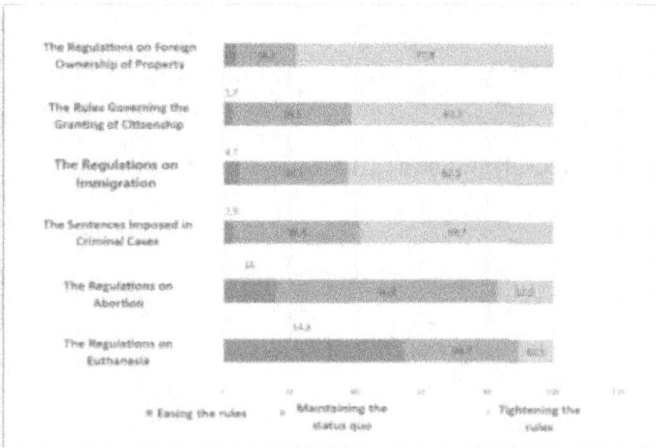

Of course, caution must be exercised in drawing generalising conclusions about the lay judges' attitudes towards the adequacy of legal regulations based on these results. A much broader investigation would have been necessary—one encompassing regulations across more areas of life. Nevertheless, we still believe that we have gained valuable insight into the structure of the lay judges' attitudes.

To illustrate the magnitude of the stricter attitudes, we created a cluster variable for each of the two life-related variables and the three "foreign-related" variables. The former was labelled as "life-attitude," while the latter was referred to as "immigration-attitude." In this way, we can assign a "judging" attitude to the regulation of each of the three areas of social life. When placed side by side, it becomes apparent that, in terms of life-attitude, the lay judges tend to lean towards easing; in terms of penalties, their attitudes are balanced; and in terms of immigration regulations, they display a distinctly stricter orientation.

However, this does not signify any specific "lay judge mentality." In fact, in relation to foreigners (immigrants, refugees), the majority of Hungarian society was characterised by a strongly distant attitude as early as the 2015[153]data collection.[154] Therefore, the lay judges merely mirrored the prevailing mental "state of being" of Hungarian society regarding foreigners.

Table 51. Life Attitude, Punishment Attitude, and Immigration Attitude

Life Attitude (Cluster Variable)		Punishment Attitude (Original Variable)		Immigration regulation Attitude (Cluster Variable)	
non-tightening	80.0	non-tightening	41.3	tightening	28.6
tightening	20.0	tightening	58.7	strictly tightening	71.4

Figure 45. Life Attitude, Punishment Attitude, and Immigration Policy Attitude (%)

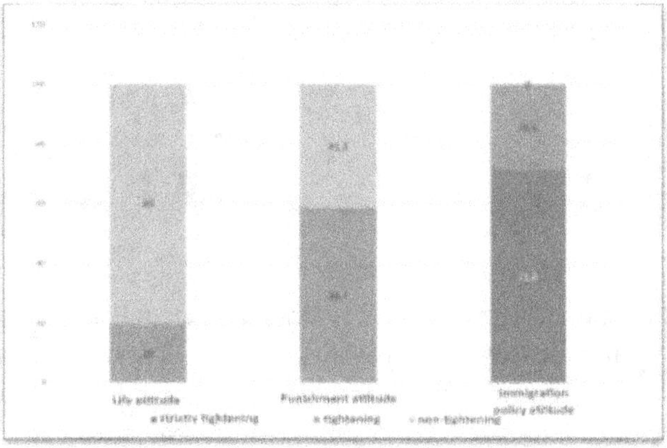

[153] This research was conducted before the autumn refugee crisis of 2015. We do not wish to address the question of how and to what extent this distant behaviour strengthened in the following years, and what factors may have contributed to it.

[154] According to the 2012 nationwide representative study conducted by the Department of Sociology at the University of Szeged (Szonda Ipsos Omnibus), a significant portion of the Hungarian population was already disturbed by the relatively high presence of foreigners in the country (39 percent) and the fact that many different nationalities live together in Hungary (40 percent). However, they were even more disturbed by the possibility of foreigners obtaining residency permits (56 percent), buying property (61 percent), taking up employment (65 percent), or purchasing land (76 percent). The 2015 Hungarian data collection of the 7th wave of the European Social Survey, which was conducted before the autumn events, again confirmed the previous waves' finding that, regarding migration, Hungarian society is among the most distant in Europe. Since the early 1990s, TÁRKI has continuously measured the population's attitudes towards asylum seekers. The proportion of those who rejected ("we should not accept anyone") fluctuated between 15 and 43 percent, but in April 2015, it reached the highest value recorded so far (46 percent).

Through cluster analysis, three relatively well-defined types were identified. One-quarter of the lay judges fall into the so-called ***"mild"*** category. They are characterised by a lenient stance on issues related to life and immigration, while adopting only a moderately strict approach in other matters. The middle group, comprising just over a third of the sample—the ***"strict"*** group—advocates a lenient position on life-related issues but takes a markedly stringent stance on all other matters. The third group, also slightly exceeding one-third—the ***"very strict"*** group—is homogeneous, consistently supporting a strict position on all issues.

The table below illustrates where the central value of each of the three types falls on the scale ranging from minus 1 to plus 1 in relation to the assessment of individual issues.

Table 52. The Mild, the Strict, and the Very Strict: Assessment of Selected Relevant Social Issues

Issue	Type 1 – "Mild"	Type 2 – "Strict"	Type 3 – "Very Strict"
Abortion	-0.13	-0.29	0.38
Euthanasia	-0.63	-0.92	0.16
Punishments	0.28	0.42	0.86
Immigration	-0.12	0.69	0.91
Citizenship	0.20	0.77	0.65
Property Acquisition	0.14	0.94	0.93
	25.3 %	37.9 %	36.8 %
	Lenient, moderately strict	Lenient, strongly strict	Strict in all areas

The distribution of these types is fairly similar across most subgroups of lay judges. The proportion of the ***strictest*** group exceeds the average (37%) in only two cases: among lay judges at the regional courts (52%) and those specialising in civil law (62%). Meanwhile, the lenient-moderately strict type deviates notably from the average (25%) only in the small subgroup (n=17) of lay judges coming from the healthcare, social services, and child protection sectors, where it accounts for 43%.

At the same time, a remarkable correlation emerged concerning the ***"length of service" of lay judges***: as their tenure increases, so does their strictness. The proportion of those who adopt a strict stance in all areas rises progressively with each term. Among first-term lay judges, this group accounts for 33%, increasing to 38% among those in their second term, 42% among those in their third term, and reaching 48% among those serving at least their fourth term.

If we focus solely on the area most closely related to the work of lay judges—***criminal justice***—the overall picture remains largely uniform. We found few instances where the proportion of those in favour of stricter measures significantly exceeded the average (59%), as this figure was fairly consistent across all groups. Nevertheless, we venture a hypothetical conclusion: it appears that lay judges from ***less favourable social backgrounds***

tend to adopt an even stricter stance than the average. One key indicator of this trend is that the proportion of the strictest group reaches 70% among those *without a university degree*. The "auxiliary indicators" are provided by small groups of lay judges: among those *without a secondary school diploma* (10 out of 13, ~77%), and among *manual workers* (11 out of 13, ~85%), the proportion of the strictest group is even higher. However, it is important to note that these categories naturally overlap.[155]

It is noteworthy that the strictest group also includes a significant proportion of lay judges from the *healthcare, social services, and child protection sectors* (13 out of 17, ~77%) as well as those *specialising in civil law* (25 out of 33, ~77%), despite the relatively small size of these groups.

In the foregoing analysis, we explored the relationship between attitudes toward stricter measures and indicators of lay judges' status and social background. However, we also observed a rather intriguing connection between these attitudes and lay judges' satisfaction with different aspects of life. This satisfaction was examined across three domains: personal life, judicial institutions, and socio-political life.

---

[155] Interestingly, however, this overlap is only partial, as just over half of the lay judges coming from manual labour backgrounds lack a secondary school diploma (8 out of 15).

What surprised us the most was that the question of leniency or strictness was least influenced by how satisfied lay judges were with the work of judicial institutions, such as the police, prosecution service, and courts.

Certain aspects of satisfaction with personal life played a significantly greater role. Small groups of lay judges who were dissatisfied with *how their lives had unfolded so far*, their *social recognition, financial situation, or standard of living* were strikingly strict on issues of punishment and immigration policy. Among them, those dissatisfied with the course of their lives were the strictest on the issue of abortion. At the same time, interestingly, these groups were far less strict than the average when it came to euthanasia.

Table 53. Opinions of Those Dissatisfied with Their Lives on Selected Relevant Social Issues

DISSATISFIED GROUP with	N	Abortion	Euthanasia	Punishments	Immigration	Citizenship	Property Acquisition
AVERAGE (-1 to +1)		**0.01**	**–0.43**	**0.56**	**0.53**	**0.57**	**0.74**
Life's Course	7	0.33	–0.90	0.76	0.83	1.00	
Standard of Living	35		–0.62	0.73		0.78	0.92
Social Recognition	16		–0.75			0.78	

The most systematic correlation, however, was observed with satisfaction regarding aspects and actors of social and political life, including the country's economic situation, the government, churches and political parties, and the functioning of the European Union.

Table 54. Opinions of Those Satisfied with Social and Political Factors on Selected Relevant Social Issues

SATISFIED GROUP with	N	Abortion	Euthanasia	Punishments	Immigration	Citizenship	Property Acquisition
AVERAGE (-1 to +1)		**0.01**	**–0.43**	**0.56**	**0.53**	**0.57**	**0.74**
Economic Situation	70	0.30	–0.71	0.71	0.81	0.70	
Government	93	0.23	–0.73	0.70	0.82	0.70	0.82
Churches	89	0.23	–0.71	0.71	0.81	0.78	
Political Parties	19	0.20	–0.56	0.71	0.81		
DISSATISFIED GROUP with							
The EU	72	0.18	–0.24	0.74	0.89	0.67	0.93

This is a highly instructive pattern. It clearly illustrates how powerfully political fault lines—particularly those centred around attitudes towards governmental actions—shape broader attitudes. Interestingly, however, the opposing groups (those dissatisfied with the economic situation, the government, churches, and political parties, and those satisfied with the EU) no longer form such a consistent bloc. They are less rigid on issues such as abortion and immigration, similarly favouring leniency on euthanasia, but when it comes to citizenship, they adopt a stance as stringent as that of the "pro-government" group.

Table 55. Opinions of Those Dissatisfied with Social and Political Factors on Selected Relevant Social Issues

DISSATISFIED GROUP with	N	Abortion	Euthanasia	Punishments	Immigration	Citizenship	Property Acquisition
AVERAGE (-1 to +1)		**0.01**	**–0.43**	**0.56**	**0.53**	**0.57**	**0.74**
Economic Situation	70	–0.17	–0.71		0.37		
Government	93	–0.24	–0.73		0.28	0.70	
Churches	89	–0.36	–0.71		0.35	0.78	
Political Parties	19		–0.56				
SATISFIED GROUP with							
The EU	72				0.39		

The cluster variable integrating the positions on the question of leniency versus strictness was able to distinguish three larger groups. The resulting group structure only reinforces our previous impression that, overall, the attitude of strictness dominates the lay judge community. While there is a lenient stance present, it only applies to regulations related to life, with a strongly strict disposition associated with the other two areas (punishments and immigration policy).

Table 56. Integrated Attitude Structures

	%
A: Lenient – Moderately Strict	25.2
B: Lenient – Strongly Strict	36.9
C: Strongly Strict in All Areas	37.9

Figure 46. Integrated Attitude Structures

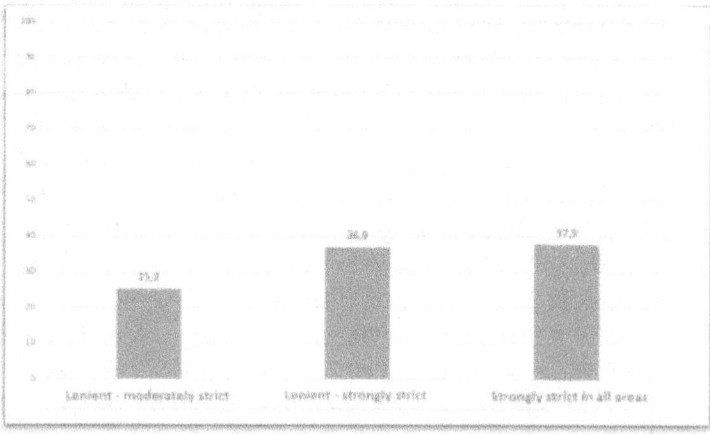

Interestingly, there is no group of lay judges where the proportion of the "A" type, representing the "mildest" individuals, is significantly higher than the average (25%). Even for the "C" type, representing the strictest, only a few smaller categories of lay judges stand out with a level of strictness above the average (38%): those from regional courts* (~52%), civil law judges*** (~62%), and those serving in at least their fourth term*** (~48%).

This type, however, is notably represented in significantly lower proportions in other smaller groups, such as those who have completed their lay judge duties** (~26%), the youngest age group (35–49 years old)*** (~22%), those with a high school diploma** (26%), physical workers*** (23%), and, interestingly, those coming from the public administration and law enforcement sector** (~30%).

Two group-forming factors showed an interesting—though statistically non-significant—relationship: with an increase in the number of lay judge terms and education level, the proportion of individuals in the "C" type slightly[156], but systematically, increased, meaning there was a strengthening of strictness.

[156] The percentage distribution according to the number of terms is as follows: 33% for one term, 38% for two terms, 42% for three terms, and 48% for more than three terms. The relative frequencies based on education level are: 30% for those without a high school diploma, 32% for those with a high school diploma, and 41% for those with a university degree.

VII.7 SUMMARY AND CONCLUSIONS

The lay judges we examined have strong attitudes regarding both personal and broader societal issues. Their attitudes toward their own lives and work can be described as positive. The majority are satisfied with their lives, their work, and their social recognition.

These attitudes do not correlate with gender, age, or even the level of education. However, it seems that whether a given lay judge has a clear political preference does influence their views. Our research did not extend to identifying specific political affiliations, so we can only state that those with a more defined political stance tend to express stronger opinions on social issues. The most interesting conclusion of our research is that we were able to identify what are known as "consistent opinions." The cluster analyses revealed that the sample can clearly be divided into three groups based on their responses. In other words, there are those who are satisfied with all areas of their life and societal environment, and those who show a completely opposite pattern, essentially dissatisfied with everything. The third group expresses dissatisfaction with their own life and the state of the country, but they experience satisfaction when it comes to the EU's direction. They could be seen as system critics or even as people with a desire to leave, as they feel things are not going well in this country, and similarly, things are not going well in their personal lives either.

It seems that the positive, negative, and EU-centric attitudes do not function as isolated viewpoints but are instead influential across multiple factors. We observed consistent, yet marked differences in direction between the three groups. This could suggest that people's opinions are not necessarily shaped by actual events but by a more general orientation, one that moves along the satisfaction–dissatisfaction axis and the home vs. EU spectrum. This orientation likely plays a role in shaping the perception of any real events, including both personal and societal occurrences, and significantly colours their interpretation. If this is the case, it can be assumed that such an orientation could also have a significant influence on the way cases in the lay judge's practice are evaluated, thereby shaping the interpretation and judgment of the cases brought before the court.

This is also evident from the fact that, for instance, the tightening of abortion regulations is advocated only by those who are satisfied with everything, while the other two groups would prefer to ease the rules, with the greatest desire for leniency coming from those who are dissatisfied with everything. Similarly, when it comes to changes in euthanasia regulations, although all three groups would favour a more lenient approach, the group most inclined to relax the rules is the EU-centric group, followed by the group most satisfied with everything, which would ease the regulations to a lesser degree. However, differences are also noticeable in the evaluation of immigration regulations, where the group most satisfied with everything would advocate for the strictest measures, while the EU-centric group would be the least strict.

VIII. SUMMARY OF THE RESEARCH

Our research group undertook the task of conducting an *empirical study* that would allow for a comprehensive evaluation of the *Hungarian lay judge system*, a task that had not been carried out in Hungary for more than fifty years. In this extensive research, which addressed several sub-questions, we focused primarily on two fundamental issues (representativeness and participation), that is, the assessment of the role and weight of lay judicial activity. Unfortunately, due to the regrettable decision of the organisation responsible for the central administration of the Hungarian judiciary, our survey turned out to be narrower than initially planned. Nonetheless, alongside gaining insights into the legal framework and uncovering the roots of the Hungarian lay court system, the opinions of judges and lay judges have enriched our understanding of the functioning of mixed courts with new knowledge.

At the beginning of our socio-legal study, we analysed the classic arguments that underpin lay participation. We found that a significant portion of the arguments listed in the legal justifications or in academic literature can only be limitedly substantiated when viewed through the lens of practice and scholarly works. Many of these arguments are closely linked to the image of a high-quality, efficient, and democratic justice system. However, in the case of different forms of lay courts, the connection between the stated goals in the arguments and their actual implementation is generally more modest than what the legislators may have intended. The particular form and functioning of lay courts in a given legal system is usually determined more by the *historical myths* associated with the institution than by the legal-political intentions aimed at improving the quality of the justice system. Nonetheless, several arguments supporting lay adjudication have found partial or full validation in the context of the various forms in which the institution appears. In light of all this, it is important to emphasise that if the Hungarian legislature were to attempt to involve more laypeople in adjudication with the aim of achieving a more democratic, transparent, efficient, and socially accountable justice system, it would be advisable to do so with consideration of empirical scientific research, and to select the appropriate form of lay courts suited to the desired goal.

Since our primary focus was on an important issue regarding judicial independence, specifically the selection of lay judges and the involvement of laypersons, we developed a *classification system for our analysis that also evaluates the methods of recruitment and participation.*

An independent *lay judge (justice of the peace-style) system* refers to a legal framework in which citizens without legal qualifications are given the opportunity to make judicial decisions, both on factual and legal issues, in civil or criminal cases, without the involvement of professional judges. In the case of an *independent jury*, the lay judges are applied as an independent body, primarily to assess factual questions that arise in civil or criminal cases, and possibly to determine the penalty. In this case, the evaluation of facts and legal issues is separated: a professional judge decides on the legal questions, while the jury, which lacks (or only randomly possesses) legal qualifications, decides on the factual questions. A *mixed jury* is referred to in those lay judicial forms where the jury is responsible for both factual and legal questions, and in the relatively larger body, there are multiple professional judges, with the number of lay judges significantly exceeding the number of professionals. Finally, a *mixed court (lay judge) system* operates in the judiciary when a small, unified body of judges makes decisions on both factual and legal issues. In this case, it may appear to be only a nominal difference from the mixed jury system, but the operational mechanism of the lay judge system differs from the jury system due to the proportion of lay judges and professional judges, which is why it can be defined as a separate type.

According to the insights gained from comparative legal research, the composition of the bodies and the mode of lay participation generally influence the method of selection. The greater the role that laypersons play in the formation of judicial decisions, the more emphasis the legislature places on the manner of selection. With regard to the *method of selection* of professional judges, it is evident that modern legal systems increasingly prioritise legal professional criteria, while the requirement for representativeness tends to appear mainly in the literature. In the case of lay judges, professionalism is of significance only in exceptional circumstances, as their role in the justice system is generally rooted in the fact that they lack legal expertise. Therefore, what is more emphasised in their case is that the judiciary should embody a broad representation of society through the institution, meaning that the composition of lay judges should adequately reflect distinct social groups. It is also noticeable that, in certain legal systems, more attention is paid to ensuring the impartiality of laypersons than to that of professional judges, as is particularly the case in the American jury system. The selection of lay judges for the French *cours d'assise*, a prime example of a mixed jury, is characterised by a precise yet more restrained selection mechanism, one that tests impartiality to a lesser extent than its American counterpart.

As far as the evaluation of the Hungarian lay judicial system, one of the main goals of our research, is concerned, the *German lay judge system* proves particularly significant. It can be concluded that the selection of jurors in Germany takes place in a multi-step, well-designed process, where, despite the distorting factors outlined – ranging from political considerations to social status – the requirement of representativeness, enshrined in law, plays a crucial role. This is evident both in the compilation of candidate lists and in the work of election committees conducted under the president's judicial leadership. However, this process does not reach the level of legislative and judicial attention observed in the selection of peace judges or jurors. A particular emphasis is placed on gender balance, and in recent decades, the distribution among jurors closely mirrors the societal distribution.

Although we have established that the involvement of lay judges in the judiciary can serve meaningful objectives, even without actual, effective participation, the legislator generally expects more than mere presence from them. According to our study, there is no lay judicial system where, apart from individual cases, active involvement by laypersons cannot be demonstrated. In smaller civil and criminal cases, lay judges in England, Scotland, or France theoretically enjoy complete freedom of decision. In the case of an independent jury, where jurors are usually responsible for assessing factual issues and possibly determining sanctions, their decision-making freedom is also considered to be complete. The situation is different in the case of mixed courts, which are also of interest from a Hungarian perspective, where laypersons, endowed with the same decision-making competence as the judge, are practically unable to become equal partners with professional judges in decision-making. Research on lay judges' participation and cooperation with professional judges largely aligns with the results of domestic studies, and it attests to the modest contribution of laypersons. However, the academic literature on popular participation does not demand professional equality or an equal level of involvement from these lay judges, but rather, beyond their legitimising and control functions, the *infiltration of societal justice* into formalised court proceedings, as evidenced by the studies on German lay judicial involvement. It is noteworthy, when comparing the German and Hungarian lay judge systems, that the number of cases in which German professional judges are persuaded by lay judges, according to Machura's survey, is much higher than in Hungary. It is also important to consider that, due to the societal demand for lay judge participation, supported by public opinion surveys, the political intent to abolish or significantly reduce popular participation, despite its unlikeliness of success, is even less probable considering that the recognition of lay adjudication in the German legal community is not higher than in Hungary.

After defining the theoretical framework and reviewing the comparative legal literature, we presented the results of our quantitative study. One of the fundamental questions of our research was to determine to what extent the *requirement for representativeness* is fulfilled during the recruitment of Hungarian lay judges, and what the opinions of both lay judges and professional judges are regarding the selection process.

Based on the comparative analysis of various selection methods and empirical studies on these methods, the starting point was the increasing emphasis on the issue of representativeness of public participation in the 20th and 21st centuries. The main reason for this is that, with adequate representativeness, lay judges participating in the judiciary can assert the values, norms, and sense of justice of their own group, and with sufficient representativeness, the impartiality and legitimacy of the judiciary are strengthened. Our hypothesis was that, since 1990, following the collapse of the monolithic state system, significant social changes should have affected the social composition of lay judges, even though no legal or policy measures were taken to improve representativeness or introduce other changes. This hypothesis seems to have been confirmed, as substantial changes occurred in the distribution of lay judges compared to the 1960s, although societal representativeness did not improve. It can be concluded that the lay judge corps *has not become younger*; rather, we observed a form of aging, which, due to the significant differences in perspectives between generations today, we regard as a serious problem. In a society that now includes Generation Z, the overrepresentation of older age groups, particularly the inactive, calls into question the original goal of public participation and, in line with Kálmán Kulcsár's observations, leads to a decline in the prestige of lay judges. Due to the nature of lay judicial activity, the overrepresentation of graduates and intellectual professionals may be less problematic. Contrary to Kulcsár's findings, which showed a higher proportion of men in the lay judge corps, our research confirmed a significant female majority. Hungarian women are also more willing to participate in the work of the judiciary, whether as lay judges or professional judges. As for minorities, the study ended with a misleadingly positive result due to significant regional disparities. In counties near the Romanian border, a substantial number of Romanian ethnic lay judges were identified, while in many other counties, there were no lay judges from any minority group. However, this does not mean that the representation of different minority groups is even minimally ensured. What can be stated is that the Roma minority, which is significant in terms of its numbers and the prejudices it creates, was almost non-existent among the respondents.

In relation to the selection procedure, our research concluded that the selection system in operation in Hungary during the research period *did not even meet the legislative goal of public participation*. Even less so did it meet the objectives outlined in international literature, which we discussed in detail in the chapter on the international perspective. Based on the nominations by social organizations, the election system of locally organised political self-governments results in lay judicial participation that does not at all meet the "*fair cross-section*" requirement. To this, we must add that the assignment of selected lay judges to specific cases is done ad hoc, based on routine or the request of judges, and lacks any systematic approach and adherence to impartiality principles. Our dissatisfaction is supported by the opinions of both lay and professional judges, as the majority of respondents do not consider the current system to be adequate. Most of them would prefer the courts to take full responsibility for the selection process. A large majority of the respondents regard life experience as the most important selection criterion, while rejecting the random element in the selection process. In contrast, we firmly believe that the foundation of properly functioning public participation could be established through a *random selection process based on civic duty*, which could then be combined with other selection techniques conducted by the courts, ensuring that the requirements for representativeness and impartiality are met, while also potentially satisfying the demands for life experience.

It can be stated *that, in terms of composition, the lay judge society differs significantly from the adult Hungarian population*: lay judges are strongly overrepresented among older individuals (over 60), women, the inactive (particularly retirees), those in intellectual professions, and those with higher education. Therefore, the composition of lay judges does not, in any sense, represent the adult Hungarian society. This is due to the selection procedure, which does not aim to enforce the requirement of representativeness either in the appointment of lay judges or in their assignment to specific cases.

In the second part of our study, we sought to answer the usual question often addressed in research on mixed courts,[157] namely, *what weight and nature of lay participation* can be observed in judicial proceedings, primarily based on the evaluations of lay judges and professional judges. Our assumption was that, based on the status-characteristics theory, despite the legislative provisions guaranteeing equal rights, this specific problem-solving group is characterised by an internal hierarchical relationship, which hinders significant lay participation. This is supported by similar empirical studies focused on mixed judicial systems. At the same time, we hypothesized that, compared to Kulcsár's study, the lay judge system in a democratic society would still result in greater participation, even if no significant legal changes have occurred since then.

If we look back at the judicial practices of the state-socialist era from today's perspective, we can see that the sociological aspect of the organisation gradually overrode the political intent in parallel with the consolidation of the communist power. One could also say that the latent function triumphed over the manifest function. This is particularly interesting in light of the fact that the political system tried to demonstrate its legitimacy by formally presenting itself as the embodiment of "people's rule." A core principle of the ruling ideology was that politics works on behalf of the "working people," symbolised by the manual workers, and it is these people who send their representatives to the legislature, as well as to the judiciary. The designation of lay participants as "people's jurors" refers to this ideological element.

Our hypothesis here was that the societal (especially value-based) changes that replaced the fading ideological-political pressure in a "post-socialist society" *created favourable conditions* for resolving the asymmetry, even though the nature of the judicial decision itself — which is the most crucial structural factor — remained unchanged. After all, it is still not "arbitrary justice," but formalised (rational) law: the judicial decision is a professional decision, one that adheres to a normative order that is legal in nature,[158] for which the judge bears responsibility regarding its consequences. This, of course, does not exclude a stronger expression of the participatory demands of lay participants.[159] However, we find

[157] The studies by Machura, Kühne, Wolfe, Jutta Gerken, Ekkehard Klausa, Kronenberger, Rennigs, Klami, and Merva also focused on this question.

[158] To this day, we consider Kulcsár's reflections on the matter (ibid., pp. 80–84) to be acceptable.

[159] Kulcsár relates this partly to organisational factors, and partly to the concept of the lay judge's 'role perception' (ibid., pp. 84–88).

it hard to disregard the influence of the condition (weakness) of civil society on this matter. Nevertheless, our study found a *higher level* of lay participation compared to the previous era (i.e., compared to the results of Kulcsár's study) in certain areas. The increase in activity, however, can only be proven in areas where opinions divergent from those of judges were formed and represented. In other areas, due to the lack of data for comparison, we can only hypothesise this increase. Today's lay participants are significantly more willing to voice their differing opinions. However, this does not substantially alter the fact that the power balance is still dominated by the professional judge, who, depending on their role perception, ensures the procedural rights of lay participants, but in substantive matters (the decision), they aim to maximise their autonomy and independence as the main rule.

Based on the results of the empirical survey, we also attempted to *categorise judicial attitudes*. In our view, the types we used (correct, correct aristocrat, reserved aristocrat, ambivalent) appropriately group the professional judges who relate to lay judges in different ways.

What can be stated with certainty is that, compared to the widespread and often derogatory opinions of lay judges held among practising lawyers, the *lay judge system presents a positive image*.[160] While the selection procedure, which fails to pay attention to representativity, may warrant strong criticism,[161] the participation (both in the procedural and decisional stages) can be regarded as distinctly good within the organisational-sociological conditions characteristic of mixed courts. The results from the completed judicial and lay judge questionnaires confirm that lay judges are not passive spectators in the trial and decision-making process, and, in contrast to the opinions formed about them, they contribute to the work of the judiciary with a much more active and often recognised role.

It is also worth highlighting among the research findings that the human relationship between judges and lay judges is fundamentally positive, which is particularly important from the perspective of the lay judges' opinions and certain arguments supporting lay adjudication. The fact that the vast majority of lay

[160] The expression "people's hypocrite" as opposed to people's lay judge (a cunning play of vowel changes on the Hungarian word components "ül" and "nök" in "ülnök" for lay judge changed into "ál" and "nok" to get "álnok" meaning a person of hypocrisy) was introduced into public discourse by Hungarian comedian Géza Hofi, and it can still occasionally be heard among lawyers today.

[161] Badó – Feleky – Lőrinczi 2016. 1–18. p.

judges were fully satisfied with the human relationship they had with the professional judges can be regarded as a possible fulfilment of the lay judge system's function in legitimising the judiciary (also from the perspective of the so-called multiplier effect). If lay judges fundamentally experience being treated as partners by professional judges, and if a good human and professional relationship can be established between them, then the role of the institution in strengthening trust in the judiciary can be considered likely.

Overall, it can still be stated that the Hungarian lay judge system, both in its pre-2017 reform state and especially in the period following the reform, plays an *extremely limited role* in fulfilling the expectations of lay adjudication. This role would primarily be expected in terms of social control over the bureaucratised judiciary and the incorporation of societal sense of justice. Lay judges represent a narrow segment of society and continue to be unable to disprove the image that causes them to be frequently referred to by practising lawyers merely as "window dressing." In parallel, they are also only marginally able to meet the expectation of controlling the bureaucratised judicial system with their dissenting opinions or perhaps through the occasional justified rejection of a professional judge's decision.

When comparing the Hungarian jury system to the most similar mixed court system, that of Germany, the potential developmental directions become more apparent in a supportive legislative environment. Taking into account the population size, during the examined period, approximately two and a half times as many lay judges were elected in the Federal Republic of Germany as in Hungary within one electoral term, which represents a significant system of mass citizen participation. The large number in Germany, beyond the various forms of lay participation, is due to the fact that the juries, which play a role in criminal cases and constitute the overwhelming majority of public participation, have a much broader scope of authority than their Hungarian counterparts, and generally more so than those in former people's democratic legal systems. Undoubtedly, it is also important to note that German lay adjudication is only partially burdened by the people's participation system of the party-state era in the former East German territories, making it more difficult to employ the arguments typically used in post-socialist countries—relating to the heavy historical legacy—to reduce the role of lay judges.

Our firm stance—contrary to measures aimed at limiting lay adjudication—is that domestic lay participation should not be abolished or restricted, but rather reformed along the lines of the German model. By precisely regulating the selection procedure, establishing guarantees for lay judges' independence and impartiality, and developing a training system for lay judges, public participation in the judiciary could have gained meaningful significance, and, of course, it could still gain meaning today.

In our opinion, lay participation still has a rightful place in European legal systems, and particular attention should be paid to the independence and impartiality of lay judges, as well as to the aspect of representativeness.

IX. Appendix

Appendix – Frequency values of the subgroups (background variables) in the weighted sample

The notation for categories with fewer than 70 cases: * = 50–69 participants; ** = 20–49 participants; *** = fewer than 20 participants.

THE INDICATORS OF LAY JUDGE STATUS	N=309
Continuity	N
those departing*	52
those continuing	257
Court Type	
Regional Court	73
Capital City District Court**	20
District Court	158
Administrative and Labour Court*	58
Headquarters, Town or City	
Capital City	73
County Seat City	69
Other City or Town	152
Cycle Number	
First Cycle	93
Second Cycle	108
Third*	59
Third or More	99
Fourth or More**	40
Area of Law	
Criminal Law	250
Civil Law**	33

INDICATORS OF LAY JUDGE STATUS	N=309
Labour law	67
(other)***	6
Number of Cases	
Beginners (1–10 cases)*	69
Relatively experienced (11–30 cases)	90
Experienced (31–100 cases)	82
Highly experienced (more than 100 cases)*	54

Membership of the Hungarian Association of Lay Judges *	55
Legal background	117

SOCIO-DEMOGRAPHIC BACKGROUND	
Gender	
male	90
female	217
Place of Residence	
capital city*	58
County-ranked city or county seat	124
Other town	107
(Other settlement)***	17
Age Group	
(35–49 years)***	19
50–59 years	72
60–64 years	103
65 years or older	113
under 60 years	91
60 years or older	216
Educational Attainment	
(No secondary school diploma)***	14
Secondary school diploma	94
Higher education degree	198
College degree	134
University degree*	64

SOCIO-DEMOGRAPHIC BACKGROUND	
Employment Status	
Active earner*	60
Retired	221
Other**	22
Occupational and Work Distribution Group	
Executive, managerial	137
Other intellectual work	83
(Manual labour)***	13
Other	70
Sector of Employment	
Production, infrastructure**	34
Services*	60
Public administration, law enforcement*	56
(Healthcare, social care, child protection)***	17
Culture, education, science, religion	101

Production and services	94
Public administration, law enforcement*	56
Human services	118
Funding Sector of Workplace	
Public sector	191
(Civil sector)***	9
Private sector	76
(Belonging to an ethnic minority group)* **	15

X. ANNEXURES

Annexure 1 – Lay Judge Questionnaire

University of Szeged Socio-Legal and Comparative Law Research Group

LAY JUDGE RESEARCH

PARTICIPATION IS VOLUNTARY

SZEGED, 2015

The Socio-Legal and Comparative Law Research Group of the University of Szeged is conducting a study aimed at gaining a comprehensive understanding of the Hungarian lay judge system.

Lay judge work constitutes a significant element of the Hungarian judiciary, and to truly understand this work, we certainly need the assistance of the lay judges themselves.

It would be particularly valuable for us to gain insight into how you perceive your role and place within the judicial system, what difficulties you encounter in your work, how you evaluate the working conditions, and how you view various issues concerning the judiciary and Hungarian society.

Such a study has not been conducted in Hungary since the 1960s, and for this reason, we would be grateful if you could contribute to the success of our research by sharing your valuable experiences and opinions.

The questionnaire is very simple to fill in: for the vast majority of questions, all you need to do is ***circle*** the number corresponding to your chosen answer.

We will indicate when you may circle more than one answer option.

In a few cases, you will be asked to provide **data** or write a ***brief text*** in the space provided.

Thanking you for your assistance,

Members of the Research Group

1.Please indicate which of the following applies to you:

1– You served as a lay judge only during the previous judicial cycle but no longer hold this position in the current one.

2– You served as a lay judge during the previous judicial cycle and continue to do so in the current one.

WE KINDLY REQUEST THAT YOU SHARE WITH US YOUR PROFESSIONAL EXPERIENCE GAINED DURING THE PREVIOUS CYCLE.

2.During the previous cycle, you served as:

1– A lay judge at a regional court
2– A lay judge at a Budapest-Capital district court
3– A lay judge at a district court
4– A lay judge at an administrative and labour court

3.In which town or city is the court located where you served as a lay judge?

…………………………………………………………………………………...……….

4.In which county is this court located?

1 Bács-Kiskun	2 Baranya	3 Békés	4 Borsod-Abaúj-Zemplén	5 Budapest
6 Csongrád	7 Fejér	8 Győr-Moson-Sopron	9 Hajdú-Bihar	10 Heves

11 Jász-Nagykun-Szolnok	12 Komárom-Esztergom	13 Nógrád	14 Pest	15 Somogy
16 Szabolcs-Szatmár-Bereg	17 Tolna	18 Vas	19 Veszprém	20 Zala

5. In which judicial cycle have you served as a lay judge?

....

6. In which areas of law have you served as a lay judge in court? (Multiple answers possible.)

1 – Criminal law
2 – Civil law
3 – Employment law

4 – Other, namely: ....

7. If you estimate, approximately how many cases have you participated in as a lay judge so far?

....

8. Were you a member of the Hungarian Association of Lay Judges during the previous cycle?

1– No, I was not a member.

2 – Yes, I was a member.

9.In your opinion, what would be the best method for selecting lay judge candidates?

1 – The municipal representative bodies should continue to make the selection.
2 – The courts should decide on the selection.

3 – Another professional organisation should be responsible for the selection.

10. For first-time applicants to the role of lay judge, which of the following selection criteria would you rank as the first, second, and third most important?

Please enter the corresponding number in the designated ranking positions.

1– The candidate's life experience
2– The candidate's relevant expertise
3– The candidate's level of education
4 – The candidate's familiarity with matters related to lay judge duties
5 – The candidate's civic engagement, public acceptance, and support
6– The candidate's adaptability
7 – The candidate's independent thinking
8– The candidate's local recognition
9– Other criterion, namely: ....
10– The best solution would be a lottery system

1st place: .... **2nd place:** .... **3rd place:** ....

11. In your view, the work of a lay judge…

1 – is merely a formality and plays no substantive role in the administration of justice.
2 – contributes to some extent to the improved functioning of the justice system.

3 – plays a significant role in enhancing the administration of justice.

12. What has being a lay judge personally meant to you? (Multiple answers are possible.)

1– It is a unique profession, a vocation for me.
2– It is a job like any other.
3– It is not work but rather a meaningful way to spend my time.
4 – It is an additional source of income for me.
5– Primarily, it is:

....

13. How willingly have you carried out your work as a lay judge?
1– Not willingly at all
2 – Rather unwillingly

3 – Indifferent
4 – Somewhat willingly
5 – Very willingly

14. Do you possess any prior legal education or training?

0 – No → Proceed to question 16. 1 – Yes

15. If so, what kind of legal background do you have?

1 – A law degree
2 – A qualification as a legal assistant
3 – A qualification in labour law and social security
4 – Legal studies undertaken during education
5 – Other, namely:...................................

16. What other (non-legal) knowledge or expertise have you found most useful in your work as a lay judge?

1 – Pedagogical
2 – Military or law enforcement
3 – Administrative
4 – Labour realtions
5 – Financial and economic
6 – Technical
7 – Other, namely:..
8 – I do not have any such expertise.

17. In your opinion, is it sufficient for a lay judge to familiarise themselves with a case only during the hearing, or do you consider it essential to prepare beforehand?

1 – It is sufficient to familiarise oneself with the case only during the hearing.
2 – It is necessary to prepare prior to the hearing

18. Do you usually prepare for hearings?

5 – Without exception, on every occasion.

4 – Generally, yes.

3 – It depends.

2 – Only rarely.

1 – I do not usually prepare.

19. In your view, have you had sufficient time to review the hearing materials in advance?

1 – Almost never had enough time.

2 – Unfortunately, in most cases, there was not enough time.

3 – It varied.

4 – In most cases, I had enough time.

5 – I always had enough time.

20. Prior to the <u>most recent case you heard</u>, did the judge provide the lay judges with the factual and legal materials of the case, or were you merely given an oral briefing?

1– We received both the case materials and an oral briefing.
2– We received only the case materials.
3– We did not receive the materials, but the judge provided an oral briefing.
4– In this case, we received neither materials nor a briefing in advance

21. Looking back at the cases you heard in your previous term, what was the <u>most typical practice</u>?

1 – We received both the case materials and oral briefings.

2 – We received only the case materials.

3 – We did not receive materials, but the judge provided oral briefings.

4 – We received neither materials nor briefings.

22. Do you generally understand the legal aspects of the cases you hear?

5 – Always.

4 – Mostly, yes.

3– It depends.

2 – Mostly not.

1 – Not at all

23. Do you read legal textbooks or journals (other than the lay judge's handbook)?

1– Not at all.
2– I have done so on occasion.
3– With some regularity.
4– Quite frequently.
5– Regularly.

24. Do you study legal statutes?

4 – Regularly.

3 – Quite frequently.

2 – Only occasionally.

1 – I do not.

25. Do you read the written judgment before signing it?

5 – Always.

4 – Mostly, yes.

3 – It depends.

2 – Mostly not.

1 – Never.

26. In your opinion, in what way can a lay judge assist the judge the most?

1 – In establishing the facts of the case.

2 – In determining guilt.

3 – In legal classification.

4 – In sentencing.

5 – Other, namely: ………………………………………..…………………

27. Based on practice, do judges usually allow lay judges to ask questions during the hearing (to the defendant, witness, expert, etc.)?

1 – Almost never.

2 – Mostly not.

3 – It varies.

4 – Mostly, yes.

5 – Always.

28. Based on practice, do judges usually seek the opinion of lay judges when assessing cases?

1 – Almost never.

2 – Mostly not.

3 – It varies.

4 – Mostly, yes.

5 – Always.

29. Based on your experience, do judges welcome the views of lay judges during deliberations?

1– Almost never.
2– Only very rarely.
3– It varies.
4 – Mostly, yes.
5– Always.

30. Have you ever had a different opinion from that of the judge regarding a case?

1– No, never.
2– There was one such instance.
3– There were a few such instances.
4– There were relatively many such instances.

31. Did you express your differing opinion?

1– I have never done so → <u>Proceed to question 33.</u>
2– Sometimes I did, sometimes I did not.
3– I did so on every occasion

32. Did the judge take your differing opinion into account?

1– Never.
2– Sometimes yes, sometimes no.
3– Always.

33. Have you ever submitted a dissenting opinion?

1– Never.
2– I did so in one case.
3– I did so in a few cases.
4– I did so in many cases.

34. In your opinion, what role do lay judges' views play in shaping judicial decisions (judgments)?

5– They are taken very seriously (almost always considered).

4 – They are considered, but the judge's professional authority prevails

3 – It varies.

2 – Lay judges' opinions carry little weight and are mostly disregarded.

1 – Lay judges' opinions are not considered at all.

35. Based on your experience, how would you characterise the relationship between judges and lay judges overall?

1 – Judges tend to see lay judges as colleagues assisting judicial work.

2 – Judges tend to regard lay judges as a hindrance to judicial work.

36. How satisfied have you been with the personal relations between judges and lay judges?

5 – Completely satisfied.

4 – Mostly satisfied.

3 – It depends.

2 – Mostly dissatisfied.

1 – Not satisfied at all.

37. How satisfied have you been with the professional work of judges?

5 – Completely satisfied in every instance.

4 – Mostly satisfied.

3 – It depends.

2 – Mostly dissatisfied.

1 – Almost never satisfied.

38. How satisfied have you been with the working conditions provided by the court for lay judges?

5 – Completely satisfied.

4 – Mostly satisfied.

3 – It depends.

2 – Mostly dissatisfied.

1 – Not satisfied at all.

39. Do you personally consider it important for lay judges to wear robes?

1 – Yes.
2 – No. → <u>Proceed to question 41.</u>
3 – I do not know → <u>Proceed to question 41.</u>

40. If you have answered 'Yes', what would be the primary reason? Because…

1 – It would enhance the personal authority of lay judges.

2 – It would enhance the prestige of the lay judge's role.

3 – It would enhance the authority of the judicial panel.

4 – Other reason, namely: ………………………………………………

……………………………………………………………………………………

41. How satisfied are you with…

	1 – not at all	**2 – rather not**	**3 – so-so**	**4 – rather yes**	**5 – entirely**
1. the course of your life so far	1	2	3	4	5
2. your social standing	1	2	3	4	5
3. Recognition of your role as a lay judge	1	2	3	4	5
4. your current financial situation and standard of living	1	2	3	4	5
5. the government's performance	1	2	3	4	5
6. the country's economic situation	1	2	3	4	5
7. the activities of the Church	1	2	3	4	5
8. the work of the police	1	2	3	4	5
9. the work of the prosecution service	1	2	3	4	5
10. the work of the courts	1	2	3	4	5

11. the activities of the National Assembly	1	2	3	4	5
12. the activities of your local government	1	2	3	4	5
13. the functioning of civil organisations	1	2	3	4	5
14. the activities of political parties	1	2	3	4	5
15. the functioning of the European Union	1	2	3	4	5

42. How would you describe the current trajectory of…

	Decidedly negative	Rather negative than positive	Rather positive than negative	Decidedly positive
1. Your personal life	1	2	3	4
2. Matters in your local community	1	2	3	4
3. Matters in the country	1	2	3	4
4. Matters in the European Union	1	2	3	4

43. In your opinion, should there be a tightening or a relaxation of regulations concerning…

	Should be relaxed	No change necessary	Should be tightened
1. The rules on abortion	1	2	3
2. The rules on euthanasia	1	2	3
3. Punishments in criminal cases	1	2	3
4. Immigration laws	1	2	3
5. The regulations on granting citizenship	1	2	3
6. The regulations on property acquisition by foreign nationals	1	2	3

44. To what extent do you agree with the statement that most people can be trusted?

1. – Entirely agree
2. – Rather agree
3. – Neutral
4. – Rather disagree
5. – Entirely disagree

45. How interested are you in politics?

1. – Not at all
2. – Rather uninterested
3. – Neutral
4. – Rather interested
5. – Very interested

46. How well-informed are you about political matters?

1– Not at all
2– Rather uninformed
3– Neutral
4– Rather well-informed 5 – Very well-informed

47. What is your stance on participation in elections?

1– It is a civic duty
2 It is a personal choice

48. Do you feel that any of the current political parties or movements are closer to your views than the others?

1– No.
2– Yes.

49. What is your gender?

1– Male
2– Female

50. In what type of settlement do you live?

1– Capital city
2– County seat or city with county rights
3– Other town
4– Village
5– Other (e.g. outlying rural area)

51. Which age group do you belong to?

1. – Under 30
2. – 30–34
3. – 35–39
4. – 40–44
5. – 45–49
6. – 50–54
7. – 55–59
8. – 60–64
9. – 65 or older

52. What is the highest level of education you have completed?

1– Primary school (8 years)
2– Vocational school or apprenticeship training
3– Technical school (without A-levels)
4– Secondary technical school (with A-levels)
5– Grammar school (with A-levels)
6– College diploma or higher technical qualification
7– University degree

53. Are you currently employed? What is your primary activity?
54. 1 – Employed full-time

3– Employed part-time
4– Employed while receiving a pension
5– Self-employed
6– Working on commission or doing occasional jobs
7– Retired (state pension)
8– Widowed pensioner
9– Disability pensioner

10– Unemployed
11– Homemaker
12– Student
13– On maternity/paternity leave (GYES, GYED, GYET)
14– Other

55. What is (or was) your current or most recent occupation/position?

1 – Senior or middle manager
2 – Junior manager or supervisor
3 – Office administrator
4 – Clerical or administrative worker
5 – Skilled worker
6 – Semi-skilled or unskilled worker
7 – Other

56. Which sector does (or did) your workplace belong to?

1 – Industry, mining, energy, manufacturing
2 – Agriculture, forestry, water management, fisheries
3 – Transport, logistics, telecommunications
4 – Trade and commerce
5 – Financial services, insurance
6 – Other services
7 – Public administration, politics
8 – Healthcare
9 – Culturc, cducation, scicncc, rcligious institutions
10 – Other (please specify):

....

57. If you are (or were) employed, where do (or did) you primarily work?

1 – Public sector (civil servant or public employee)
2 – Non-profit sector (foundation, charity, association, etc.)
3 – Private sector (business, corporation, limited company, etc.)

58. Do you belong to any ethnic minority group in Hungary?

1– No
2– Yes, I belong to the following minority group::...

1. Roma
2. German
3. Slovak
4. Croatian
5. Romanian
6. Ukrainian
7. Rusyn
8. Serbian
9. Slovenian
10. Polish
11. Greek
12. Bulgarian
13. Armenian
14. Jewish
15. Bunjevac
16. Other (please specify):

……………..…………………………………

THANK YOU FOR YOUR VALUABLE INPUT!

Annexure 2 – Judicial Questionnaire

University of Szeged

Socio-Legal and Comparative Law Research Group

JUDGES ON LAY JUDGE WORK

PARTICIPATION IS VOLUNTARY

The Socio-Legal and Comparative Law Research Group of the University of Szeged is conducting a study aimed at obtaining a comprehensive portrayal of the Hungarian lay judge system, for which the opinions of professional judges are also of particular interest.

No such inquiry has been undertaken in Hungary since the 1960s, and for this reason, among others, we would be most grateful if you could contribute to the success of our research by sharing your valuable experiences and perspectives.

Completing the questionnaire is exceedingly straightforward: in the vast majority of cases, you need only click to ***select*** the number corresponding to your chosen response.

Where multiple responses may be selected for a given question, this will be clearly indicated.

In some instances, you will be required to enter specific ***data*** or a ***brief textual response*** in the space provided.

We sincerely appreciate your assistance!

1.Which court does he/she currently work at?

1– district court
2– Budapest-Capital district court
3– labour court
4 – regional court
5– regional court of appeal
6– Curia

2.In which county?

1 Bács-Kiskun	2 Baranya	3 Békés	4 Borsod-Aba-új-Zemplén	5 Budapest
6 Csongrád	7 Fejér	8 Győr-Moson-Sopron	9 Hajdú-Bihar	10 Heves
11 Jász-Nagykun-Szolnok	12 Komárom-Esztergom	13 Nógrád	14 Pest	15 Somogy
16 Szabolcs-Szatmár-Bereg	17 Tolna	18 Vas	19 Veszprém	20 Zala

3.In which settlement is the court located?

…………………………………………………………………………………

4.How many years have you worked as a judge?

1– 1–5 years
2– 6–10 years
3– 11–15 years
4– 16–20 years
5– 21–25 years
6– 26–30 years
7– more than 30 years

5.In the course of his/her career, in which areas of law have you performed judicial duties?

1– criminal

2– civil

3– labour

4– other, namely: ....

6.Have you ever worked with lay judges in the course of his/her judicial duties?

1– never worked with lay judges

2– yes, but only rarely

3– yes, quite regularly (often)

7.Do you think it is worthwhile to involve laypeople in the judicial process?

1– yes

2– no → proceed to question 9

8.In your opinion, why is it worthwhile to involve laypeople in the judicial process?

Please write the number corresponding to the appropriate selection criterion in the blank ranking space.

1– in order to improve the quality of justice

2– in order to make justice more democratic

3 – in order to increase the legal knowledge of society

4– due to the "more eyes see more" or "fresh eyes notice more" phenomenon

5– in order to channel societal sense of justice

6– for budgetary reasons

7– other:...

9.How do you view the role of lay judges in the judicial process?

1– it is primarily a formality, with no substantive role in the administration of justice

2– it somewhat contributes to the better functioning of justice

3– it plays a substantive role in the better functioning of justice

10. Do you agree with the view that serving as a lay judge should be a civic duty?

1– agree

2– disagree

11. Which solution would you consider the best for selecting lay judge candidates?

1– local government representative bodies should continue to decide on the selection

2– courts should decide on the selection

3– some other professional organisation should decide on the selection

4– selection should be made in some other manner, namely:

....

12. Among the following selection criteria for lay judge applicants, which would you place in first, second, and third position? *Please enter the appropriate selection criterion number in the blank ranking space!*

a) – the candidate's life experiences
b) – the candidate's useful professional expertise
c) – the candidate's level of education
d) – the candidate's knowledge of issues related to lay judge duties
e) – the candidate's public activity, acceptance, and support
f) – the candidate's adaptability
g) – the candidate's independent thinking
h) – the candidate's local recognition
i) – other, namely:

....

1st place: 2nd place: 3rd place:

13. Would you agree with the idea that the selection of lay judges should be done by random draw, without considering various criteria?

1– agree

2– disagree

14. Regarding the assignment of lay judges to specific court cases (panels), which solution would you prefer?

1– appointment by the court leader

2– selection by the presiding judge

3– selection based on joint decisions of the parties involved (the opposing parties) and the judge

4– rotation according to the fixed schedule of the trial panels
5– simple random draw

15. We would now like your opinion on the four models of lay adjudication. Which do you think is the most appropriate?

1. **The justice of the peace system.** In the English legal system, 95% of criminal cases are decided by non-legally qualified justices of the peace, without the involvement of professional judges.
2. **The jury system in the Anglo-Saxon form.** In the United States, the jury decides on factual matters, while the judge decides on legal issues.
3. **Mixed panels.** In many legal systems, like Hungary, professional judges and lay judges form mixed panels, making decisions on all matters with equal rights (e.g., the lay judge system, or the French and Italian jury systems).
4. **The absence of lay participation.** In some legal systems, there is no lay participation in justice (e.g., as a justice of the peace, jury member, or lay judge).

***16. How willingly do you work (or have you worked) with lay judges?**

1– not at all willingly
2– rather not, than yes
3– rather willingly
4– very willingly

***17. In your judicial work, have you ever benefited from the non-legal knowledge, education, or abilities of lay judges?**

1 – yes, rarely
2 – yes, frequently
3 – no

***18. What (non-legal) knowledge, abilities, or qualifications of lay judges have you found most useful?**

1 1 – pedagogical
2 – military, law enforcement
3 – administrative
4 – labour-related
5 – economic-financial
6 – technical

7 – common sense
8 – observational skills
9 – other, namely:..

***19. Do you think it is sufficient for a lay judge to become familiar with a case only at the hearing, or do you believe they must be prepared beforehand?**

1 – it is sufficient to learn about the case only at the hearing
2 – it is necessary to prepare beforehand

***20. Before <u>the last case you tried with lay judges</u>, did you provide them with the factual and legal materials of the case or did you only inform them?**

1 – they received both the case materials and information
2 – they only received the case materials
3 – they did not receive materials, but I provided them with information
4 – I provided neither materials nor information beforehand

***21. How do you view it, do lay judges generally understand the legal connections in the cases they try?**

5 – always
4 – mostly yes
3 – sometimes
2 – mostly no
1 – never

***22. In your opinion, in what way can lay judges assist the judge the most?**

1 – they do not really assist in any way
2 – in establishing the facts
3 – in determining guilt
4 – in legal qualification
5 – in sentencing
6 – in other areas, namely:

....

***23. Do you provide opportunities for lay judges to ask questions of the persons being heard at the trial (defendant, witness, expert, etc.)?**

1 – almost never
2 – mostly not
3 – sometimes, varies
4 – mostly yes
5 – always

***24. Do you ask for lay judges' opinions on the cases being tried?**

1 – almost never
2 – mostly not
3 – sometimes, varies
4 – mostly yes
5 – always

***25. Do you enjoy hearing lay judges' opinions in the deliberation regarding a case?**

1 1 – almost never
2 – very rarely
3 – sometimes, varies
4 – mostly yes
5 – always

***26. Have lay judges ever had a different opinion from yours on a substantive issue in a case?**

1 1 – no, never → proceed
2 – this happened once
3 – this happened a few times
4 – this has happened quite often

***27. In such cases, did you take the lay judge's opinion into account?**

1 1 – yes, generally yes
2 – sometimes yes, sometimes no
3 – no, generally not

***28. Has there ever been a vote in your panel during the decision-making process?**

1 1 – it has never occurred
2 – this happened once
3 – this has happened a few times
4 – this has happened quite often

***29. Have lay judges ever submitted a dissenting opinion in a case?**

1 1 – no, never
2 – this happened once
3 – this has happened a few times
4 – this has happened quite often

***30. In your opinion, how much influence do lay judges' opinions have on judicial decisions (on the merits of the case)?**

5 – they are very important (almost always)
4 – they are important, but the judge's professional authority dominates
3 – sometimes yes, sometimes no
2 – lay judges' opinions have little weight, they generally do not count
1 – lay judges' opinions do not count at all

31. The law grants lay judges the same decision-making rights as professional judges. Do you think this status should be reflected in the following areas as well?

	1 – yes	2 – no
1 – wearing a robe		
2 – provision of chambers		
3 – access to a computer		

32. What is your gender?

1– Male
2– Female

33. What settlement do you live in?

1 – capital city
2 – county town, administrative centre
3 – other town
4 – village
5 – other (e.g., outlying area)

34. Which age group do you belong to?

1 1 – under 30
2 – 30–34
3 – 35–39
4 – 40–44
5 – 45–49
6 – 50–54
7 – 55–59
8 – 60–64
9 – 65 or older

35. If you believe that the current lay judge system should be reformed, we would be honoured if you could share your valuable thoughts on how this reform might be implemented.

....

....

THANK YOU FOR YOUR VALUABLE ASSISTANCE!

Annexure 3a – Judges on Lay Judge Work – Responses

What court are you currently working at?	
	Valid Percentage
1 – District Court	40.4
2 – Regional Court	11.9
3 – Labour Court	6.4
4 – Tribunal	33.9
5 – Court of Appeal	5.5
6 – Curia	1.8
Total:	100

In which county?[162]	
	Valid Percentage
1 – Bács-Kiskun	4.7
2 – Baranya	5.7
3 – Borsod-Abaúj-Zemplén	9.4
4 – Budapest	25.5
5 – Csongrád	2.8
6 – Fejér	2.8
7 – Győr-Moson-Sopron	5.7
8 – Hajdú-Bihar	4.7
9 – Heves	2.8
10 – Jász-Nagykun-Szolnok	4.7
11 – Komárom-Esztergom	10.4
12 – Nógrád	1.9
13 – Pest	3.8
14 – Somogy	3.8
15 – Szabolcs-Szatmár-Bereg	4.7
16 – Vas	0.9
17 – Veszprém	5.7
Total:	100

162 No responses from Békés, Tolna, and Zala counties.

Which town or city is the court located in?	
	Valid Percentage
	22.9
Balassagyarmat	0.9
Budaörs	0.9
Budapest	15.6
Debrecen	0.9
Debrecen	3.7
Eger	1.8
Encs	1.8
Esztergom	2.7
Győr	3.7
Hatvan	0.9
Kaposvár	2.8
Kazincbarcika	2.8
Kecskemét	1.8
Kiskunfélegyháza	1.8
Komárom	0.9
Komló	0.9
Miskolc	2.8
Mohács	0.9
Monoron	0.9
Nyíregyháza	3.7
Pécs	2.8
Salgótarján	0.9
Sopron	0.9
Szeged	2.8
Székesfehérvár	2.8
Szolnok	3.7
Szombathely	0.9
Tapolca	1.8
Tatabánya	4.6
Other county seats	0.9
Due to an abundance of data and the small size of the court, personal identification is not practically challenging, so further completion of the questionnaire is not pursued.	0.9
Veszprém	1.8
Total:	100

How many years have you worked as a judge?	
	Valid Percentage
1 – 1–5 years	15.1
2 – 6–10 years	15.1
3 – 11–15 years	15.1
4 – 16–20 years	18.9
5 – 21–25 years	17
6 – 26–30 years	10.4
7 – More than 30 years	8.5
Total:	100

In which areas of law have you performed judicial work?

[Criminal law]	
	Valid Percentage
1 – Not selected	40.4
2 – Yes	59.6
Total:	100

[Civil law]	
	Valid Percentage
1 – Not selected	62.4
2 – Yes	37.6
Total:	100

[Labour law]	
	Valid Percentage
1 – Not selected	88.1
2 – Yes	11.9
Total:	100

[Other]	
	Valid Percentage
1 – Not selected	90.8
2 – Yes	9.2
Total:	100

What other areas of law?	
	Valid Percentage
None in “Other” areas	91.7
Economic	0.9
Economic, non-litigious	0.9
Administrative	0.9

Non-litigious, enforcement	2.7
Offences	0.9
Enforcement	0.9
None in "Other" areas	0.9
Total:	100

Have you ever worked with lay judges in your judicial work?	
	Valid Percentage
1 – Never worked with lay judges	12
2 – Yes, but only rarely	15.7
3 – Yes, relatively regularly	72.2
Total:	100

Do you think it is worth involving laypeople in the adjudication process?	
	Valid Percentage
1 – No	60.7
2 – Yes	39.3
Total:	100

Why do you think it is worth involving laypeople in adjudication?

[To improve the quality of justice]	
	Valid Percentage
1 – Not selected	95.4
2 – Yes	4.6
Total:	100

[To make the justice system more democratic]	
	Valid Percentage
1 – Not selected	87.2
2 – Yes	12.8
Total:	100

[To increase legal awareness in society]	
	Valid Percentage
1 – Not selected	81.7
2 – Yes	18.3
Total:	100

[Due to the phenomenon of "more eyes see more" or "fresh eyes notice more"]	
	Valid Percentage
1 – Not selected	77.1
2 – Yes	22.9
Total:	100

[To channel the sense of social justice]	
	Valid Percentage
1 – Not selected	79.8
2 – Yes	20.2
Total:	100

[For budgetary reasons]	
	Valid Percentage
1 – Not selected	99.1
2 – Yes	0.9
Total:	100

[For other reasons]	
	Valid Percentage
1 – Not selected	98.2
2 – Yes	1.8
Total:	100

For other reasons?	
	Valid Percentage
	98.2
For instance, professional expertise can significantly assist in the assessment of a case, in the conduct of the hearing, and in formulating questions for the accused and witnesses	0.9
Professional knowledge and experience help to understand life situations, which facilitates the establishment of facts	0.9
Total:	100

How do you perceive the role of lay judges in judicial work?	
	Valid Percentage
1 – Mainly just a formality, with no real role in justice	65.1

2 – Somewhat contributes to the better functioning of the justice system	31.2
3 – Plays a significant role in the better functioning of the justice system	3.7
Total:	100

Do you agree that being a lay judge should be an obligation of citizenship?	
	Valid Percentage
1 – Disagree	84.1
2 – Agree	15.9
Total:	100

Which solution would you consider the best for selecting lay judge candidates?	
	Valid Percentage
1 – Continue to have local government representative bodies make the decision	20.4
2 – Courts should make the decision	62
3 – A professional organisation should make the decision	14.8
4 – It should be done in another way	2.8
Total:	100

Among the following selection criteria for lay judge candidates, which would you rank as the most important?	
	Valid Percentage
1 – The candidate's life experience	37.6
2 – The candidate's useful expertise	37.6
3 – The candidate's educational background	9.2
3– The candidate's knowledge of issues related to lay judge work	4.6
5 – The candidate's public engagement, acceptability, and support	0.9
7 – The candidate's independent thinking	7.3
8 – The candidate's local recognition	0.9
9 – Other criteria	1.8
Total:	100

Among the following selection criteria for lay judge candidates, which would you rank as the second most important?	
	Valid Percentage
1 – The candidate's life experience	20.4
2 – The candidate's useful expertise	22.2
3 – The candidate's educational background	22.2
4 – The candidate's knowledge of issues related to lay judge work	1.9
5 – The candidate's public engagement, acceptability, and support	2.8
6 – The candidate's adaptability	4.6
7 – The candidate's independent thinking	25
8 – The candidate's local recognition	0.9
Total:	100

Among the following selection criteria for lay judge candidates, which would you rank as the third most important?	
	Valid Percentage
1 – The candidate's life experience	17
2 – The candidate's useful expertise	10.4
3 – The candidate's educational background	14.2
4 – The candidate's knowledge of issues related to lay judge work	18.9
5 – The candidate's public engagement, acceptability, and support	5.7
6 – The candidate's adaptability	5.7
7 – The candidate's independent thinking	23.6
8 – The candidate's local recognition	2.8
9 – Other criteria	1.9
Total:	100

What other selection criteria do you consider important?	
	Valid Percentage
	96.3

Participation in special training for lay judges and passing the final examination.	0.9
Human insight	0.9
I do not consider it justified to maintain the system of lay judges	0.9
Psychological suitability; a clean record; basic legal and procedural knowledge (may be required for direct questioning)	0.9
Total:	100

Would you agree with the selection of lay judges being resolved by a simple lottery, without consideration of various selection criteria?	
	Valid Percentage
1 – Disagree	89
2 – Agree	11
Total:	100

Regarding the assignment of lay judges to specific cases (councils), which solution do you prefer (or would prefer)?	
	Valid Percentage
1 – Selection by the court leader	9.2
2 – Selection by the presiding judge	31.2
3 – Selection by mutual decision of the involved (opposing) parties and the judge	7.3
4 – Rotation based on the fixed order in the judicial councils	40.4
5 – Simple lottery	11.9
Total:	100

Now, regarding the four models of lay adjudication, we would like your opinion. Which solution do you consider the most appropriate?	
	Valid Percentage
1 – The magistrate system. In the English justice system, 95% of criminal cases are decided by lay magistrates without the assistance of professional judges.	0.9

2 – The jury system in the Anglo-Saxon form. In the United States, a separate jury decides facts, while the judge decides legal questions.	10.1
3 – Mixed councils. In several legal systems, including Hungary, professional judges and laypeople form mixed councils, making decisions on all matters with equal rights.	38.5
4 – Absence of the lay element. In some legal systems, lay judges do not participate in the judicial process.	50.5
Total:	100

How willingly do you work (or have worked) with lay judges?	
	Valid Percentage
1 – Not at all willing	9.5
2 – Rather unwilling	31.6
3 – Somewhat willing	47.4
4 – Very willing	11.6
Total:	100

In the course of your judicial work, have you ever found the non-legal knowledge, expertise, or skills of lay judges to be of use?	
	Valid Percentage
1 – Not at all	43.2
2 – Yes, but only on rare occasions	46.3
3 – Yes, frequently	10.5
Total:	100

Which area of non-legal knowledge, expertise, or skills of lay judges have you found most useful?	
	Valid Percentage
1 – Pedagogical expertise	18.5
2 – Economic or financial acumen	22.2
3 – Technical proficiency	18.5
4 – Practical wisdom	24.1
5 – Acute observational skills	14.8
6 – Other	1.9
Total:	100

Have you found any additional areas of expertise among lay judges to be useful?	
	Valid Percentage
No additional expertise identified	99.1
Medical knowledge	0.9
Total:	100

In your opinion, is it sufficient for a lay judge to become acquainted with a case solely during the hearing, or do you consider prior preparation essential?	
	Valid Percentage
1 – It suffices for them to familiarise themselves with the case solely during the hearing	61.7
2 – Prior preparation is essential	38.3
Total:	100

Before the hearing of the last case you adjudicated with lay judges, did you provide them with the case facts and legal materials, or did you only brief them?	
	Valid Percentage
1 – Provided with both case materials and a briefing	9.6
2 – Supplied only with case materials	1.1
3 – Not given case materials but received a briefing on the case	81.9
4 – Received neither case materials nor a briefing	7.4
Total:	100

How well do lay judges generally understand the legal aspects of the cases they adjudicate?	
	Valid Percentage
1 – Not at all	5.3
2 – For the most part, no	25.3
3 – Mixed	26.3
4 – For the most part, yes	41.1
5 – Entirely	2.1
Total:	100

In your opinion, in what way can lay judges provide the greatest assistance to judges?	
	Valid Percentage
1 – In truth, in no aspect	42.1
2 – Establishing the facts of the case	30.5
3 – Determining culpability	4.2
4 – Sentencing	11.6
5 – Other	11.6
Total:	100

In what other ways have lay judges been of assistance?	
	Valid Percentage
No additional contributions identified	90.8
Monitoring the conduct of the hearing	0.9
Applying relevant professional expertise	0.9
Addressing supplementary matters (e.g., criminal costs, confidentiality of sensitive data)	0.9
Providing an external perspective, as strict adherence to legal provisions may, at times, render judgments excessively technical	0.9
Introducing novel viewpoints that may enrich judicial reasoning and the formulation of rulings	0.9
Offering insights into workplace-specific conditions	0.9
Drawing upon non-legal expertise	0.9
Imparting knowledge from outside the legal sphere	0.9
Bringing specialist knowledge from fields such as engineering or architecture	0.9
Assisting with technical matters	0.9
Total:	100

Do you permit lay judges to ask questions of those being heard in the trial (defendant, witness, expert, etc.)?	
	Valid Percentage
1 – Almost never	5.3
2 – Mostly not	6.4
3 – Mixed, varies	6.4
4 – Mostly yes	27.7
5 – Always	54.3
Total:	100

Do you welcome the opinions of lay judges during deliberations on a case?	
	Valid Percentage
1 – Almost never	3.2
2 – Only very rarely	9.7
3 – Mixed, varies	17.2
4 – Mostly yes	29
5 – Always	40.9
Total:	100

Have lay judges ever held a substantive opinion differing from your own?	
	Valid Percentage
1 – Never	43
2 – On one occasion	19.4
3 – On several occasions	35.5
4 – On relatively many occasions	2.2
Total:	100

In such cases, did you take the lay judge's opinion into account?	
	Valid Percentage
1 – No / generally not	30.8
2 – Sometimes yes, sometimes no	44.2
3 – Yes / generally yes	25
Total:	100

Has a vote ever taken place in your panel during decision-making?	
	Valid Percentage
1 – Never occurred	62.4
2 – On one occasion	9.7
3 – On several occasions	17.2
4 – On relatively many occasions	10.8
Total:	100

Have lay judges ever submitted a dissenting opinion in a case?	
	Valid Percentage
1 – Never occurred	95.7
2 – On one occasion	4.3
Total:	100

In your opinion, what role do lay judges' opinions play in judicial decision-making (judgments)?	
	Valid Percentage
1 – Lay judges' opinions do not matter at all	9.5
2 – Lay judges' opinions carry little weight and are mostly insignificant	52.6
3 – Mixed, varies	8.4
4 – Lay judges' opinions are taken into account, but the professional authority of judges predominates	27.4
5 – Lay judges' opinions are taken very seriously and almost always matter	2.1
Total:	100

The law theoretically grants lay judges equal decision-making rights with professional judges. In your opinion, should this status also be reflected in the following?

[Wearing a judicial robe]	
	Valid Percentage
1 – Nem	63.9
2 – Yes	36.1
Total:	100

[Being provided with chambers]	
	Valid Percentage
1 – Nem	80.6
2 – Yes	19.4
Total:	100

[Access to a computer for judicial work]	
	Valid Percentage
1 Nem	63.9
2 Yes	36.1
Total:	100

What is your gender?	
	Valid Percentage
1 – Male	44.4
2 – Female	55.6
Total:	100

What type of settlement do you live in?	
	Valid Percentage
1 – Capital city	24
2 – County-rank city	45.2
3 – Other town or city	24
4 – Village	6.7
Total:	100

Which age group do you belong to?	
	Valid Percentage
1 30–34 years	3.7
2 35–39 years	15.7
3 40–44 years	19.4
4 45–49 years	21.3
5 50–54 years	17.6
6 55–59 years	12
7 60–64 years	9.3
8 65 years or older	0.9
Total:	100

Annexure 3b – Judges on the Lay Judge System – Written Responses

In 2016, the Ministry of Justice proposed a reform of the Hungarian lay judicial system as part of the broader reform of criminal procedure.[163]The intention, which since 2018 has aimed at significantly reducing the role of laypersons without legal qualifications in the judiciary, fits into the broader process that has characterised post-socialist countries since the 1990s. During the era of the one-party system, the jury courts, modelled on the Soviet system, did little to strengthen the belief among lawyers that popular participation served any meaningful purpose. Lay participation would remain limited to military criminal proceedings and cases involving minors. In practice, the reform implies that, henceforth, the legislator seeks to exploit the special knowledge of laypersons (in military, pedagogical, and psychological fields), rather than their general life experience, in judicial decision-making. While the arguments supporting the significant limitation of lay participation seem rather uncertain, and the reference to historical roots appears strained, given the similar mixed judicial systems functioning in numerous democratic states, there is no doubt that it aligns with the expectations of a significant portion of the Hungarian legal community. In post-socialist countries, very similar arguments are used to justify the reduction of the role of laypersons. (In his 2011 article on the Czech reform concerning lay judges, Michael Bobek also enumerates legislative justifications for the reduction of lay elements, which include the passivity of laypersons, their modest contribution, and the technical difficulties associated with operating the jury system).[164]

Before becoming aware of this reform proposal, our research group decided to conduct a comprehensive empirical study in Hungary, exploring the views of both lay judges and professional judges. Through our investigation, we aimed to gain

---

[163] 300 Draft ME/163/2015. Proposal to the Government on the Regulatory Principles of the New Criminal Procedure Code. Prepared: 30 January 2015. Budapest: Ministry of Justice, 2015, p. 32. Available online:
http://www.kormany.hu/download/1/21/40000/20150219%20IM%20el%C5%91terjeszt%C3%A9s%20az%20%C3%BAj%20b%C3%BCntet%C5%91elj%C3%A1r%C3%A1si%20t%C3%B6rv%3%A9ny%20 szab%C3%A1lyoz%C3%A1si%20elveir%C5%91l.pdf (2016.10.10.)

[164] 301 Michael bobek „Judicial Selection, Lay Participation and Judicial Culture in the Czech Republic: A Study in a Central European (Non) Transformation" Research Paper in Law 2014/3. 27. http://aei.pitt.edu/63516/ (2017.02.07.)

insight into the jury system, as no such research had been carried out in over fifty years. We believed that the often negative perception of lay judges' activities was largely shaped by myths, the professional superiority of lawyers, and similarly negative statements made in other countries, rather than by the opinions of those who, whether as laypersons or professional judges, had an actual understanding of the system's true functioning.

The online questionnaire for judges was returned by 109 judges. As with the lay judges, we cannot speak of the representativeness of the sample in this case either. However, it was reassuring for us that the composition of the responding judges demonstrated diversity in terms of the most important characteristics: (a) ***from an organisational perspective***, we found judges from district courts (44), regional courts (13), labour courts (7), regional courts (37), appellate courts (6), and the Curia (2); (b) based on ***the location of their court***, there were judges from the capital (22), county seats (45), and other urban areas (20); with regards to ***gender***, the sample was fairly balanced, with 60 female judges and 48 male judges; and in terms of ***judicial experience***, the distribution was nearly even: 32 judges had 1-10 years of experience, 36 had 11-20 years, 29 had 21-30 years, and 9 had over 30 years of experience. An interesting feature of the sample was that 13 judges completed the questionnaire who had never worked with lay judges before. Of the remaining respondents, 17 had worked with lay judges only occasionally, while 78 had regularly served alongside them.

Among the responding judges, the majority (61%) were of the opinion that it was not worthwhile to involve laypersons in judicial decision-making. However, it was flattering for us that both those who opposed the jury system and those who accepted it (38 judges in total) expressed their evaluations and suggestions regarding the system in written form.[165] Some provided brief responses, while others elaborated on their viewpoints in greater detail. Below, we present these shorter and longer evaluative opinions and suggestions, indicating each respondent's overall position on the jury system (affirmative or negative), their judicial status, years of judicial experience (the data collection took place in December 2015 and January 2016), and their gender.

[165] Our request in this regard was phrased as follows: *"If you believe that the current jury system should be reformed, we would be honoured if you could express your valuable thoughts on this matter in one or two sentences."*

POSITION	JUDICIAL STATUS	JUDICIAL EXPERIENCE	GENDER
Negative	district judge	6-10 years	Male
OPINION/SUGGESTION			
In light of the current appellate expectations, lay judges' involvement is unnecessary concerning the detailed reasoning of substantive judgments (fact-finding, scope, evaluation of evidence, balancing, and legal argumentation related to qualifications) and in terms of case management. The reason for this is that the work of the first-instance judge will be reviewed by an appellate panel consisting of three professional judges, whose criteria differ markedly from those of laypersons.			

POSITION	JUDICIAL STATUS	JUDICIAL EXPERIENCE	GENDER
Negative	labour court judge	21-25 years	female
OPINION/SUGGESTION			
The presentation of all the case documents at every hearing is done because of the lay judges, not the parties, which leads to significant time delays at each session. This diverts the judge's attention from managing the hearing, and creates the impression among the parties that the judge is being tested on their case. The time required for pre-judgment consultation and voting is disproportionate to the soundness and professionalism of the lay opinions, and instead limits the judge's ability to focus on the case. The legal decision slowly caters to both the judge and the lay judges and their opinions, as they can overrule the judge. The judge must justify why they decided according to the legal rules. The jury system does not assist but rather hinders the timely, well-founded decision-making process. The judge must be aware of all the facts and connections, which the lay judges cannot help with. The lack of preparation by the judge cannot be compensated by the lay judge.			

POSITION	JUDICIAL STATUS	JUDICIAL EXPERIENCE	GENDER
Negative	**labour court judge**	**16-20 years**	**female**
OPINION/SUGGESTION			
If the legislature deems the participation of laypersons in judicial decision-making necessary, it should clearly define the qualifications, professional knowledge, and experience required for lay judges to potentially work effectively. I consider educational background to be crucial in the selection process, and it would also be beneficial if the lay judges have some understanding of the law. In the current selection process, I believe that, apart from age, nothing else is taken into account. Most often, retired judges—who are available in the mornings—are appointed or volunteer. There have been instances where a lay judge had only completed eight years of primary school education. The court is willing to provide the lay judge with access to case files before the hearing. However, it has never happened that any lay judge was interested in the case to the extent that they would request to review the files. Naturally, in accordance with the legal requirements, the case documents are presented before the hearing, so the lay judge is aware of the subject of the case. Given that the lay judge must be given the opportunity, the question is presented accordingly. However, it is very rare that the questions asked are based on the case at hand; it is more typical that their sympathies are evident in the way the question is posed. For example: "Why did they have to dismiss this poor, inexperienced, young girl?" There have been occasions when I had to call for a break because a lay judge fell asleep. Maintaining the court's authority becomes quite difficult under these circumstances. I consider the participation of laypersons in judicial decision-making to be a high-cost system that does not positively influence (and in fact, may hinder) the decision-making process, at least in labour law cases.			

POSITION	JUDICIAL STATUS	JUDICIAL EXPERIENCE	GENDER
Negative	district court judge	6-10 years	Male
OPINION/SUGGESTION			
The complete abolition of the jury system is justified.			

POSITION	JUDICIAL STATUS	JUDICIAL EXPERIENCE	GENDER
Negative	district court judge	6-10 years	male
OPINION/SUGGESTION			
It could be abolished with complete ease: on numerous occasions, hearings cannot be held due to their illness or other commitments; if one is absent, the evidence must be repeated with a new lay judge... public participation in the legal process is a completely outdated legal institution.			

POSITION	JUDICIAL STATUS	JUDICIAL EXPERIENCE	GENDER
Negative	Budapest-Capital district court judge	11-15 years	female
OPINION/SUGGESTION			
The current lay judge system unquestionably requires reform and thorough reconsideration. In practice, lay judges do not engage meaningfully in the professional work. The number of lay judges who at least request the indictment or any information regarding the case is negligible. It is not the judges who exclude the lay judges, but rather they, regrettably, mostly present the image of bored retirees. In this form, the current lay judge system fails to achieve its intended purpose. The participation of laypersons in the administration of justice is not necessarily desirable. The fundamental shortcomings can be traced back to deficiencies in education, as laypersons are entirely unfamiliar with and fail to understand the system of justice. Therefore, the involvement of lay judges should begin with a reform of education.			

POSITION	JUDICIAL STATUS	JUDICIAL EXPERIENCE	GENDER
Negative	**regional court judge**	**26-30 years**	**Male**
OPINION/SUGGESTION			
For 24 years, I adjudicated first-instance cases at the regional court, always with lay judges. The law obliges the judge, and therefore I always listened to the opinions of the lay judges, without limiting their rights. My response to the question of "providing the case materials" should be understood in the sense that, if the lay judge had come in the previous week, they could freely study the case file, but they could not be compelled to do so. The opportunity for studying the files was rarely utilised. Today, I chair a second-instance panel, so I also have experience in professional judicial collaboration. It has always been my opinion – since the selection process and individual preparation of lay judges cannot be monitored – that lay judging should be abolished. Perhaps the system of teacher lay judges could be retained, provided there were specialised courts for juvenile cases.			

POSITION	JUDICIAL STATUS	JUDICIAL EXPERIENCE	GENDER
Negative	**regional court judge**	**11-15 years**	**female**
OPINION/SUGGESTION			
Lay adjudication should be abolished.			

POSITION	JUDICIAL STATUS	JUDICIAL EXPERIENCE	GENDER
Negative	**district court judge**	**26-30 years**	**female**
OPINION/SUGGESTION			
Lay judging had its historical role. Today, it holds little relevance, as other forms of oversight are more effective.			

POSITION	JUDICIAL STATUS	JUDICIAL EXPERIENCE	GENDER
Negative	**labour court judge**	**26-30 years**	**male**
OPINION/SUGGESTION			
I do not consider the lay judge system necessary. In any case, the only meaningful alternative might be a system of professional lay judges, in which trained representatives of employer and employee interest groups participate in the proceedings.			

POSITION	JUDICIAL STATUS	JUDICIAL EXPERIENCE	GENDER
Negative	**district court judge**	**21-25 years**	**Female**
OPINION/SUGGESTION			
There is no point in maintaining the current system in its present form. I do not consider the system of justices of the peace or the American jury system to be bad, but if the lay judge is to make the decision, then it should not be the judge who is required to provide the reasoning. At present, as the judge bears the responsibility of justifying the verdict, it is clear that they cannot rely on the lay judge's opinion in the decision-making, especially if it is one that cannot be justified by a professional judge.			

POSITION	JUDICIAL STATUS	JUDICIAL EXPERIENCE	GENDER
Negative	**regional court of appeal judge**	**26-30 years**	**female**
OPINION/SUGGESTION			
In its current form, it is merely formal.			

POSITION	JUDICIAL STATUS	JUDICIAL EXPERIENCE	GENDER
Negative	**district court judge**	**11-15 years**	**male**
OPINION/SUGGESTION			
I would abolish it; it is formal, costly, and unnecessary due to their lack of preparation, and indifference.			

POSITION	JUDICIAL STATUS	JUDICIAL EXPERIENCE	GENDER
Negative	**district court judge**	**11-15 years**	**male**
OPINION/SUGGESTION			
I see the exclusion of the lay element as the only acceptable solution in the current legal and societal context.			

POSITION	JUDICIAL STATUS	JUDICIAL EXPERIENCE	GENDER
Negative	**district court judge**	**11-15 years**	**female**
OPINION/SUGGESTION			
Abolition.			

POSITION	JUDICIAL STATUS	JUDICIAL EXPERIENCE	GENDER
Negative	**regional court judge**	**16-20 years**	**Female**
OPINION/SUGGESTION			
The participation of two lay judges does not constitute meaningful involvement, especially due to the composition of the panel. Very often, they are unable to contribute any specialised knowledge to the subject of the case, essentially just being present. If lay adjudication is to be considered, I could only envision the successful involvement of a larger number of laypersons, such as in the case of a jury.			

POSITION	JUDICIAL STATUS	JUDICIAL EXPERIENCE	GENDER
Negative	**regional court judge**	**N/A**	**female**
OPINION/SUGGESTION			
Lay judges are neither professionally prepared nor equipped with the psychological skills, behavioural culture, or the ability to apply logical reasoning, nor do they possess knowledge of procedural law. Their individual knowledge, life experience, expertise, and character are the sole factors that determine their behaviour and actions.			

POSITION	JUDICIAL STATUS	JUDICIAL EXPERIENCE	GENDER
Negative	**regional court judge**	**6-10 years**	**male**
OPINION/SUGGESTION			
In my view, the lay judge system should be completely abolished, and instead, legally qualified individuals who provide genuine assistance to judges should be appointed on a permanent basis (such as the so-called "Rechtshilfer" in Germany). For questions requiring expertise, I would make it possible for judges to consult professional advisors. Until these changes are realised, I would ensure that lay judges undergo mandatory legal training and account for the knowledge they have acquired. In its current form, the lay judge system is hypocritical, with the "lay" element only playing a formal role. While a professional judge studies law and judicial practice for at least 5+3+1 years, regularly demonstrating their knowledge, lay judges, based on my experience, are often lacking even the most basic legal knowledge. In such cases, granting them the same rights while they have no interest in preparation (and would mostly be incapable of doing so) is a dangerous move. Rights and responsibilities are disproportionate, as their substantial work essentially boils down to signing the final			

decision. Just as we would not allow lay individuals into a surgeon's operating room without professional qualification and without delegating authority to intervene in the surgery, we must acknowledge that law is a learned profession that requires thorough preparation, commitment, and certain essential competencies. The lay element is more susceptible to manipulation and misdirection, stemming from a lack of legal reasoning (and often education) in particular.

POSITION	**JUDICIAL STATUS**	**JUDICIAL EXPERIENCE**	**GENDER**
Negative	**district court judge**	**above 30 years**	**female**
OPINION/SUGGESTION			
In the early period of my career, we discussed many cases in a panel – divorce, maintenance agreements, etc. In civil cases, the presence of a lay judge is unnecessary. In criminal cases, perhaps it would be appropriate if, in cases involving family-related issues, a teacher and/or a woman were part of the panel. Fundamentally, I do not consider the lay judge system to be necessary.			

POSITION	**JUDICIAL STATUS**	**JUDICIAL EXPERIENCE**	**GENDER**
Negative	**district court judge**	**16-20 years**	**male**
OPINION/SUGGESTION			
It should be abolished.			

POSITION	**JUDICIAL STATUS**	**JUDICIAL EXPERIENCE**	**GENDER**
Negative	**Budapest-Capital district court judge**	**26-30 years**	**female**
OPINION/SUGGESTION			
I believe it should be abolished, particularly in civil proceedings, as the "lay" knowledge and experience have no significant value in labour court adjudication, where lay judges are still involved. The only instance in which I consider the involvement of a lay judge to be important is in cases involving juvenile offenders, where a teacher's participation is essential. In such cases, the knowledge and experience of a professional trained in pedagogy and psychology are crucial, especially when considering mitigating or aggravating circumstances and determining the sentence.			

POSITION	JUDICIAL STATUS	JUDICIAL EXPERIENCE	GENDER
Negative	**district court judge**	**6-10 years**	**male**
OPINION/SUGGESTION			
Lay judges have no role whatsoever: in any other profession requiring specialised training, there is no room for lay involvement. It only generates costs and organisational difficulties, and should not be maintained.			

POSITION	JUDICIAL STATUS	JUDICIAL EXPERIENCE	GENDER
Negative	**district court judge**	**16-20 years**	**female**
OPINION/SUGGESTION			
There is no need for the lay judge system.			

POSITION	JUDICIAL STATUS	JUDICIAL EXPERIENCE	GENDER
N/A	**regional court judge**	**26-30 years**	**female**
OPINION/SUGGESTION			
Involving lay judges with specialised knowledge and basic legal understanding would be useful, for example, by providing them with foundational legal training. It would also be beneficial to include judges with technical, pedagogical, or healthcare expertise in first-instance procedures. As a municipal judge, I have worked alongside lay judges for approximately 20 years. Based on my experience, lay judges with specialised knowledge have been helpful in my work.			

POSITION	JUDICIAL STATUS	JUDICIAL EXPERIENCE	GENDER
Affirmative	**regional court judge**	**above 30 years**	**female**
OPINION/SUGGESTION			
The selection process should make impartiality, objectivity, absence of criminal records, and the avoidance of conflicts of interest mandatory.			

POSITION	JUDICIAL STATUS	JUDICIAL EXPERIENCE	GENDER
Affirmative	judge at the Curia	above 30 years	female
OPINION/SUGGESTION			
In labour disputes, I believe it is justified to involve "specialist lay judges" who are not experts but possess significant professional knowledge, such as in engineering, etc. Their explanations could contribute to the acceleration of proceedings – not everything requires an expert, if the lay judge can clearly explain how the machine works.			

POSITION	JUDICIAL STATUS	JUDICIAL EXPERIENCE	GENDER
Affirmative	Budapest-Capital district court judge	1-5 years	female
OPINION/SUGGESTION			
I would subject the candidates to a thorough introductory training. They are not fully aware of the seriousness of the work.			

POSITION	JUDICIAL STATUS	JUDICIAL EXPERIENCE	GENDER
Affirmative	district court judge	6-10 years	male
OPINION/SUGGESTION			
The method of selection should definitely be reconsidered, and some form of motivation (or obligation) should be introduced, so that the lay judges are not solely retirees or former court employees.			

POSITION	JUDICIAL STATUS	JUDICIAL EXPERIENCE	GENDER
Affirmative	regional court of appeal judge	16-20 years	Female
OPINION/SUGGESTION			
A questionnaire should be completed by those applying to be lay judges, through which their actual intelligence can be measured, as well as the motivation behind their application—whether it is driven by mere curiosity, boredom at home, or a sense of dedication.			

POSITION	JUDICIAL STATUS	JUDICIAL EXPERIENCE	GENDER
Affirmative	**regional court judge**	**N/A**	**male**
OPINION/SUGGESTION			
Political bodies should not play a role in the selection process.			

POSITION	JUDICIAL STATUS	JUDICIAL EXPERIENCE	GENDER
Affirmative	**district court judge**	**11-15 years**	**male**
OPINION/SUGGESTION			
I would prioritise the professional qualifications of lay judges, considering the types of cases that frequently occur in different areas of law.			

POSITION	JUDICIAL STATUS	JUDICIAL EXPERIENCE	GENDER
Affirmative	**regional court judge**	**21-25 years**	**female**
OPINION/SUGGESTION			
The system of lay judges is necessary because, on the one hand, their presence assists the judge, and on the other hand, their participation in society can help gain acceptance for certain decisions.			

POSITION	JUDICIAL STATUS	JUDICIAL EXPERIENCE	GENDER
Affirmative	**Budapest-Capital district court judge**	**N/A**	**female**
OPINION/SUGGESTION			
The courts should have a greater say in the selection of lay judges so that the appropriate judges can continue their work and ongoing cases do not need to be restarted. Judges should not be re-elected if their work, appearance, or behaviour is unworthy of participation in the administration of justice, or if they are over the age of 66, as their age may prevent them from fulfilling their duties as lay judges during the four-year term.			

POSITION	JUDICIAL STATUS	JUDICIAL EXPERIENCE	GENDER
Affirmative	labour court judge	21-25 years	female
OPINION/SUGGESTION			
Lay judges should be selected by the court based on nominations from professional organisations. The lay judge lists should be compiled according to professional knowledge and qualifications. This way, lay judges with the relevant expertise related to the subject matter of the case could be called upon. It would also have a cost-reducing effect, as for less significant technical questions, the use of experts could be dispensed with, or at least a more concise opinion would suffice for the adjudication of the case.			

POSITION	JUDICIAL STATUS	JUDICIAL EXPERIENCE	GENDER
Affirmative	regional court judge	above 30 years	Female
OPINION/SUGGESTION			
I believe the institution of the justice of the peace should be introduced. In villages and district areas of towns, they could adjudicate less weighty cases – with some level of preparation – on a designated day each week in the local government office, for example, in the courtroom. This would not require new investments or extravagant spending, yet it would reduce the burden on the courts and speed up the administration of justice, among other benefits.			

POSITION	JUDICIAL STATUS	JUDICIAL EXPERIENCE	GENDER
Affirmative	regional court judge	11-15 years	female
OPINION/SUGGESTION			
The scope of the affected cases could be expanded to include certain types of lawsuits, such as those concerning parental custody rights, where the involvement of teacher lay judges would be beneficial.			

POSITION	JUDICIAL STATUS	JUDICIAL EXPERIENCE	GENDER
Affirmative	district court judge	11-15 years	male
OPINION/SUGGESTION			
Judges should be made aware of the advantages of lay judging, so that they do not view lay judges as an obstacle to their work. Greater transparency should be ensured during the selection of lay judges, both for society and for the judges themselves, perhaps by posting the list of candidates on the court's website along with a brief overview of their professional background. The selection process should place increased emphasis on the lay judge's professional qualifications and personal attributes. I would not rule out the possibility of conducting a suitability test or having candidates complete an assessment. It is also crucial to improve their financial compensation. Additionally, I consider it important and necessary to reintroduce the wearing of judicial robes.			

POSITION	JUDICIAL STATUS	JUDICIAL EXPERIENCE	GENDER
Affirmative	regional court of appeal judge	21-25 years	Female
OPINION/SUGGESTION			
In family law cases, I would reinstate the lay judge system.			

Annexure 4 – Lay Judge Research – Responses

Please kindly indicate whether you...	
	Valid Percentage
1 – Only carried out judicial duties during the previous lay judge cycle, but not in the current one	15
2 – Carry out judicial duties in both the previous and current cycles	75.4
3 – Only carry out judicial duties in the current cycle	9.5
Total:	100

In the previous cycle, were you...?	
	Valid Percentage
1 – A lay judge at a regional court	14.6
2 – A lay judge at a Budapest-Capital district court	4.9
3 – A lay judge at a district court	52.1
4 – A lay judge at an administrative and labour court	28.5
Total:	100

In which municipality is the court located where you serve or have served as a lay judge?	
	Valid Percentage
Not specified	5.5
Balassagyarmat	0.3
Battonya	1.7
Békés	0.9
Békéscsaba	3.7
Central District Court of Buda 2007–2011, Budapest Regional Court 2011–2015	0.3
BKKB. Budapest, Budakeszi út	0.3
Budapest Districts II and III	0.3
Budai	0.3
Central District Court of Buda	0.6
Budaörs	0.9
Budapest	21.3

Budapest, appointed as a lay judge in summer 2015, yet to participate in a hearing.	0.3
Budapest II	0.3
Budapest Distrcits II and III	0.3
Budapest, Markó Street	0.3
Budapest Courts for Districts XX, XXI, and XXIII	0.3
Budapest District Courts for Districts XX, XXI, and XXIII	0.3
Budapest District XXI, Csepel	0.3
Budapest, Budapest Regional Court	0.3
Budapest, Districts XX., XXI., and XXIII.	0.3
Budapest, Districts XX., XXI., and XXIII.	0.3
in Budapest	0.6
Budapest	0.3
Cegléd, Districts Court	0.3
Csongrád	2.9

Debrecen	0.3
Eger	5.5
Encs	0.3
the Capital City	0.3
Gödöllő	0.6
Gyöngyös	0.3
Győr	3.2
Gyula	8.9
Heves	0.3
Budapest, Districts IV to XV	0.3
Kaposvár	0.3
Kazincbarcika	0.3
Miskolc	11.8
Mosonmagyaróvár	1.4
Nyírbátor	0.3
Nyíregyháza	1.4
Orosháza	1.4
Ózd	1.1
Central District Court of Pest (Budapest)	0.3
Sopron	1.4
Szarvas	2
Szeged	4.6

Szeged, county-rank city	0.3
Szeged	0.3
Szeghalom	1.4
Székesfehérvár	0.9
Szentendre	0.3
Szentes	4
Szerencs	0.6
Szikszó	1.4
Tatabánya	1.4
Vác	0.3
Total:	100

In which county is the court located?	
	Valid Percentage
1 – Békés	22.2
2 – Borsod-Abaúj-Zemplén	16.1
3 – Budapest	23.4
4 – Csongrád	14
5 – Fejér	1.2
6 – Győr-Moson-Sopron	5.8
7 – Hajdú-Bihar	0.3
8 – Heves	5.8
9 – Komárom-Esztergom	1.5
10 – Nógrád	0.3
11 – Pest	6.7
12 – Somogy	0.3
13 – Szabolcs-Szatmár-Bereg	2.3
Total:	100

In which cycle did you serve as a lay judge?	
	Valid Percentage
1	31
2	35.6
3	18.2
4	8.6
5	3.3
6	1.3
7	0.3
8	1
9	0.3
10	0.3
Total:	100

Have you ever served as a lay judge in [criminal] areas of law?	
	Valid Percentage
1 – Not selected	35.1
2 – Yes	64.9
Total:	100

Have you ever served as a lay judge in [civil] areas of law?	
	Valid Percentage
1 – Not selected	90.8
2 – Yes	9.2
Total:	100

Have you ever served as a lay judge in [labour] areas of law?	
	Valid Percentage
1 – Not selected	73
2 – Yes	27
Total:	100

Have you ever served as a lay judge in [other] areas of law?	
	Valid Percentage
1 – Not selected	96.8
2 – Yes	3.2
Total:	100

In which other areas of law have you served as a lay judge?	
	Valid Percentage
Not specified	96.8%
Juvenile cases	0.3%
Juveniles	0.6%
Criminal cases involving juveniles	0.3%
First-instance cases	0.3%
KGYK	0.3%
Public administrative	1.1%
Private prosecution cases	0.3%
Total:	100.0%

If you estimate, in approximately how many cases have you participated as a lay judge?

	Valid Percentage
1	0.3
2	2
3	2
4	4.4
5	1.4
6	2.4
7	0.7
8	2
9	1.7
10	4.4
11	1
12	2.4
13	0.3
14	1
15	4.4
17	0.7
18	1
19	0.3
20	7.1
21	0.3
24	0.3
25	3.4
29	0.3
30	5.8
35	0.7
36	0.3
37	0.3
40	4.8
45	0.7
49	0.3
50	6.5
52	0.3
55	0.3
60	3.1
65	0.3
70	1
80	1.7
90	0.7
100	5.1

110	0.3
115	0.3
120	3.4
140	0.3
150	2
160	0.3
170	0.3
174	0.3
180	0.7
190	0.7
200	2.7
216	0.3
220	0.3
300	2
350	0.3
400	1.4
500	2
545	0.3
600	0.7
700	0.7
800	1
830	0.3
900	0.3
1500	0.7
2000	0.3
3000	0.3
6000	0.3
8000	0.3
15000	0.3
Total:	100

In the previous cycle, were you a member of the Hungarian Association of Lay Judges?	
	Valid Percentage
1 – I was not a member	83.9
2 – I was a member	16.1
Total:	100

Which solution would you consider the best for selecting lay judge candidates?	
	Valid Percentage
1 The local government representative body should continue to decide on the selection:	40.1
2 The courts should decide on the selection	54.6
3 Some other professional organisation should decide on the selection	5.3
Total:	100

The MOST important criterion for selecting candidates for lay judge work:	
	Valid Percentage
1 The candidate's life experience.	35.5
2 The candidate's useful professional expertise.	24.5
3 The candidate's level of education.	11.6
4 The candidate's knowledge of issues related to lay judge work.	6.7
5 The candidate's public activity, acceptability, and support.	4.9
6 The candidate's adaptable personality.	3.1
7 The candidate's independent thinking.	12.5
8 The candidate's local recognition.	0.6
9 Other considerations.	0.6
Total:	100

The SECOND most important criterion for selecting candidates for lay judge work:	
	Valid Percentage
1. The candidate's life experience.	19
2. The candidate's useful professional expertise.	18.7

3. The candidate's level of education.	19.3
4. The candidate's knowledge of issues related to lay judge work.	12.5
5. The candidate's public activity, acceptability, and support.	7.2
6. The candidate's adaptable personality.	5
7. The candidate's independent thinking.	17.1
8. The candidate's local recognition.	0.9
9. Other considerations.	0.3
Total:	100

The THIRD most important criterion for selecting candidates for lay judge work:	
	Valid Percentage
1. The candidate's life experience.	14.7
2. The candidate's useful professional expertise.	11.6
3. The candidate's level of education.	17.2
4. The candidate's knowledge of issues related to lay judge work.	12.9
5. The candidate's public activity, acceptability, and support.	5.6
6. The candidate's adaptable personality.	8.2
7. The candidate's independent thinking.	25.4
8. The candidate's local recognition.	2.2
9. Other considerations.	1.9
10. The best solution would be random selection.	0.3
Total:	100

What are the other considerations?	
	Valid Percentage
No other considerations specified.	97.4%
The candidate's emotional intelligence, empathy.	0.3%
The candidate's willingness to act, commitment.	0.3%
The completion of lay judge work should not encounter obstacles.	0.3%
Empathy.	0.3%
Decisiveness.	0.3%
Intelligence, behaviour culture.	0.3%

Belonging to a Christian church, religiousness, Bible knowledge, spiritual life.	0.3%
Psychological suitability, or cultural level should qualify as a 4-6 hour public service activity, with reimbursement for travel and meal expenses.	0.3%
Competence.	0.3%
Total:	100.0%

How do you see lay judge work...?	
	Valid Percentage
1. Mostly a formality, with no significant role in the justice system.	8.6
2. Somewhat contributes to the better functioning of the justice system.	55.5
3. Has a significant role in the better functioning of the justice system.	35.9
Total:	100

What did lay judge work mean for you? [This is a special job for me, a vocation.]	
	Valid Percentage
1 – Not selected	20.4
2 – Yes	79.6
Total:	100

What did lay judge work mean for you? "This is the same kind of work as any other for me."	
	Valid Percentage
1 – Not selected	98.6
2 – Yes	1.4
Total:	100

What did lay judge work mean for you? "This is not work for me, but a useful pastime."	
	Valid Percentage
1 – Not selected	80.2
2 – Yes	19.8
Total:	100

What did lay judge work mean for you? "This is an additional opportunity to earn income for me."

	Valid Percentage
1 – Not selected	90.8
2 – Yes	9.2
Total:	100

What did lay judge work mean for you? "This means something else for me."	
	Valid Percentage
1 – Not selected	88.5
2 – Yes	11.5
Total:	100

For me, this primarily means...	
	Valid Percentage
	88.8%
A limited, but specific insight into the practical side of legal work. (But I would consider it most appropriate to select full-time lay judges between the ages of 35 and 65.)	0.3%
Continuation of my previous legal career.	0.3%
I was able to apply the knowledge I gained in this work to my job.	0.3%
It signifies the fulfilment of what I was preparing for during my university years, though life 'swayed' me towards another area.	0.3%
It should signify contributing somewhat to the better functioning of the justice system, which is difficult in continental law systems. I believe that the justice system would function with fewer mistakes in the Anglo-Saxon system, where social oversight is nearly all-encompassing. Unfortunately, Hungarian society is not yet ready, nor are the judges, for the Anglo-Saxon legal system. Most of Europe, especially former socialist countries, is in the same position. A discussion of this would be the subject of a separate study, which this form is unsuitable for.	0.3%
Insight into the Hungarian justice and appeal system.	0.3%
Insight into a specific segment of social life (personal and organisational aspects of judicial activity, prosecutor's role, investigation quality, defence work, forms of criminal society's appearance).	0.3%
Partial continuation of my previous career, for pension purposes.	0.3%
Getting to know an unknown field.	0.3%

A special job for me, considering my 40 years of experience in public administration and education. This is moral recognition, a useful and fulfilling use of my retirement years.	0.3%
The use of my life experience (with minors).	0.3%

After becoming acquainted with human fates and issues, I consider the evaluation of potential solutions before responding.	0.3%
Responsibility, which also provides an enriching experience.	0.3%
Gaining useful information and experiences.	0.3%
I believe in the deterrent power of the law.	0.3%
Utilising my knowledge and experience for the benefit of the community.	0.3%
Developing my knowledge and expertise.	0.3%
A new field has opened up to me.	0.3%
The continuation of my previous activities in another phase of the Code of Criminal Procedure.	0.3%
I take part in community work, feel useful, and can assist with my knowledge.	0.3%
I have gained a deeper understanding of another branch of power.	0.3%
I have encountered a different world within this field.	0.3%
Having been a company director and employer for nearly 30 years, and since the proceedings predominantly involve employee lay judges, I found it essential that practical professionals from the other side also be involved in the proceedings. I apply the same reasoning to public administration.	0.3%
Activities connected to my work.	0.3%
As a retiree, I am still a valuable member of society.	0.3%
As a retiree, it provides me with both an occupation and an opportunity to utilise my life experience. Additional income is not a consideration as the remuneration is far too demeaning.	0.3%
Opportunities for participation in public life.	0.3%
Maintaining my professional knowledge.	0.3%
It signifies professional experience.	0.3%
The application of my professional knowledge.	0.3%
I assist in solving problematic cases with my expertise.	0.3%
Keeping my intellectual abilities sharp and acquiring important knowledge.	0.3%

Gaining experience.	1.2%
Social work.	0.3%
Social engagement.	0.3%
The possibility of influencing society.	0.3%
Total:	100.0%

How much did you enjoy the work of a lay judge?	
	Valid Percentage
1 – Rather willingly	12.5
2 – Particularly willingly	87.5
Total:	100

Do you possess any legal qualifications?	
	Valid Percentage
1 – Nem	60.7
2 – Yes	39.3
Total:	100

What type of legal qualifications do you have?	
	Valid Percentage
1 – Law degree	6.1
2 – Legal assistant qualification	2.3
3 – Qualifications in labour law and social security	24.2
4 – Took legal subjects during my studies	47.7
5 – Other	19.7
Total:	100

What other legal qualifications do you hold?	
	Valid Percentage
None indicated for other qualifications	92.5%
Public administration college	0.3%
In my banking career, I also worked in a legal presentation role and developed processes based on legal compliance.	0.3%

Court staff	0.3%
Court expert (subject) for a long time	0.3%
Security guard	0.3%
Construction authority work	0.3%
Advanced foreign trade law in goods circulation	0.3%

As an entrepreneur	0.3%
Child protection and family law	0.3%
Management organiser	0.3%
Experience in institutional leadership	0.3%
Law student, final exams pending (The role of the lay judge should be more prominent. The principle of trial by jury could be applied in every first-instance procedure, at least in criminal cases, due to its ultima ratio nature. It might even close the gap between so-called paper law and living law [...] by more actively involving those willing to participate in adjudicating activities, non-lawyers with no professional legal qualifications. I think the practice of sentencing could be made stricter in line with societal demands for justice. A lay judge – if not merely ornamental – would push the verdict in this direction ("if guilty, the person should receive the maximum sentence, unless this is their only transgression and they have not murdered anyone").)	0.3%
Basic legal knowledge	0.3%
Law degree, years 1–4	0.3%
Legal librarian	0.3%
Accountant	0.3%
Nearly 30 years of experience as an executive director	0.3%
Labour law specialist consultant	0.3%
Local government work	0.3%
Police experience	0.3%
Police criminal law specialist	0.3%
Police academy	0.3%
RTF	0.3%
Studied legal subjects during my studies; as a security organiser	0.3%
Worked at the Prosecutor's Office for 38 years, possessing basic legal knowledge	0.3%
Final-year law student	0.3%
Total:	100.0%

What other (non-legal) knowledge or qualifications have you found most useful in your work as a lay judge?	
	Valid Percentage
1 – Pedagogical	28.4
2 – Military, law enforcement	7.1
3 – Administrative	8.8
4 – Labour law	14.5
5 – Economic-financial	12.5
6 – Technical	6.1
7 – Other	14.9
8 – I do not possess such specialised knowledge	7.8
Total:	100

Other (non-legal) knowledge:	
	Valid Percentage
No other (non-legal) knowledge indicated	87.6%
Everyday life experience	0.3%
Public administration matters	0.3%
Drug prevention	0.3%
Knowledge in drug prevention	0.3%
Medical qualifications	1.2%
Food industry engineering qualification	0.3%
Life experience	1.1%
Human and leadership experience	0.3%
Knowledge of human nature	0.3%
Knowledge of human nature, experience (Hospitality, trade)	0.3%
Occupational rehabilitation expert	0.3%
Special education qualification	0.3%
Administrative, labour law, economic-financial knowledge	0.3%
Administrative; cultural sector	0.3%
Judicial service	0.3%
Many years of work in supervisory bodies	0.3%
Handwriting expert, graphologist	0.3%
Handwriting expert qualification	0.3%
Legal knowledge, significantly higher than general level, but without a formal qualification	0.3%
Minority life experience	0.3%
Administrative work	0.3%

Criminology	0.6%
Occupational safety	0.6%
Pedagogical, administrative, economic-financial	0.3%
Pedagogical, military, law enforcement, technical	0.3%
Involvement with civil guard, crime prevention, law enforcement, drug prevention	0.3%
Psychological	0.3%
Psychological, pedagogical	0.3%
Psychological, sociological	0.3%
Psychological-healthcare	0.3%
Social worker qualifications and experience	0.3%
Social pedagogy	0.3%
Studied psychology	0.3%
Extensive knowledge as a secretary	0.3%
Decades of leadership and pedagogical experience	0.3%
Total:	100.0%

Do you think it is sufficient for a lay judge to become acquainted with the case during the hearing itself, or is it necessary for them to prepare before the hearing?	
	Valid Percentage
1 – It is sufficient to become acquainted with the case during the hearing	44.1
2 – It is necessary to prepare before the hearing	55.9
Total:	100

Do you usually prepare for hearings?	
	Valid Percentage
1 – I do not usually prepare	20.2
2 – Only occasionally	10.7
3 – Sometimes	15.3
4 – Generally, yes	37.8
5 – Without exception, every time	16
Total:	100

Do you feel that you had enough time to review the case materials before the hearing?	
	Valid Percentage
1 – I almost never had enough time	9.5
2 – Unfortunately, I did not have enough time in most cases	11.9

3 – Sometimes, it varied	28.2
4 – I had enough time in most cases	33
5 – I always had enough time	17.3
Total:	100

Before the last case hearing, did the judge provide you with the case's factual and legal materials, or did they merely inform you?	
	Valid Percentage
1 – We received the case materials and also information	27.1
2 – We only received the case materials	3.9
3 – We did not receive materials, but the judge provided information about the case	63.9
4 – In this case, we did not receive materials or information in advance	5.2
Total:	100

If you reflect on the cases you have heard in your previous term, what was the most typical situation?	
	Valid Percentage
1 – We received the case materials and also information	25.9
2 – We only received the case materials	2.6
3 – We did not receive materials, but the judge provided information	67.6
4 – We received neither materials nor information	3.9
Total:	100

Do you generally understand the legal context of the cases you hear?	
	Valid Percentage
1 – Sometimes	5.1
2 – Mostly yes	51.6
3 – Always	43.3
Total:	100

Do you ever read legal textbooks or journals (other than the lay judge handbook)?	
	Valid Percentage
1 – Never	10.9
2 – There has been an occasion	40.1
3 – With more or less regularity	22.8
4 – Quite frequently	19.2

5 – Regularly	7.1
Total:	100

Do you ever study statutes?	
	Valid Percentage
1 – I do not usually do so	10.6
2 – Only occasionally	42.3
3 – Quite frequently	29.4
4 – Regularly	17.7
Total:	100

Do you read the written decision before signing it?	
	Valid Percentage
1 – Never	1.3
2 – Mostly not	4.5
3 – Sometimes	6.4
4 – Mostly yes	27.8
5 – In every case	60.1
Total:	100

In your opinion, in what area can the lay judge be of most help to the judge?	
	Valid Percentage
1 – Establishing the facts of the case	37.7
2 – Determining guilt	30.1
3 – Legal qualification	1.7
4 – Determining the sentence	20.9
5 – Other areas	9.6
Total:	100

What other areas?	
	Valid Percentage
No other areas selected	92.0%
All of 1 to 4	0.3%
1., 2., and 4.	0.3%
1., 2., 4., extenuating and aggravating circumstances	0.3%
All of the above	0.3%
Along with the above, also in administration	0.3%
Experience gained in economic life	0.3%
Decision-making in questions based on evaluation	0.3%
Recalculating and verifying police records	0.3%

The authenticity of testimonies [...] discussing the connections, directing the judge's attention to aspects that may be important (details), body language, etc.	0.3%
By expressing one's standpoint	0.3%
Presenting the general assessment	0.3%
In the discovery and representation of the truth	0.3%
Determining guilt; mitigating or aggravating circumstances	0.3%
In determining the sentence; human factors, empathy	0.3%
In determining the sentence; whether to place the defendant under house arrest or not	0.3%

With his life experience and the broad perspective it provides	0.3%
Can ask questions to the parties during the trial before the decision is made	0.3%
Monitors the course of the trial	0.3%
Application of practical rules in the economic and financial field	0.3%
Mentioning humanitarian factors	0.3%
From a lay perspective	0.3%
All four	0.3%
In every issue related to the case, and naturally, in the imposition of a just and reasonable sentence	0.3%
By forming an objective opinion	0.3%
I paid attention to every small detail during the hearings, and there were instances where the judge overlooked something	0.3%
In establishing the facts, determining guilt, and imposing a sentence	0.3%
Reality in practical life, in everyday practice, with examples from daily life	0.3%
In expressing an opinion	0.3%
Total:	100.0%

In practice, do judges provide opportunities for lay judges to ask questions during the hearing (e.g. of the defendant, witness, or expert)?

	Valid Percentage
1 – Rarely	7.7
2 – Usually not	10.3
3 – Sometimes	18.6
4 – Mostly yes	25.3
5 – Always	38.1
Total:	100

In practice, do judges usually ask for the opinion of lay judges on the case's evaluation?	
	Valid Percentage
1 – Rarely	1
2 – Usually not	4.2
3 – Sometimes	11
4 – Mostly yes	32.9
5 – Always	51
Total:	100

Based on your experience, do judges tend to listen to the opinions of lay judges during the deliberation?	
	Valid Percentage
1 – Rarely	1.3
2 – Only very rarely	3.8
3 – Sometimes	14.1
4 – Mostly yes	40.1
5 – Always	40.7
Total:	100

Have you ever had an opinion different from the judge's on a case?	
	Valid Percentage
1 – No	42
2 – This has happened once	20.8
3 – This has happened several times	36.2
4 – This has occurred quite often	1
Total:	100

Have you voiced your opinion when it differed from the judge's?	
	Valid Percentage
1 – I have never done so	10.7
2 – There were occasions when I did, and occasions when I did not	37.6
3 – I have done so every time	51.7
Total:	100

Did the judge take your opinion into account?	
	Valid Percentage
1 – Never	5.8
2 – Sometimes yes, sometimes no	52.6
3 – Always	41.7
Total:	100

Have you ever submitted a dissenting opinion?	
	Valid Percentage
1 – No, not yet	96.6
2 – I have once	1.7
3 – I have done so a few times	1.7
Total:	100

In your opinion, what role do lay judges' opinions play in the formation of judicial decisions (judgments)?	
	Valid Percentage
1 – Lay judges' opinions do not matter at all.	1.3
2 – Lay judges' opinions carry little weight and are mostly disregarded.	9.9
3 – They matter to some extent.	4.8
4 – Lay judges' opinions matter, but the professional authority of the judges prevails.	58.7
5 – Lay judges' opinions matter greatly (almost always).	25.3
Total:	100

Based on your experience, how do you perceive the relationship between judges and lay judges overall?	
	Valid Percentage
1 – Judges primarily see you as assistants in the judicial process.	95.1
2 – Judges perceive the work of lay judges as an obstacle to their duties.	4.9
Total:	100

How satisfied are you with the human relationship between judges and lay judges?	
	Valid Percentage
1 – Not at all.	1
2 – Rather not.	0.3
3 – To some extent.	3.2
4 – Mostly yes.	15.3
5 – Completely.	80.2
Total:	100

How satisfied are you with the professional work of the judges?	
	Valid Percentage
1 – To some extent.	1.6
2 – Mostly satisfied.	29.2
3 – Completely satisfied in all cases.	69.2
Total:	100

How satisfied are you with the working conditions provided by the court for the lay judge's work?	
	Valid Percentage
1 – Not at all.	0.6
2 – Rather not.	4.8
3 – To some extent.	9.4
4 – Mostly yes.	26.1
5 – Completely.	59
Total:	100

Would you personally consider it important for lay judges to wear robes?	
	Valid Percentage
1 – No	62.7
2 – Yes	37.3
Total:	100

Why would this be beneficial? Because...	
	Valid Percentage
1 – It would increase the personal authority of lay judges.	5.2
2 – It would enhance the prestige of the lay judges' work.	26.7
3 – It would enhance the prestige of the judicial panel.	61.2

4 – For other reasons.	6.9
Total:	100

Other reasons:	
	Valid Percentage
No other reasons provided.	97.7%
It would enhance the prestige of the judicial panel, making the judgments more unified both internally and externally.	0.3%
Various attire.	0.3%
Due to appropriate appearance.	0.3%
It would increase the prestige of the lay judge's work; it would reduce financial concerns over "dress."	0.3%
Our attire would be uniform.	0.3%
The attire of the judicial panel would be more uniform.	0.3%
It would make the appearance of the panel more elegant.	0.3%
All three.	0.3%
Total:	100.0%

How satisfied are you with the way your life has developed so far?	
	Valid Percentage
1 – Not at all.	0.6
2 – Rather not.	1.9
3 – To some extent.	17.6
4 – Mostly yes.	54.2
5 – Completely.	25.7
Total:	100

How satisfied are you with your social recognition?	
	Valid Percentage
1 – Not at all.	1.6
2 – Rather not.	5.3
3 – To some extent.	26.6
4 – Mostly yes.	44.7
5 – Completely.	21.9
Total:	100

How satisfied are you with the recognition of your work as a lay judge?	
	Valid Percentage
1 – Not at all.	2.2
2 – Rather not.	4.7
3 – To some extent.	18.5

4 – Mostly yes.	40.4
5 – Completely.	34.2
Total:	100

How satisfied are you with your current financial situation and standard of living?	
	Valid Percentage
1 – Egyáltalán nem	5.2
2 – Inkább nem	8
3 – Is-is	32.7
4 – Inkább Yes	43.2
5 – Teljes mértékben	10.8
Total:	100

How satisfied are you with the government's activities?	
	Valid Percentage
1 – Not at all.	11.6
2 – Rather not.	20.6
3 – To some extent.	34.2
4 – Mostly yes.	23.2
5 – Completely.	10.3
Total:	100

How satisfied are you with the country's economic situation?	
	Valid Percentage
1 – Not at all.	9.6
2 – Rather not.	30.4
3 – To some extent.	36.5
4 – Mostly yes.	19.9
5 – Completely.	3.5
Total:	100

How satisfied are you with the activities of the churches?	
	Valid Percentage
1 – Not at all.	7.9
2 – Rather not.	16.4
3 – To some extent.	43.3
4 – Mostly yes.	23.3
5 – Completely.	9.2
Total:	100

How satisfied are you with the work of the police?	
	Valid Percentage
1 – Not at all.	1.9
2 – Rather not.	12.4
3 – To some extent.	49.8
4 – Mostly yes.	31.1
5 – Completely.	4.8
Total:	100

How satisfied are you with the work of the prosecution service?	
	Valid Percentage
1 – Not at all.	1
2 – Rather not.	6.7
3 – To some extent.	34.1
4 – Mostly yes.	46.5
5 – Completely.	11.8
Total:	100

How satisfied are you with the work of the courts?	
	Valid Percentage
1 – Not at all.	0.3
2 – Rather not.	2.5
3 – To some extent.	19.2
4 – Mostly yes.	53.1
5 – Completely.	24.8
Total:	100

How satisfied are you with the activities of the National Assembly?	
	Valid Percentage
1 – Not at all.	12.2
2 – Rather not.	21.2
3 – To some extent.	42.8
4 – Mostly yes.	19
5 – Completely.	4.8
Total:	100

How satisfied are you with the activities of your local municipal government?	
	Valid Percentage
1 – Not at all.	2.2
2 – Rather not.	9.9
3 – To some extent.	41.7

4 – Mostly yes.	37.2
5 – Completely.	9
Total:	100

How satisfied are you with the functioning of civil society organisations?	
	Valid Percentage
1 – Not at all.	4.6
2 – Rather not.	12.4
3 – To some extent.	50.7
4 – Mostly yes.	28.8
5 – Completely.	3.6
Total:	100

How satisfied are you with the activities of political parties?	
	Valid Percentage
1 – Not at all.	18.7
2 – Rather not.	35.1
3 – To some extent.	39.3
4 – Mostly yes.	4.3
5 – Completely.	2.6
Total:	100

How satisfied are you with the functioning of the European Union?	
	Valid Percentage
1 – Not at all.	11.6
2 – Rather not.	15.8
3 – To some extent.	46.1
4 – Mostly yes.	25.2
5 – Completely.	1.3
Total:	100

What would you say is the current direction of your personal life?	
	Valid Percentage
1 – Definitely bad.	0.9
2 – Rather bad than good.	14.1
3 – Rather good than bad.	66.6
4 – Definitely good.	18.4
Total:	100

What would you say is the current direction of the local affairs of where you live?	
	Valid Percentage
1 – Definitely bad.	2.2
2 – Rather bad than good.	20.3
3 – Rather good than bad.	65.4
4 – Definitely good.	12.1
Total:	100

What would you say is the current direction of the country's affairs?	
	Valid Percentage
1 – Definitely bad.	9.6
2 – Rather bad than good.	34.7
3 – Rather good than bad.	47.3
4 – Definitely good.	8.4
Total:	100

What would you say is the current direction of the European Union's affairs?	
	Valid Percentage
1 – Definitely bad.	9.4
2 – Rather bad than good.	35.5
3 – Rather good than bad.	52.6
4 – Definitely good.	2.6
Total:	100

Do you believe the rules on abortion should be made stricter or more lenient?	
	Valid Percentage
1 – They should be made more lenient.	17.4
2 – There should be no change.	67.4
3 – They should be made stricter.	15.2
Total:	100

Do you believe the rules on euthanasia should be made stricter or more lenient?	
	Valid Percentage
1 – They should be made more lenient.	56.2
2 – There should be no change.	34.4
3 – They should be made stricter.	9.4
Total:	100

Do you believe the sentences in criminal cases should be made stricter or more lenient?	
	Valid Percentage
1 – They should be made more lenient.	2.9
2 – There should be no change.	38.5
3 – They should be made stricter.	58.6
Total:	100

Do you believe the rules on immigration should be made stricter or more lenient?	
	Valid Percentage
1 – They should be made more lenient.	5.8
2 – There should be no change.	34.9
3 – They should be made stricter.	59.3
Total:	100

Do you believe the rules on granting citizenship should be made stricter or more lenient?	
	Valid Percentage
1 – They should be made more lenient.	2.9
2 – There should be no change.	37.8
3 – They should be made stricter.	59.3
Total:	100

Do you believe the rules on foreign ownership of property should be made stricter or more lenient?	
	Valid Percentage
1 – They should be made more lenient.	3.8
2 – There should be no change.	21.2
3 – They should be made stricter.	75
Total:	100

To what extent do you agree with the opinion that people can generally be trusted?	
	Valid Percentage
1 – Not at all.	4.7
2 – Rather not.	17.6
3 – To some extent.	43.5
4 – Mostly yes.	29.1

5 – Completely.	5
Total:	100

How interested are you in politics?	
	Valid Percentage
1 – Not at all.	5.6
2 – Rather not than yes.	17.8
3 – To some extent.	30.3
4 – Rather yes than no.	35.3
5 – Very interested.	11
Total:	100

How informed are you about political issues?	
	Valid Percentage
1 – Not at all.	1.8
2 – Rather not than yes.	10.7
3 – To some extent.	33.1
4 – Rather yes than no.	43.6
5 – Very informed.	10.7
Total:	100

What is your stance on citizen participation in elections?	
	Valid Percentage
1 – It is a civic duty.	70.1
2 – It is a personal decision for everyone.	29.9
Total:	100

Are there any political parties or organisations that are closer to you than others?	
	Valid Percentage
1 – None.	57.8
2 – Yes.	42.2
Total:	100

What is your gender?	
	Valid Percentage
1 – Male	29.2
2 – Female	70.8
Total:	100

What type of settlement do you live in?

	Valid Percentage
1 – Capital city.	24.5
2 – County town, city seat.	37
3 – Other town or city.	32.9
4 – Village.	5.2
5 – Other (e.g., outlying area).	0.3
Total:	100

Which age group do you belong to?	
	Valid Percentage
1 – 35–39 years	0.9
2 – 40–44 years	1.8
3 – 45–49 years	3.8
4 – 50–54 years	6.1
5 – 55–59 years	14.9
6 – 60–64 years	38
7 – 65 years or older	34.5
Total:	100

What is your highest level of education?	
	Valid Percentage
1 – Primary school education.	0.9
2 – Vocational school, vocational training.	0.9
3 – Vocational school.	2.6
4 – Secondary school diploma from a technical school.	14.7
5 – Secondary school diploma (secondary grammar school).	16.8
6 – College diploma or higher vocational education.	43.2
7 – University degree.	20.9
Total:	100

Are you currently employed? What is your primary activity?	
	Valid Percentage
1. Full-time employment	12.1
2. Part-time employment	3
3. Working alongside a pension	11.8
4. Working in one's own business	1.8
5. Performing work for a fee or occasional tasks	1.8
6. Retired with an old-age pension	55.3
7. Widowed pensioner	1.5

8. Disqualified, disabled pensioner	5.6
9. Unemployed	1.5
10. Other	5.6
Total:	100

What is (or was) your current (most recent) occupation or position?	
	Valid Percentage
1. Senior executive or middle management	28.9
2. Lower management, supervisor	17.3
3. Subordinate clerk	19.9
4. Administrative worker	7.1
5. Skilled worker	3.9
6. Semi-skilled or unskilled worker	0.6
7. Other	22.3
Total:	100

What sector does (or did) your workplace belong to?	
	Valid Percentage
1. Industry, mining, energy, manufacturing	6
2. Agriculture, forestry, water management, fishing	2.7
3. Transportation, logistics, telecommunications	3.9
4. Commerce	7.8
5. Financial services, insurance	6.3
6. Other services	5.4
7. Public administration, politics	20.9
8. Healthcare	6.9
9. Culture, education, science, religion	30.1
10. Other	10.1
Total:	100

Other sectors:	
	Valid Percentage
No other sector indicated	90.8%
Ministry of the Interior employee	0.3%
Food industry	0.6%
Armed forces	0.3%
Child protection	0.3%
Child care institution	0.3%
Child protection services	0.3%
Professional soldier	0.3%

Defence	0.3%
Tourism business	0.3%
Justice	0.6%
Real estate rental, operation	0.3%
Legal	0.3%
Printing industry	0.3%
Printer	0.3%
Law enforcement	0.3%
Police	0.3%
Social services	0.6%
Social sector	0.9%
Social care	0.3%
Social services – child protection	0.6%
Services	0.3%
Fire brigade	0.3%
Entrepreneur	0.3%
City management	0.3%
Chemistry	0.3%
Hospitality	0.3%
Total:	100.0%

Which sector do you belong to?	
	Valid Percentage
1. Public sector (as a public servant, civil servant)	68.4
2. Civil sector (such as foundation, company limited by shares, association, etc.)	3.6
3. Private sector (such as a company, limited liability company, etc.)	28
Total:	100

Do you belong to any ethnic minority group in Hungary?	
	Valid Percentage
1 – No	95.2
2 –Yes	4.8
Total:	100

Which ethnic minority group in Hungary do you belong to?	
	Valid Percentage
1. Roma	12.5
2. German	18.8
3. Slovak	18.8
4. Croatian	6.3

5. Romanian	25
6. Serbian	6.3
7. Armenian	6.3
8. Other	6.3
Total:	100

Other national, ethnic minorities:	
	Valid Percentage
No other national, ethnic minority indicated	99.7
Yes	0.3
Total:	100

BIBLIOGRAPHY

Aaseng, Nathan: You are the Juror. The Oliver Press, Minneapolis, 1997.
Abadinsky, Howard: An Introduction to the American Legal System. Nelson-Hall Inc., Chicago, 1991.

Ablonczy Zsuzsanna: A laikus bíráskodás problémájának bemutatása a magyarországi esküdtszéki ítélkezés történetén keresztül. In: Iustum aequum salutare 5., 2009/4. 167–188. p.

Alker, H. R. – Hosticka, H. – Mitchell, M.: Jury Selection as a Biased Social Process. In: Law and Society 11., 1976/1. 9–41. p.Anderson, Stanley: Lay Judges and Jurors in Denmark. In: The American Journal of Comparative Law 38., 1990/4. 839–864. p.

Andoor, George: Laien in der Strafrechtsprechung. Eine vergleichende Betrachtung der Laienbeteiligung an deutschen und englischen Strafgerichten. Berliner Wissenschafts-Verlag, Berlin, 2013.

Antal Tamás: A 19. századi brit laikus bíráskodás magyar szemmel: Szilágyi Dezső az angol esküdtszékről. In: Ünnepi kötet Dr. Tóth Károly címzetes egyetemi tanár 70. születésnapjára. = Acta Jur. et Pol. Szeged. Tom. 78. Szeged, 2015. 339–353. p.

Antal Tamás: A bírói hatalom gyakorlásának jogszabályi változásai a dualiz- mus korában (1890–1914). In: Homoki-Nagy Mária. (Ed.:) Konferen- cia a bírói hatalomról és az állampolgárságról. Szeged, 2011. 9–21. p.

Antal Tamás: A Szegedi Királyi Ítélőtábla története 1914 és 1921 között. = Bíróságtörténeti könyvek. Fejezetek a Szegedi Ítélőtábla történetéből II., Szegedi Ítélőtábla, Budapest–Szeged, 2015.

Antal Tamás: Árnyékország. A Harmadik Birodalom politika- és alkotmánytörténete. In: Belvedere Meridionale, 2001. február. (1–2. sz.) 104–123. p.

Antal Tamás: Az angliai esküdtszéki rendszer kritikája és reformja a 19. század elején. In: Jogtudományi Közlöny, 2015/2. 79–89. p.

Antal Tamás: Az angol esküdtszék fejlődése a közép- és a koraújkorban – a Magna Chartától Morus Tamás peréig. In: Jogtudományi Közlöny 70., 2015/10. 477–486. p.

Antal Tamás: A bírák helyzete a középkori német jogkönyvekben és az angol szokásjogban. In: Jogtudományi Közlöny 67., 2012/5. 233–239. p.

Antal Tamás: Az angol esküdtszék történetének rövid foglalata. In: FORVM Acta Juridica et Politica 3., 2013/2. 5–29. p.

Antal Tamás: Ranulf Glanvill jogkönyve és az angol esküdtszék felemelkedé- se. In: Jogtudományi Közlöny, 2014/9. 401–410. p.

Antal Tamás: Törvénykezési reformok Magyarországon (1890–1900). Ítélőtáblák, bírói jogviszony, esküdtszék. = Dél-alföldi évszázadok 23. Csong- rád Megyei Levéltár, Szeged, 2006.

Antal, Tamás: The Codification of the Jury Procedure in Hungary. In: The Journal of Legal History 30. December 2009/3. 279–297. p.

Antal, Tamás: Lessons and Criticism of the Criminal Jury in the History of Hungary. In: Canadian Social Science 11., 2015/6. 215–220. p.

Antal, Tamás: The Jury in Hungary. In: Зборник Радова (Collected Papers), 2008/1–2. Novi Sad, 2008. 927–939. p.

Badó Attila – Bencze Mátyás: Reforming the Hungarian Lay Justice System. In: Cserne Péter [et al.] (Ed.): Theatrum legale mundi: symbola Cs. Varga oblata = Bibliotheca iuridica. Libri amicorum 24. Szt. István Tár- sulat, Budapest, 2007. 1–13. p.

Badó Attila – Feleky Gábor – Lőrinczi János: Reprezentativitás a magyar ülnökrendszerben (2016). Egy empirikus vizsgálat alapkérdése I. = MTA Law Working Papers 3. Budapest, 2016/16. 1–18. p.

Badó Attila: A francia esküdtszékkel kapcsolatos dilemmák. In: Acta Jur. et Pol., 1999. Tom. 57., Fasc.1. 1–26. p.

Badó Attila: A laikus bíráskodás létjogosultságának korlátairól a tudományos vizsgálatok tükrében. In: Állam- és Jogtudomány 57., 2016/2. 3–15. p.

Badó Attila: A laikus bíráskodás. In Badó – Loss – H. Szilágyi – Zombor (Ed.): Bevezetés a jogszociológiába. = Prudentia Iuris. Bíbor Kiadó, Miskolc, 1997. 183–208. p.

Badó Attila: A magyar ülnöki rendszer vizsgálata. 2015. (Kézirat)

Badó Attila: Az angol jogászság. In: Badó – Loss – H. Szilágyi – Zombor (Ed.): Bevezetés a jogszociológiába. = Prudentia Juris, Bíbor Kiadó, Miskolc, 1997. 220–267. p.

Badó Attila: Az angolszász típusú esküdtszék kritikai elemzése. In: Acta Jur. et Pol. 1996. Tom. 50., Fasc.1. 1–52. p.

Badó Attila: Hungarian Mixed Court without Representativity: An Empirical Research. In: Зборник Радова 50., 2016/4. 1415–1436. p.

Badó Attila: Laikus bíráskodás és reprezentativitás: a „fair cross section" doktrína. In: Acta Jur. et Pol., 2000. Tom. 58. Fasc.1. 7–14. p.

Badó Attila: Pszichológiai vizsgálatok az esküdtszékkel kapcsolatban: Hogyan dönt 12 dühös ember? In: Magyar Jog 45., 1998/8. 479–481. p.

Badó Attila: Társadalomtudósok a bíróságon. A média hatása. (Út a pártatlan ítélők felé) In: Jogtudományi Közlöny 49., 1994/1. 28–37. p.

Bailey F. – Rothblatt H.: Fundamentals of Criminal Advocacy. The lawyers Cooperative Publishing Co., New York, 1974.

Baker, J. H.: An Introduction to English Legal History. Third Edition. Butterworth, London, 1990.

Balch, R. W. – Griffith, C. T. – Hall, E. L. – Winfree, L. T.: The Socialization of Jurors. The Voir Dire as a Rite of Passage. In: Journal of Criminal Justice 4. 1976. 271–283. p.

Baldwin, John – McConville, Michael: Jury Trials. In: The Modern Law Review 42., 1983/6. 726–727. p.

Bermant, G.: The Psychology of Evidence and Trial Jury Procedure. Beverly Hills, 1985.

Bloomstein, M. J.: Verdict – The Jury System. New York, Dodd, Mead Co., 1968.

Boehme-Nessler, Volker: Unabhängige Richter in der Mediengesellschaft? Überlegungen zum Einfluss der Medien auf die Gerichte. Archive für Presserrecht, 2010.

Bonnieu, Michel: The Presumption of Innocence and The Cour d'Assises: Is France Ready for Adversarial Procedure? In: Revue Internationale de Droit Pénal. vol.72. 2001/1–2. 559–577. p.

Bonora, B. – Crauss, E.: Jurywork. Systematic Techniques. National Jury Project, Oakland, CA., 1979.

Boot, Max: Out of Order. Arrogance, Corruption and Incompetence on the Bench. Basic Books, New York, 1998.

Both Ödön: Küzdelem az esküdtbíráskodás bevezetéséért Magyarországon a reformkorban és az 1848. április 29-i esküdtszéki rendelet. In: Uő.: Reform és forradalom. Egybegyűjtött írások Magyarország alkotmány- és jogtör- ténetéből, 1790–1849. Ruszoly József, Antal Tamás (Ed.:) = A Pólay Elemér Alapítvány könyvtára 26. Pólay E. Alapítvány, Szeged, 2009. 83–131. p.

Boudreaux, Donald J. – Pritchard, A.C.: Reassessing the Role of the Inde- pendent Judiciary in Enforcing Interest-Group Bargains. In: Constitutional Political Economy, 1994/5. Winter. 1–21. p.

Böttges, W.: Die Laienbeteiligung an der Strafrechtspflege. Ihre Geschichte und heutige Bedeutung. [s.n.], Bonn, 1979.

Brenner, Susan W.: The Voice of the Community. In: Virginia Journal of Social Policy & The Law. 67. 1995. Fall. 11–61. p.

Broeder, D. (1965) Voir Dire Examinations. An empirical study. In: Southern California Law Review 38. 503–528. p.

Broeder, D.: The Functions of the Jury. Facts or fictions. In: Chicago Law Review21. 1954/3. 386–424 p.

Broeder, D.: The University of Chicago Jury Project. In: Nebraska Law Review 38., 1959/38. 744–746. p.

Brunner, Heinrich: Die Entstehung der Schwurgerichte. Weidman, Berlin, 1872.

Bryan, William J.: The Chosen Ones. The Art of Jury Selection. Westwood Publishing Company, California 1985. 438 p.

Buchnan, R. W. – Pryor, B. – Taylor, K. P. – Strawn, D. V.: Legal Communication. An Investigation of Juror Comprehension of Pattern Jury Instructions. In: Communications Quarterly 26., 1978/4. 31–35. p.

Burbank, Stephen B.: Alternative Career Resolution. An Essay on the Removal of Federal Judges. In: Kentucky Law Journal 76. 1988/3, 643–700. p.

Burgess, Pete W. – Corby, Susan – Latreille, Paul L.: Lay Judges and Labor Courts. A Question of Legitimacy. In: Comparative Labor Law & Policy Journal 35. 2014. 191–216. p.

Casper, Gerhard – Zeisel, Hans: Der Laienrichter im Strafprozess. Vier empirische Studien zur Rechtsvergleichung. C. F. Müller Juristischen Verlag, Karlsuhe, 1979.

Casper, Gerhard – Zeisel, Hans: Lay Judges in the German Criminal Court. Journal of Legal Studies 1., 1972/1. 135–191. p.

Catz, Robert S.: Removal of Federal Judges by Imprisonment. In: Rutgers Law Journal, 1986. Fall. 103–122. p.

Charvet, Dominique: Une ou deux magistratures? Recueil Dalloz, 2007. Chase, Harold W.: The Warren Court and Congress. In: Minnesota Law Review

44. 1959/60. 595–638. p.

Clermont, Kevin M. – Eisenberg, Theodore: Trial by Jury or Judge. Transcending Empiricism. In: Cornell Law Review 77., 1992/5. 1124– 1177. p.

Cloran, H. J.: Jury System. Book. on Demand Ltd. 2013.

Corey, Zachary – Hans, Valeria P.: Japan's New Lay Judge System. Deliberative Democracy in Action? Cornell Law Faculty Publications, 2010. Paper 636.

Costanini, E. – King, J.: The Partial Juror. Correlates and Causes of Prejudgement. In: Law and Society Review 15. 1980/1981/1. (15). 9–40. p.

Csizmadia Andor: Az esküdtbíróság Magyarországon a dualizmus korában. In: : Jogtörténeti tanulmányok I. Közgazdasági és Jogi Könyvkiadó, Bu- dapest, 1966. 131–147. p.

Dawson, John P.: The History of Lay Judges. Harvard University Press, Cambridge Mass., 1960.

Devlin, Patrick: Trial by Jury. Stevens & Sons Limited, London, 1956.

Dexter, H. R.: In Search of the Fair Jury. Does Extended "Voir Dire"? Remedy the Effects of Pretrial Publicity? International University, Florida, 1956. Diamond, Shari Seidman – Vidmar, Neil: Jury Room Ruminations on

Forbidden Topics. In: Virginia Law Review 87., 2001/8. 1857–1915. p.

Diamond, Shari Seidman: Revising Images of Public Punitiveness. Sentencing by Lay and Professional Magistrates. In: Law and Social Inquery 15. 1990/2. 191–221. p.

Diesen, Christian: Lay Judges in Sweden. A Short Introduction. In: Interna- tional Review of Penal Law 72. 2001/1–2. 313–315. p.

DiPerna, P.: Juries on trial. Faces of American Justice. Dembner Books, New York, 1984.

Donner, Ted A.: Jury Selection. Strategy & Science. 3d (Trial Practice Series), Thomson Reuters, 2015–2016.

Dubber, Markus – Pihlajamäki, Heikki: Introduction. Lay Participation in Modern Law. A Comparative Historical Analysis. In: Comparative Legal History 3., 2015/2. 224–230. p.

Fagan Ginger, Ann: Jury Selection in Criminal Trials. LawPress in Tiburon. California, 1977.

Fahidi Gergely: Laikus bíráskodás: magánítélkezők. HVG. 1997/45 (963). 115–117. p.

Fahringer, Herald Price: In the Valley of the Blind. A Primer on Jury Selection in a Criminal Case, 3. In: Diplomacy Journal, No2. 1980. 116–136. p.

Forston, R. F.: Research in Jury Structure and Function. Paper presented at Convention of the Speech Communication Association, Chicago, 1972. Forston, R. F.: The Decision-making Process in the American Civil Jury. A Comparative Methodological Investigation. PhD. thesis, University of Minnesota. 1968.

Francis, Philip: How to Serve on a Jury. = LegalAlmach Series No 31. Oceana Publications, New York, 1953.

Frank, J. – Frank, B. – Hoffmann, H. M.: Law and the Modern Mind. New York, Garden City, 1957.

Frank, J.: Courts on Trial. Myth and Reality in American Justice. Princeton University Press, 1949.

Frank, J.: Law and the Modern Mind. Stevens, London, 1930.

Frankel, Jack E.: Judicial Conduct and Removal of Judges For Cause in California. Southern California Law Review 36., 1962/1. 72–87. p.

Frankel, Jack E.: Judicial Discipline and Removal. In: Texas Law Review, 1966. 1177–1135. p.

Frederick, J. T.: The Psychology of the American Jury. Charlottesville, Virgi- nia, 1987.

Freedman, Monroe H.: The Threat to Judicial Independence by Criticism of Judges. A Proposed Solution to the Real Problem. In: Hofstra Law Review 25., 1997/3. Spring. 729–743. p.

Friedman, L. M.: A History of American Law. Simon and Schuster, New York, 1973.

Garde, Peter: The Danish Jury. In: Revue Internationale de Droit Pénal 72. 2001/1–2. 87–120. p.

Glöckner, Andreas – Dickert, Stephan – Landsberg, Marie – Scholz, Selina – Schönfeldt, Kristina: Entscheidungsverhalten von Schöffen. Forschungsbericht. Max-Planck-Institut zur Erforschung von Gemeinschaftsgütern, Bonn Forschungsgruppe Intuitive Experten, 2008.

Gobert, James: Justice, Democracy and the Jury. Dartmouth, Ashgate, 1997.
Goldbach, Toby Susan – Hans, Valerie: Juries, Lay Judges, and Trials. In: Bruinsma, Gerben and Weisburd, David (Eds.): Encyclopedia of Criminology and Criminal Justice. = Cornell Legal Studies Research Paper, 2013. 13–87. p.

Griffit, J.: Simulated Jury Decision. Influence of Jury Defendant Attitude, Similarity-dissimilarity. In: Social Behavior and Personality 1., 1973/1. 1–7. p.

Hans, V. P. – Vidmar, N.: Judging the Jury. Plenum Press, New York – London, 1986.

Hans, V. P.: The jury system. Aldershot, England, Burlington; VT, Ashgate, 2006.

Harrington, D. C. – Dempsey, J.: Psychological Factors in Jury Selection. In: Tennessee Law Review 73., 1969. 173–178. p.

Helmholz, R. H.: The Early History of the Grand Jury and the Canon Law. In: University of Chicago Law Review 50. 1983. 613–627. p.

Hennenberg, M. C. – DeVan, M. R.: Conducting a Defense Jury Voir Dire through the Judge in Federal District Court. Champion, 1987.

Horowitz, I. A. – Willging, T. E.: Changing Views of Jury Power. The Nullification Debate, 1787–1988. In: Law and Human Behavior 15., 19912/., special issue (April) 165–182. p.

Hunt, M.: Putting Juries on the Couch. In: New York Times Magazine, November 28, 1982. 70–88. p.

Hyman H. M. – Tarrant, C. M.: Aspects of American Trial Jury History. In James Simon, R.J. (Ed.): The Jury System in America. A Critical Overview. Sage Publications, Beverly Hills–London, 1975.

Iontcheva, Jenia: Jury Sentencing as Democratic Practice. In: Virginia Law Review, 2003/2. 311–383. p.

Kalven, Harry – Zeisel, Hans: The American Jury. Little Brown and Company, Boston, 1966.

Kassin, S. M. – Wrightsman L. S.: The American Jury on Trial. Psychological Perspectives. Hemisphere P. C., New York, 1988.

Kennebeck, E.: From the Jury Box. In: James Simon, R. (Ed.): The Jury System in America. A Critical Overview. Sage Publications, Beverly Hills–London, 1975. 233-244 p.

Kessler, J. B.: Techniques of Jury Research. Presented to Central States Speech Association, Milwaukee, 1974. April.

Kessler, J.: An Empirical Study of Six- and Twelve-member Jury Decision-making Processes. In: University of Michigan Journal of Law Reform 6., 19733. 712–734. p.

Klami, Hannu Tapani – Hämäläinen, Merva: Lawyers and Laymen on the Bench. A Study of Comparative Legal Sociology. Suomalainen Tiedeakatemia, Helsinki, 1966.

Klausa, Ekkehard: Ehrenamtliche Richter. Ihre Auswahl und Funktion – empirisch Untersucht. Athenäum, Frankfurt am Main, 1972.

Köbler, Ralf: Professioneller IT-Betrieb für die Dritte Gewalt – Kein unzulässiger Eingriff in die Unabhängigkeit. In: Deutsche Richterzeitung, 2012. 162–164. p.

Kronenberger, Franz Rudolph: Laien in der Strafrechtspflege? In: Jung, Heike (Hrsg.:) Alternativen zur Strafjustiz. Verlag Forum, Bonn, 1989. 189–191. p.

Kulcsár Kálmán: A népi ülnök a bíróságon. = Szociológiai tanulmányok. Akadémiai Kiadó, Budapest, 1971.

Kulcsár Kálmán: A bírósági szervezet fejlesztéséről. In: Magyar Jog 37., 1990/1. 1–10. p.

Kutnjak, Ivkovic Sanja: Lay Participation in Criminal Trials. The Case of Croatia. Austin & Winfield, Lanham, Md., 1999.

Kutnjak, Ivkovic: Exploring Lay Participation in Legal Decision-making. Lessons from Mixed Tribunals. In: Cornell International Law Journal 40. 2007/2. 429–453. p.

Lempert, R.: A Jury for Japan? In: The American Journal of Comparative Law 40., 1992/1. Winter. 37–71. p.

Lempert, Richard: Citizen Participation in Judicial Decision Making. Juries, Lay Judges and Japan. St. Louis–Warsaw Transatlantic Law Journal. 2001/1. 1–14. p.

Lesser, Maximus A.: The Historical Development of the Jury System. WilliamS. Hein & CO., INC. Buffalo–New York, 1992.

Levy, Leonard W.: The Palladium of Justice. Origins of Trial by Jury. Ivan R. Dee, Chicago, 1999.

Liao, Kuang-sheng: People's Supervision and Communist China's Legal System. In: Issues & Studies, 1988. August. 34–58. p.

Lieber, Hasso – Sens, Ursula: Fit fürs Schöffenamt. Eine Orientierungshilfe zur gleichberechtigten Teilnahme an der Hauptverhandlung. Band 1: Aufgaben, Rechte und Pflichten der Schöffen. Berliner Wissenschafts- Verlag, Berlin, 2013, 148. p., Band 2: Das Strafverfahren: Grundlagen, Beweisaufnahme, Strafen. Berliner Wissenschafts-Verlag, Berlin, 2014, 127. p.

Lieber, Hasso: Die Anteile von Frauen und Männer an den gewählten Hauptschöffen der Amtsperiode 2009 bis 2013. In: RohR 1/11. 3–5. p.

Machura, Stefan: Eine Kultur der Kooperation zwischen Schöffen und Berufsrichtern. In: Richter ohne Robe, 2000/12. 111–116. p.

Machura, Stefan: Fairness und Legitimität. Nomos Verlagsgesellschaft, Ba- den-Baden, 2001.

Machura, Stefan: Interaction Between Lay Assessors and Professional Judges in German Mixed Courts. Revue Internationale de Droit Pénal, 2001/1. 451–479. p. = https://www.cairn.info/revue-internationale-de-droit-penal- 2001-1-page-451.htm (2016.02.15.)

McCabe, S. – Purves, R. (eds.): The Jury at Work. A Study of a Series of Jury Trials in which the Defandant was Acquitted. Oxford University Penal Research Unit, Occasional Paper Nr. 4. 1972.

Pap András László: Döntsön a nép? Laikus bíráskodás a tengeren innen és túl. In: Beszélő, 2008/6. 22–35. p.

Papier, David J: Insulating Incumbent Judges from the Vicissitudes of the Political Arena. Retention Elections as a Viable Alternative. In: Fordham Urban Law Journal 15., 1986/87/3. 743–766. p.

Penrod, S. – Linz, D.: Voir Dire: Uses and Abuses. In: Kaplan, M. F. (Ed.): The Impact of Social Psychology on Procedural Justice. Springfield, Il., 1984. 135–163. p.

Perron, Walter: Lay Participation in Germany. In: Revue Internationale de Droit Pénal 72., 2001/1–2. 181–195. p.

Rasicot, J.: Jury Selection, Body Language and the Visual Trial. AB Publications, Minneapolis, 1983.

Rennig, Christoph – Machura, Stefan: Die Zusammenarbeit zwischen Schöffen und Berufsrichtern. In: Lieber, Hasso – Sens, Ulla (Hrsg.): Ehrenamtliche Richter – Demokratie oder Dekoration am Richtertisch? Kommunal- und Schul Verlag, Wiesbaden, 1999. 65–70 p.

Rennig, Christoph: Influence of Lay Assessors and Giving Reasons for the Judgement in German Mixed Courts. In: Revue Internationale of Penal Law, 2001/1–2. 481–494. p.

Renning, Christoph: Die Entscheidungsfindung durch Schöffen und Berufsrichter in rechtlicher und psychologischer Sicht. Empirische, rechtsdogmatische und psychologisch-theoretiche Untersuchungen zur Laienbeteiligung an der Strafgerichtsbarkeit. N. G. Elwert, Marburg, 1993. Sage, W.: Psychology and the Angela Davis Jury. In: Human Behavior Magazine,1973. January. 56–61. p.

Sams, Murray Jr.: Persuasion in the voir dire: The Plaintiff 's Approach. In: Persuasion: The Key to Damages. G. Holmes ed. Ann Arbor: The Insti- tute of continuing Legal Education, 1969. 3–8. p.

Schmid, Niklaus: Das amerikanische Strafverfahren. Eine Einführung. C. F. Müller, Heidelberg, 1986.

Sealy, A. P. – Cornish, W. R.: Jurors and their Verdicts. In: Modern Law Review 36., 1973/5. 496–508. p.

Seligson, Milton: Lay Participation in South Africa from Apartheid to Majority Rule. In: Revue Internationale de Droit Pénal 72. 2001/1–2. 273–284. p. Smoke,

W. H. – Zajonc, R. B.: On the Reliability of Group Judgements and Decisions. In: Criswell, J. J. – Solomon, H. – Suppes, P. (Eds.): Mathematical Methods in Small Group Processes. = Stanford Mathematical Studies in

the Social Sciences. Stanford University Press, Stanford, 1962. 322–333. p.

Stephan, C. – Tully, J. C.: The Influence of Physical Attractiveness of a Plaintiff on the Decisions of Simulated Jurors. Paper read at the meetings of the North Central Sociological Association, Cincinatti, 1973.

Stewart, E.: Defendant's Attractiveness as a Factor in the Outcome of Criminal Trials. An observational study. In: Journal of Applied Social Psychology. 1980/4. 348-361. p.

Strandbakken, Asbjorn: Lay Participation in Norway. In: Revue Internationale de Droit Pénal 72. 2001/1–2. 225–251 p.

Strodtbeck, F. – James, R. – Hawkins, C.: Social Status in Jury Deliberations. In: American Sociological Review, 1957. December. 713–719. p.

Strodtbeck, F. L. – Hook, L. H.: The Social Dimensions of a Twelve-Man Jury Table. In: Sociometry 24. 1961/4. 397–415. p.

Strodtbeck, F.: Social Process, the Law and Jury Functioning. In: Evan, N. (Ed.): Law and Sociology. 1962.

Strodtbeck–Mann: Sex Role Differentiation in Jury Deliberations. In: Sociometry 19. 1956/1. 3–11. p.

Szikinger István: Esküdtszék. Képviseleti egyenlőség alapján. In: Beszélő, 2001. 6. évf. 4. sz, 41–42. p.

Thaman, Stephen C.: Europe's New Jury Systems. The Cases of Spain and Russia. In: Law and Contemporary Problems 62., 1999/2. Spring. 233–260. p.

Thaman, Stephen C.: Spain returns to Trial by Jury. In: Hastings International and Comparative Law. Review 21. 1998. 241–537, p.

Thaman, Stephen C.: Japan's New System of Mixed Courts. Some Suggestions Regarding Their Future Form and Procedures. In: St. Louis–Warsaw Transatlantic Law Journal, 2001. 89–117. p.

Thaman, Stephen C.: The Resurrection of Trial by Jury in Russia. In: Stanford Journal of Iternational Law 31. 1995/61. 166–274. p.

Tocqueville, Alexis de: A demokrácia Amerikában. Válogatás. [ford.: Frémer Jusztina]. = Politikai gondolkodók. Gondolat, Budapest, 1983.

Tóth László: Az esküdtszék a kül-államokban. In: Jogtudományi Közlöny, 1901/37. 261–263. p.

Vidmar, Neil: The Performance of the American Civil Jury An Empirical Perspective. Arizona Law Review 40., 1998. 849–899. p.

Villmov, Bernhard – TerVeen, Heino – Walkowiak, Anett – Gerken, Jutta: Die Mitwirkung von Laien in der (Jugend-) Strafgerichtsbarkeit. Rechtsprechung zwischen Professionalität und Bürgernähe. In: Ostendorf, Heribert: Integration von Strafrechts – und Sozialwissenschaften. Festschrift für Lieselotte Pongrats. J. Schweitzer, München, 1986. 306–361. p.

Volcansek, Mary L.: Judicial Impeachment. None Called for Justice. Univer- sity of Illinois Press, Chicago, 1993.

Wachtler, S.: Grand Juries. Wasteful and Pointless. New York Times, 1990. Jan. 6. = http://www.nytimes.com/1990/01/06/opinion/grand-juries- wasteful-and-pointless.html

Warner, H. C.: Development of Trial by Jury. In: Tennesse Law Review, 1959. 26. 459–467. p.

Werding, K.: Schwurgerichte in den USA. Verlag Schneider und Weber, Kassel, 1975.

Williams, G.: The Proof of Guilt. A Study of the English Criminal Trial. Stevens and Sons Limited, London, 1955.

Wishman–Seymour: Anatomy of a Jury. The System on Trial. Times Books, New York, 1986.

Wittreck, Fabian: Erledigungszahlen unter (Dienst-)Aufsicht? In: Deutsche Richterzeitung, 2013. 60–61. p.

Wittreck, Fabian: Anwälte als Richter? Anmerkungen zur jüngsten Novellierung des Richtergesetzes und der Neubesetzung der Richterdienstgerichte. In: Neue Juristische Wochenschrift, 2004. 3011– 3015. p.

Younger, Richard D.: The People's Panel. The Grand Jury in the United States, 1634–1941. In: American History Research Center, Providence, 1963.

Zeisel, H. – Diamond, S. S.: The Jury Selection in the Mitchell-Stans Conspiracy Trial. In: American Bar Foundation Research Journal, 1974. 151–174. p. Zeisel, H.: What Determines the Amount of Argument per Juror? In: American Sociological Review. 28, 1963. 279. p.

Zuklie, M.S. Rethinking the Fair Cross-Section Requirement. In: California Law Review, 1996. 101–150. p.

Zweigert, Konrad – Kötz, Hein: Einführung in die Rechtsvergleichung auf dem gebiete des Privatrechts. J. C. B. Mohr, Tübingen, 3. Auflage, 1996. 729. p.

www.ingramcontent.com/pod-product-compliance
Lightning Source LLC
LaVergne TN
LVHW052306200926
848481LV00002B/480

* 9 7 9 8 8 9 9 6 6 0 2 6 9 *